MW01673042

CLOTHING-INDUSTRY ADJUSTMENT IN DEVELOPED COUNTRIES

Clothing-industry Adjustment in Developed Countries

BY

José de la Torre

Professor of International Business
Institut Européen d'Administration des Affaires
Fontainebleau, France

St. Martin's Press New York

© Trade Policy Research Centre, 1984, 1986

All rights reserved. For information, write:
St. Martin's Press, Inc., 175 Fifth Avenue, New York, NY 10010
Printed in Hong Kong
Published in the United Kingdom by The Macmillan Press Ltd
First published in the United States of America in 1986

ISBN 0–312–14492–X

Library of Congress Cataloging-in-Publication Data
De la Torre, José R.
Clothing-industry adjustment in developed countries.
Bibliography: p.
Includes index.
1. Clothing trade. 2. Textile industry. 3. Clothing trade—Developing countries. 4. Textile industry—Developing countries. 5. International economic relations.
I. Title.
HD9940.A2D4 1986 338.4'7677'0091722 85–18381
ISBN 0–312–14492–X

Contents

List of Tables

List of Figures

Biographical Note

JOSE DE LA TORRE has been Professor of International Business at the Institut Européen d'Administration des Affaires, Fontainebleau, France, since 1974 where he has been responsible for research and teaching on industrial policy and international competition. Professor de la Torre has been a consultant to the World Bank, the Organisation for Economic Cooperation and Development, the United Nations and the Inter-American Development Bank, chiefly advising on foreign investment in developing economies.

After obtaining his doctorate from the Harvard Business School in 1970, Professor de la Torre joined the Institute of International Business at Georgia State University, Atlanta, and his research and writings since have dealt mainly with the impact of foreign direct investment in host and home countries and with the problems of adjustment in declining industries. He is co-author of *The US Apparel Industry: International Challenge — Domestic Response* (1982), *Corporate Responses to Import Competition in the US Apparel Industry* (1978) and *Nine Investments Abroad and their Impact at Home* (1976).

Preface

PUBLIC discussion, never mind policy formation, on international trade in textiles and clothing has been seriously hampered down the years by a lack of empirical research and analysis of the issues posed by government intervention. Work is nearing completion on a study on 'textiles and clothing in world trade' which is being conducted in the Secretariat of the General Agreement on Tariffs and Trade (GATT) with a view to examining 'expeditiously, taking into account the results of such a study, modalities of further trade liberalisation in textiles and clothing, including the possibilities of bringing about the full application of GATT provisions to this sector of trade'.

The quoted passages are from the declaration issued after the ministerial meeting in November 1982 of the countries which are contracting parties to the General Agreement, the instrument which has governed, since 1948, the institutional environment of international trade among market-oriented economies. Although the GATT ministerial meeting failed to make a confidence-building impact on business expectations about the determination of governments to halt and reverse protectionist trends in the world economy, it did authorise an extensive 'work programme' which has served to keep governments engaged, focussing their attention on the complex issues that have bedevilled international economic relations for the last decade or so.

Indeed, the GATT ministerial meeting in November 1982, the first since the one in September 1973 which formally launched the Tokyo Round of multilateral trade negotiations, might be said, in retrospect, to have initiated preparations for a new GATT round. At the Economic Summit meeting held in Williamsburg, Virginia, at the end of May 1983, the heads of government of the seven leading Western countries undertook 'to halt protectionism and as [economic] recovery proceeds to reverse it by dismantling barriers to trade'. Six months later, the Prime Minister of Japan, Yasuhiro Nakasone, urged that preparations for a new GATT round should be advanced, thereby stimulating more intensive discussions on the subject at inter-governmental level.

Thus, since November 1982, work has been proceeding in the GATT framework on a wide range of topics including not only textiles and clothing but also 'structural adjustment and trade policy', 'existing quantitative restrictions and other non-tariff measures' and, more generally, 'the prospects for increasing trade between developed and developing countries'. Since the inception of the work programme, it has become increasingly evident that what is required to help promote a sustained, which is to say a non-inflationary, recovery in economic activity and to help overcome the 'debt crisis' is a concerted effort to restore the momentum of trade liberalisation in the world economy that was lost in the late 1960s and 1970s. It is expected, therefore, that the review of the GATT's work programme at its annual meeting in November 1984 will further concentrate attention on what is important to the credibility, strength and vitality of the international trading system.

In 1981 the Trade Policy Research Centre published the report of a study group which concluded that 'the most important benefit that developed countries can bestow on the developing countries is the maintenance of stable growth and an open trading system. By comparison with these achievements, all the "concessions" the developed countries may make to the "demands" of the Group of 77 can do little towards alleviating the plight of poor peoples in the Third World.'

If the liberal principles of the international trading system, as expressed in the GATT, are to be preserved for the benefit of all, the report added, merely verbal reassertions by the governments of the developed countries of their commitment to these principles will not be enough. Governments have to demonstrate that they mean what they say. They have to repudiate the precedents for departures from those principles. They have to convey, thereby, clear signals to non-protected industries. In short, they have to start dismantling restrictive trade measures such as the Multi-fibre Arrangement (MFA), 'voluntary' export-restraint agreements, sectoral pacts of a cartel character and non-tariff devices which distort trade. Such were some of the conclusions of the report, entitled *Global Strategy for Growth*, which had been prepared for the Centre by an international group of businessmen and economists under the chairmanship of Lord McFadzean of Kelvinside.

Trade in textiles between developed and developing countries is a particularly important case in point. Given that the Arrangement Regarding International Trade in Textiles, the formal title of the MFA, represents a major departure from GATT principles and rules, and most significantly from the principle of non-discrimination, it has been important to illumine what exactly is involved in the whole arrangement. Accordingly, in May 1980, the Trade Policy Research Centre and the International Chamber of Commerce convened a conference in Brussels on international trade in textiles and clothing. Shortly afterwards, the Centre published a Thames Essay, *Textile Quotas against Developing Countries*, by Donald B. Keesing and Martin Wolf which has been widely acknowledged as an authoritative analysis of the MFA and the issues it poses.

In a review of *Textile Quotas against Developing Countries*, K.C. Jackson wrote in *The Textile Institute and Industry*, published in Manchester: 'Rarely are the interpretation of trade arguments and the analysis of the import-control issues [posed by the MFA] treated with the objectivity they deserve. Dr Keesing and Mr Wolf, however, have provided the scholarly perspective that is needed and their book is a welcome addition to the literature... The book is to be recommended for its balanced and logical approach to a major issue.'

On the conditions of public debate on the MFA, Dr Keesing and Mr Wolf remarked in their Thames Essay that 'it is important to note that as more and more of the significant decisions [on trade in textiles and clothing] are taken within bureaucracies and involve the manipulation of an incredibly complex, highly opaque and — to the outsider — extremely uninteresting structure of import quotas, the lobbyists of the developed countries come increasingly into their own. They are eternally interested, unceasingly helpful and, not least, always available. They find little difficulty, moreover, in grappling with this Frankenstein monster. [The MFA] is, in part, their own creation' (page 176).

With growing concern over precedents for departures from GATT principles and rules, the Centre has been conducting a programme of studies on Neo-protectionism and Managed Trade which, apart from dealing with general questions of structural adjustment in the industrialised countries, has focussed on steel, footwear and textiles and clothing.

Studies in the programme which deal with managed trade in textiles and clothing include: Gerard Curzon, José de la Torre, Juergen B. Donges, Alasdair I. MacBean, Jean Waelbroeck and Martin Wolf, *MFA*

Forever? Future of the Arrangement for Trade in Textiles, International Issues No. 5 (1981); Geoffrey Shepherd, *Textile-industry Adjustment in Developed Countries*, Thames Essay No. 30 (1981); and Martin Wolf, Hans Hinrich Glismann, Joseph Pelzman and Dean Spinanger, *Costs of Protecting Jobs in Textiles and Clothing*, Thames Essay No. 37 (1984). Two other studies in the programme which bear on trade in textiles and clothing have been Deepak Lal, *Resurrection of the Pauper-labour Argument*, Thames Essay No. 28 (1981), and Brian Hindley and Eri Nicolaides, *Taking the New Protectionism Seriously*, Thames Essay No. 34 (1983).

In order to understand the background to the regulation of international trade in textiles and clothing it is important to grasp what is going on in the industries of the developed countries themselves. It was for that reason that the Centre invited Dr Geoffrey Shepherd, of the European Research Centre at the University of Sussex, to prepare the essay on the textile industry that was published in 1981. At the same time, the Centre invited Professor José de la Torre, of the Institut Européen d'Administration des Affaires (INSEAD) in Fontainebleau, to prepare a parallel essay on the clothing industry. As the reader will observe, this last has grown into a substantial, and also an authoritative, volume on private and public responses to change in the clothing industries of developed countries.

It is widely believed that, under the threat of low-cost competition from developing countries, the clothing industries of developed countries face a future of irreversible decline unless they are afforded stringent protection. Professor de la Torre's essay indicates that this is too simplistic a view. While true of those who produce for the more functional end of the market, where competition from developing countries would quickly prove overwhelming if unchecked, there is also an increasingly international and fashion-oriented segment of the market characterised by the high quality of its output and an ability to incorporate new trends and designs. In this rapidly growing segment of the industry, Professor de la Torre shows, the bulk of the value added will continue to accrue to citizens of developed countries. Moreover, opportunities for successful adjustment in this direction are plentiful.

Under any plausible assumptions, employment — especially of unskilled workers — will continue to decline in these industries. It is for this reason that public policies in developed countries have consisted largely of protection and other forms of resistance to change, but this, Professor de la Torre argues, is a dangerous response. Public assistance should instead induce companies to make those choices that are in tune with global market trends. A key element in such policies would be a carefully-planned, long-term programme of trade liberalisation among all major producers, both developed and developing. In such a context, a leaner, more competitive and ultimately healthier industry will emerge in developed countries. 'Having failed to prevent change,' Professor de la Torre concludes, 'it is perhaps time for governments to show confidence in the ability of private firms to manage it.'

The scale and thoroughness of the research which has led to those conclusions reflects the fact that the essay is the synthesis of work over nearly ten years by Professor de la Torre on the processes which have accompanied change and adjustment in the clothing industries of developed countries. As in any attempt to summarise complex phenomena, the essay borrows heavily from the work of others, often carried out in partnership or in close cooperation with the author, but other parts are the product of Professor de la Torre's independent research. Sources of ideas are acknowledged in the numerous notes and references at the end of each chapter.

Professor de la Torre wants recorded here his debt to colleagues and co-authors in a number of previous studies on various aspects of competition and policy responses in the world clothing industry. Professor Jeffrey Arpan and Mr Brian Toyne, of the University of South Carolina, Professor Michael Jedel, of Georgia State University, and Mr Michel Bacchetta, of Telesis (a private consulting firm in Paris), all made major contributions to his thoughts, analyses and conclusions in this field. To Mr Nicholas Plessz, formerly of the Organisation for Economic Cooperation and Development in Paris, he is grateful for the opportunity to contribute to the OECD study of the textile and clothing industries conducted in 1980 from which he has borrowed liberally. Ms Sheila Sutherland husbanded the manuscript through countless versions until it was transferred to the printers' hands.

Unfortunately, so substantial a volume could also not have been prepared without cost to the author's family and, therefore, he has dedicated the essay to his children, Christina and José Ramón, in recognition of all the time it robbed from them.

As usual, it has to be stressed that the views expressed in this Thames Essay do not necessarily reflect the views of members of the Council or those of staff and associates of the Trade Policy Research Centre which, having general terms of reference, does not represent on any particular issue a consensus of opinion. The purpose of the Centre is to promote independent analysis and public discussion of international economic policy issues.

HUGH CORBET
Director
Trade Policy Research Centre

London
May 1984

List of Abbreviations

ACP	Countries in Africa, the Caribbean and the Pacific which are associated with the European Community under the Lomé Convention
CAM	computer-aided manufacturing
CETIH	Centre d'Etudes Techniques des Industries de l'Habillement, a publicly-financed research institute in France
CIDS	Clothing Industry Development Scheme, introduced in the United Kingdom in 1975 to improve efficiency without increasing capacity
CIPI	Comité Interministeriale de Politica Industriale, an inter-ministerial body in Italy created in 1977 to administer certain aspects of industrial policy
CIPRA	Clothing Industry Productivity Resources Agency, established in the United Kingdom in 1978 to harness and develop technical research
CIRIT	Centre Interprofessionel de Recherche des Industries Textiles, a publicly-funded organisation in France created to provide assistance on projects aimed at modernisation and improved productivity

Dfl.	Dutch florins (guilders)
EC	European Community
EDA	Economic Development Administration, established by the Department of Commerce of the United States to administer regional aid programmes
EDC	Economic Development Committee(s) of the National Economic Development Council (NEDC) in the United Kingdom
EEC	European Economic Community, one of the components of the European Community, the other two being the European Coal and Steel Community (ECSC) and the European Atomic Energy Community (Euratom)
ENI	Ente Nazionale d'Idrocarburi, a state holding company in Italy concerned with the petrochemical industry
ERP	Economic Recovery Programme Development Law in the Federal Republic of Germany which grouped together all government intervention in industry
ETA	Eastern Trading Area, a United Nations category covering all centrally-planned economies (excluding Yugoslavia and developing countries)
EUA	Units of account used in the European Community for budgetary, statistical and related purposes

FSAI Fond Spécial pour l'Adjustment Industriel, a publicly-funded body in France formed to link public assistance to productive investment

GARB Garment and Allied Industries Requirements Board, established in the United Kingdom in 1975 by the government to provide financial assistance and to conduct research into user requirements

GATT General Agreement on Tariffs and Trade, the instrument which, since 1948, has regulated trade among market-oriented economies, although its membership of 90 countries includes a number of state-socialist ones

GEPI Gestioni e Partecipazioni Industriali, a holding company in Italy established to enter into 'salvage' operations in the textile industry, particularly in the *Mezzogiorno* (southern part of the country)

GNP gross national product

GSP Generalised System of Preferences, preferential trading schemes between developed and developing countries benefiting the exports of the latters' manufacturer and semi-manufactures

IMI Istituto Mobiliare Italiano, an organisation in Italy created to provide aid to industrial firms in difficulty

IRI Istituto per la Ricostruzione Industriali (state holding company in Italy)

ISIC International Standard Industrial Classification

LDC less developed country(ies)

LTA Long Term Arrangement Regarding International Trade in Cotton Textiles, an agreement negotiated in 1962 between importing and exporting countries regulating international trade in cotton textiles for five years from the expiry of the STA

MFA Multi-fibre Arrangement (popular name for the Arrangement Regarding International Trade in Textiles first negotiated in 1973)

MITI Ministry of International Trade and Industry, Government of Japan, Tokyo

NEDC National Economic Development Council, a tripartite forum in the United Kingdom, with representatives from government, business and labour with some independent members, which meets under the chairmanship of the Chancellor of the Exchequer

NEDO National Economic Development Office, the body in the United Kingdom which services the NEDC and its Economic Development Committees (EDCs)

NEHEM Nederlandse herstructureringsmaatschappij, a tripartite body comprising representatives of government, employers and employees financed and empowered by the Netherlands Government to promote and restructure Dutch industry

OECD	Organisation for Economic Cooperation and Development, based in Paris, which succeeded the Organisation for European Economic Cooperation (OEEC) established to administer Marshall Plan aid
SBA	Small Business Administration, an independent government corporation in the United States
SITC	Standard International Trade Classification
STA	Short Term Agreement Regarding International Trade in Cotton Textiles negotiated in 1961
TAA	Trade Adjustment Assistance, a scheme in the United States created by the Trade Expansion Act of 1962 (TEA)
TEA	Trade Expansion Act of 1962 which provided the negotiating authority for the President of the United States in the Kennedy Round of multilateral trade negotiations under the auspices of the GATT
TES	Temporary Employment Subsidy, used in the United Kingdom in the mid-1970s to defer threatened redundancies; now abolished
UNCTAD	United Nations Conference on Trade and Development, the first session of which was held in Geneva in 1964, subsequently becoming a permanent body of the United Nations
VER	'voluntary' export-restraint agreement, usually negotiated between two countries, sometimes on an industry-to-industry basis, not always publicly notified

CHAPTER ONE

Evolutionary Struggle in World Industry

'Owing to this struggle [for life], variations, however slight and from whatever cause proceeding, if they be in any degree profitable to the individuals of a species, in their infinitely complex relations to other organic beings and to their physical conditions of life, will tend to the preservation of such individuals and will generally be inherited by the offspring... As new species in the course of time are formed through natural selection, others will become rarer and rarer and finally extinct. The forms which stand in closest competition with those undergoing modification and improvement will naturally suffer most'

— Charles Darwin, *The Origin of Species* (1859)

'It is my impression that no one really likes the new. We are afraid of it... Even in slight things the experience of the new is rarely without some stirring of foreboding... In the case of drastic change the uneasiness is of course deeper and more lasting. We can never be really prepared for that which is wholly new. We have to adjust ourselves and every radical adjustment is a crisis in self-esteem: we undergo a test, we have to prove ourselves. It needs inordinate self-confidence to face drastic change without inner trembling'

— Eric Hoffer, *The Ordeal of Change* (1964)

CHANGE is often a threatening phenomenon. Adjusting to change — whatever its causes — is a trying process which often taxes one's reserves of energy and fortitude. Where change has also resulted in the weakening of an individual's strength or of his willingness to resist and adapt to whatever new conditions prevail, adjustment will be rendered even more difficult. Sapped of stamina, fearful of the new forces that are being encountered and inexperienced in what may or may not succeed in dealing with them, a threatened individual or species must either summon the courage to adjust and evolve or run the risk of becoming a 'footnote' to history.

The pattern of evolution and survival for social organisations resembles that of animal species. Faced with rapidly changing economic conditions, any industrial corporation must constantly assess the nature of the threat to its established position and endeavour to take whatever measures are deemed necessary to enhance its ability to compete and survive. To procrastinate and postpone action is to provide a newcomer with an opportunity to gain ground on and weaken the established firm, thus making any subsequent adjustment more painful and less likely to succeed; the magnitude of the necessary changes becomes larger with the passage of time while the scope for successful adjustment policies will narrow.

Survival Strategies for the Private Firm

In an open system — whether in the realm of industry worldwide or in that of Darwin's South American flora — any change in the conditions governing life and competition will give an immediate advantage to those organisms which were bred and developed under conditions similar to those now prevailing. Industrial organisations facing competition from better-adapted variants have only two options before them. The first is to adapt to the new competition by undertaking a series of defensive and offensive actions. These may include (depending on the source and nature of the threat): an increase in investment to improve efficiency and productivity; better product design and larger marketing expenditure aimed at improving market position or gaining brand-name loyalty; shifts in product lines by moving into areas which are more profitable and in which competitive advantage can be maintained; moving to less costly locations to exploit lower factor costs; mergers and acquisitions leading to structural rationalisation; and, more often than not, a change in management that will force the organisation to accept and implement the necessary action in the least possible time. Alternatively, the company faced with the need to adjust may decide that present costs are too high relative to future benefits or that the chances of success do not merit the required investment. In this case, operations will be closed and labour made redundant unless other activities exist within the organisation that can utilise part of the capital and human resources released by this decision. The diversifed firm is, in this situation, more capable of internalising the adjustment process without incurring great social costs and with minimum friction. But, in the majority of cases, it is up to the mechanisms operating in the capital, labour and managerial markets to recycle these resources back into productive employment after a minimum period of time has elapsed and, obviously, some personal or social costs have been incurred.

One should note that these choices remain the same, irrespective of the source of competition or disruption to the established order. The implications for the existing firm are not altered whatever the causes of shifts in demand, be they demographic forces, lower rates of economic growth or changes in lifestyles and tastes. It is also immaterial whether the disruption is brought about by breakthroughs in technology affecting either product design or production processes or by variations in the relative prices of inputs, such as result from sudden and drastic differences in the availability of raw materials. Nor does it matter to the established firm if the loss of relative bargaining power is due to structural changes in industry or the introduction of collective-bargaining systems or to improvements in the availability and dissemination of information that attracts new or potential competitors. In all cases, the firm must either adapt to the new conditions and fight this new competition or abandon the field.

Thus far two abstractions have been mentioned that deserve further scrutiny. One concerns the possible disparity that may exist between private and social costs and benefits in the adjustment process; the other, the degree of openness of the economy to external forces. The state — whether motivated by social considerations regarding equity and welfare or by market imperfections inherent, for example, in the degree of accuracy and the speed of transmission of information relevant to decision making — will play a role that influences the adjustment process in ways which are easy to anticipate but more difficult to evaluate.

State Intervention: Resisting Decline or Assisting Growth?

There is inherent potential for conflict between national policies aimed at easing or facilitating the process of industrial adjustment and the achievement of an optimal international division of labour, which is both efficient in static (that is, efficient *per se*) and dynamic (in the sense of providing ample opportunity for growth and specialisation) economic terms. To avert such conflict the Organisation for Economic Cooperation and Development (OECD) held a Council meeting at ministerial level in June 1978, where a broad programme of concerted action was agreed upon. A key element of this agreement was a set of general orientations calling on the member countries (essentially the developed countries of Western Europe, North America, Oceania and Japan) to facilitate structural adjustment away from declining sectors to new competitive lines of production and to do so in such a way as to offset growing demands for protection from injured sectors and avoid sectoral, regional and labour policies destined to preserve inefficient economic structures.[1]

The following year, the OECD Council established a Special Group on Positive Adjustment Policies and gave it a mandate to examine the international consequences of national adjustment policies and to identify those which stimulated private adjustment at minimum social cost to the world. Meanwhile, the culmination of the Tokyo Round of multilateral trade negotiations in 1979, carried out under the auspices of the General Agreement on Tariffs and Trade (GATT), included a Code on Subsidies and Countervailing Duties. While recognising the importance of domestic subsidies for structural adjustment purposes, the code set up standards and complaint procedures to deal with the possible adverse effects that such subsidies could have on the trade and domestic interests of other signatories.[2]

A broad range of public-assistance measures is offered by most governments in the developed countries. Such measures may be classified according to their scope as programmes of general industrial promotion, regional development or as intervention in specific sectors of industry. In addition, one can further differentiate these measures by assessing the degree to which they influence or distort market mechanisms in the process of resource allocation. In descending order according to the degree of direct market intervention, one finds, first, a series of policies designed to improve the function of market mechanisms and reduce friction and rigidities to the greatest possible extent. Second, there is a broad range of fiscal and manpower policies whose aim is to influence the costs of allocating resources in certain desirable ways, but which leave the ultimate responsibility for economic decisions to the private sector. Third, there are more interventionist measures, including investment in industry by state capital, which attempt to restructure, directly, the functioning of the economy or a specific sector to suit social or competitive goals. Finally, governments have occasionally enacted series of highly differentiated policy measures designed to provide the economy in general, or specific sectors and firms, with relief from direct competitive pressures.

The range of policy orientations and objectives available to government officials is illustrated in Table 1.1. From the standpoint of the OECD's call for positive adjustment policies, those measures found in the upper left-hand corner of the table are greatly preferable to those in the bottom right-hand corner. As might be expected, however, the policy mix selected by any government at any particular time will be an outcome of the specific political, social and economic conditions which prevail, of the flexibility and efficacy of its public and private institutions and of the historical and ideological context in which business-government relations in that country are set.[3]

The experience of the last decade shows that the industrialised market-oriented economies have felt obliged to take a more active part in promoting structural adjustment. Years of uninterrupted growth have affected the capacity of Western society to make the sacrifices required by change, certainly to the extent necessary in the brief time span dictated by the rapid rise of competitors from industrialising countries. The diminished capacity or willingness of labour, capital and management to respond to changing competitive conditions has weakened industry in many industrialised countries. When compounded with the slow economic growth experienced since 1974 and by persistently high levels of unemployment and over-capacity, the favoured response of many elements of society is to call for protection from change.

Resisting Adjustment: Pressures for Protection

Perhaps a remarkable aspect of the economic crisis gripping the world economy since the early 1970s is that

TABLE 1.1 A Classification of Public-assistance Measures to Industry

Policy objectives	*Policy orientation*		
	General promotion of industrial development	*Regional development*	*Sector specific*
Improve the functioning of markets	Competition and anti-trust policies Regulatory environment National investments in infrastructure	Improve insfrastructure and other basic services Remove or reduce cost disadvantages	Sponsor the collection and dissemination of information Promote joint industry research and productivity centres
Influence resource allocation	Incentives for industrial research and development Accelerated depreciation allowances Labour training schemes	Investment grants and concessions Fiscal advantages Mobility and training grants	Subsidies and special grants for research and development Government procurement schemes Defence spending
Industrial restructuring and modernisation	General merger policy Investment and dividend tax policy Early retirement and shorter working week Retraining and relocation grants	Added incentives for relocation of facilities Exemptions from crisis measures applicable elsewhere	State ownership and rationalisation Capacity-reduction schemes Promotion of mergers and takeovers
Relief from competitive pressures	Employment subsidies Investment grants tied to employment maintenance Competitive devaluation	Income-maintenance schemes Support for continuing wage differentials	Trade protection Creation of crisis cartels Wage and employment freezes

it has not yet deteriorated into a defensive brawl involving mutually escalating import restrictions. As economic growth has remained flat and unemployment has surpassed the 30 million level throughout the OECD countries, the pressures for isolating domestic industries from external competition have mounted in all countries. Here lies the alternative 'solution' to the adjustment dilemma posed earlier. Faced with the choice of undertaking costly adjustment measures, both private and public, and the spectre of unemployment and bankruptcy, labour and capital will collude to convince government of the need to postpone or, at best, to avoid the choice altogether.

While the level of tariff protection has not increased in response to these developments, except in isolated cases,[4] there has been a serious deterioration in trade relations since the early 1970s, primarily through the use of 'voluntary' export-restraint agreements (VERs), the so-called 'monitoring' of import levels undertaken by various countries, the rise in bilateral (and sometimes multilateral) 'reciprocal' trade accords and the growth of domestic subsidy programmes for declining and 'crisis' industries. All of these measures effectively circumvent the GATT and erode the order that the GATT brought to international trade relations for over a quarter of a century.

There are two main reasons for the deterioration in trade relations. The first is the contention that increasing rates of government intervention (in other words, subsidisation of investments and operating expenditures) have rendered international competition 'unfair' in a large number of key sectors. The second is the use of non-tariff measures such as quality inspections, certification requirements, import licensing regulations *et cetera*. The outlook for international agreement on limiting these distortions to the allocation of resources is grim. As one negotiator has stated:

> 'Industrial adjustment and related government intervention in support of this dynamic process is one of the most sensitive issues in the context of national development. It touches the very core of nation-building and social mobilisation for the pursuit of improved national welfare. Its emergence as an international issue raises fundamental questions about the supremacy of national sovereignty over global interdependence unlike any other economic issue such as trade liberalisation, development assistance, monetary policy or foreign investment, which have traditionally dominated international economic relations.'[5]

The best one can hope for in this context is that the threat of applying the GATT Code on Subsidies and Countervailing Duties will deter or remedy the most flagrant violations and that support for transparency (that is, full disclosure of government measures in trade and industry) — a major part of the OECD programme to promote positive adjustment policies[6] — will gain strength over the next few years. In any event, the advanced industrialised economies all have much to lose and little to gain by directly challenging each other's major industrial activities. The capacity for any one of the OECD countries to retaliate against a deviant member is both serious and real. Thus, while much skirmishing will undoubtedly occur at the margins, particularly against such successful exporters as Japan, the fundamental principle of open trade is not likely to be brought into question, barring a major crisis. Whatever disagreements arise (and they will in areas such as steel, agriculture, automobiles and shipping), considerable effort will be spent to prevent them from escalating or spreading to other fields.

This is not necessarily the case in North-South economic relations. Table 1.2 summarises the success that several industrialising countries and other developing

TABLE 1.2

Import Shares of the Newly Industrialising and Developing Countries in Total OECD Imports of Manufactures

	(%)				Total OECD imports (US$ billion)	
	1963	*1970*	*1976*	*1979*	*1963*	*1979*
Clothing	20.3	28.6	47.7	47.5	1.5	30.8
Leather, footwear and travel goods	14.8	23.1	40.5	40.1	1.0	16.6
Wood and cork products	21.0	26.7	29.3	36.5	0.6	6.8
Textiles	17.1	15.0	20.4	21.1	4.0	33.2
Electrical machinery	1.3	5.8	13.4	18.0	3.8	56.6
Metal manufactures	1.9	2.3	7.7	10.5	1.7	20.9
Rubber manufactures	1.2	7.1	6.7	10.0	0.5	7.4
Non-metallic mineral manufactures	6.0	8.2	9.5	9.6	1.8	28.3
Iron and steel	2.1	3.6	6.6	8.9	4.2	38.1

Chemicals	5.6	5.3	4.7	4.5	5.5	82.5
Non-electrical machinery	0.6	1.3	3.0	3.7	9.1	100.9
Transport equipment	1.8	1.0	2.3	3.5	5.5	107.1
Paper products	0.6	1.0	2.8	2.9	2.0	17.8
Miscellaneous finished products	5.0	8.7	11.9	13.1	4.1	68.9
All Manufactures	4.9	6.2	10.2	11.5	45.3	615.3
% from:						
OECD NICs	0.8	1.1	1.8	2.1		
Brazil and Mexico	0.3	0.5	1.0	1.1		
Far Eastern NICs	1.2	2.5	4.7	5.3		
Other developing countries	2.3	1.8	2.3	2.6		

SOURCES: *The Impact of the Newly Industrialising Countries on Production and Trade in Manufactures*, Report by the Secretary-General (Paris: OECD Secretariat, 1979); and 'updated tables' published in 1981.

countries have had in penetrating OECD markets for manufactured goods. In certain traditional lines (clothing, leather and footwear, wood products), penetration levels have risen significantly in recent years and now account for more than 35 per cent of imports of these products into OECD countries. The share of their textile exports, also a traditional source of earnings for developing countries, in total OECD imports remained stable throughout the twenty years since 1963. Other categories (electrical machinery, metal products, iron and steel, and rubber manufactures) have been subject to more rapid increases, although in none of the cases has the share of imports from developing countries exceeded 10 per cent. In a large number of categories (non-electrical machinery and chemicals, for example) the developing countries play almost no role at all in OECD imports. Given the large disparities in the total volume of OECD imports among these categories (see the two columns on the right of Table 1.2), it is clear that the domestic impact of a certain import share will be significantly different in, say, clothing and textiles than transport equipment. Furthermore, the relatively small share of developing-country exports in total OECD imports of manufactures is rendered even smaller when compared with total consumption in the industrialised countries. Thus, for manufactured goods as a whole, imports from developing countries rose from less than 0.9 per cent of consumption in the European Community, Canada, the United States and Japan in 1968 to less than 2 per cent in the mid-1970s and to no more than 2.5 per cent by 1980. Even in clothing, where their relative success is greatest, the developing countries' share of total consumption in industrialised countries does not exceed 15 per cent, although it was less than 2 per cent in 1968.[7]

Why then is there this growing concern with competition from the developing countries and the ensuing rapid proliferation of non-tariff measures and other restrictions against their imports? For one, the relatively rapid rate of growth of imports from both the industrialising countries and other 'second-tier' developing countries (see Table 1.3) in a stagnant or low-growth market results in potentially large labour redundancies and idle capacity. Also, since time is a major determinant of the likelihood of success and of the costs associated with any attempt at adjustment, rapid 'surges' in the penetration levels of certain product categories lead domestic producers to claim that severe 'market disruption' is occurring at a rate that makes adjustment difficult or impossible to achieve. Clearly, both the absolute level and the growth rate of imports are critical to this argument. Using data from the United Nations Conference on Trade and Development (UNCTAD), a recent study by the International Labour Office (ILO) examined 347 individual commodity categories of imports into the European Community. The authors concluded that

> 'in more than two thirds of the categories the LDCs [less developed countries] increased their share of imports between 1970 and 1977; in most cases the growth rate of imports from LDCs was greatly in excess of the growth rate of imports from all sources. Nonetheless, it should be stressed that even now the number of products in which the LDCs supply a significant proportion of the developed countries' imports is still quite small. In more than half of the 347 product categories examined, LDCs supplied less than 1 per cent of the European Community's imports, and in nearly 80 per cent of the categories they supplied less than 5 per cent. Only in 10 per cent of the categories did they supply more than 20 per cent of the Community's imports.'[8]

It should be added that by focussing attention on such measurements of economic disruption as import penetration, share of imports or growth of imports, the potential for real adjustment through greater international specialisation is ignored. What if a greater level of imports relative to domestic consumption is accompanied by a rapid development of the domestic industry's penetration of foreign markets in other related product categories? For this reason (as will be argued later in more detail), a preferable measure of performance would be the ratio of net trade to domestic consumption.

Leaving aside the validity of the case for market disruption as a justification for protectionist measures, there remain many other arguments in the arsenal of domestic interests threatened by competitive changes of this nature.[9] For example, those who cite 'social dumping' as a rationale for protection focus attention on the low wages and often poor working conditions prevalent in many developing countries and do not wish to contribute to this form of exploitation.[10]

There is also the issue of subsidisation of exports by many developing countries; and the 'reciprocity' argument, by which access to the industrialised countries' markets will be granted only when, and to the same extent as, the developing countries open their own protected markets to external competition. This last point clearly does not apply to Hong Kong and Singapore, two of the world's most open economies, nor to the really poor countries of the 'Fourth World', and can be subject to a degree of flexibility depending on the level of each developing country.

It is also argued that the industries subject to competition from developing countries are often those least capable of dealing with it in terms of the poor adjustment capacity of their management and labour. The preponderance of small firms employing certain categories of workers — low-skilled, immigrant, female

TABLE 1.3

Exports of Manufactured Goods by 37 Developing Countries[a] (US$)

Value of 1979 exports in current prices and exchange rates	*Annual growth rate of manufactured exports, 1972-78 (in terms of constant 1975 prices)*		
	Less than 6.9%[b]	*6.9-13%*	*Over 13%*[c]
$100 million-$1 billion	Colombia Dominican Rep. Egypt El Salvador Guatemala	Bangladesh Costa Rica Ivory Coast Kenya Turkey	Chile Cyprus Haiti Indonesia Jordan Macau Malta Mauritius Morocco Peru Sri Lanka Tunisia Uruguay
$1-$2 billion	Pakistan	Argentina	Malaysia Philippines Thailand
$3-$6 billion	Yugoslavia[d] Mexico[d]	India Israel	Brazil[d] Singapore[d]
Over $10 billion		Hong Kong[d]	South Korea[d] Taiwan

SOURCE: *OECD Observer*, OECD Secretariat, Paris, November 1982, p. 27.

[a]Countries with over $100 million in exports of manufactures. Not included in the table are: China, Iran, Jamaica, Kuwait, Lebanon, Liberia, Nigeria, Saudi Arabia, Trinidad and Tobago, Venezuela and Vietnam. OECD newly industrialising countries (Greece, Portugal and Spain) are also excluded.

[b]World average for the period.

[c]Average growth rate of non-OECD newly industrialising countries' exports for the period.

[d]Newly industrialising countries.

or older workers — often concentrated in regions characterised by a lack of alternative employment opportunities, raises the private costs of adjustment to very high levels and encourages government intervention in the name of social equity. Thus a strong case can be made for allowing a certain 'breathing space' during which industry can be modernised or, if not possible nor profitable to do so, resources transferred to alternative uses through training, mobility or regional development programmes.

Finally, there is the argument of national security which, although often abused, remains a credible justification in many cases for preserving a proportion of domestic production. Whether protection is the best means to achieve this is another question, since a direct subsidy may yield the same results, perhaps at the same cost, but in a more transparent manner.

The fact remains that the incidence and level of restrictions on the exports of developing countries to the industrialised market-oriented economies have increased in recent years. After the imposition of restrictions on textiles and clothing exports from Hong Kong during the 1950s, quantitative restrictions on footwear imports were imposed by the European Community in 1972 and by the United States five years later. Since then, in addition to the steel and shipbuilding sectors where the crisis measures adopted by most member countries of the OECD apply to all producers indiscriminately, a number of successful developing-country exporters have learned the virtues of restraint in electronic consumer goods, iron and steel manufactures, wood products, processed foods and, more recently, electronic watches from Hong Kong and commuter aircraft from Brazil.

Most of these restrictions have taken the form of 'voluntary' export-restraint agreements — quotas self-imposed by exporting countries under pressure from the threat by the importing country to impose an official tariff or quota — which are difficult to monitor and whose cost is almost impossible to assess. When one considers that most multilateral tariff reductions have been negotiated by and for the benefit of the industrialised countries, the impact of these quantitative restrictions is further aggravated. In these cases, the world does not benefit from the self-control which the threat of effective retaliation imposes upon the way in which industrialised countries manage trade relations among themselves. Protection against developing-country imports can be implemented with relative impunity. Discriminatory behaviour is thus possible and represents an attractive alternative to the discipline of adjustment.

North-South Interdependence

The growing interdependence of world economic relations may be changing this attitude. From 1963 to 1979, OECD exports of manufactures to developing countries rose from 21.9 billion American dollars to $242.7 billion. The fastest rise occurred in the years following the 1974-75 recession when the volume of OECD exports to these countries rose at an annual rate of 21 per cent. This meant that the surplus of trade in manufactured goods for the OECD countries with the developing world increased from $19.1 billion in 1963 to $52.4 billion in 1973 and to $160.1 billion in 1979. When considering only the industrialising countries, the results are equally impressive. While imports of their manufactures by the OECD countries increased dramatically in the same period, the net trade surplus remained positive for the OECD and increased from $4.3 billion in 1963 to $13.8 billion in 1973 and $24.5 billion in 1979. In fact, it may be argued that developing countries in general — and the industrialising countries in particular — provided the only bright spot during the 1970s in terms of their sustained demand for many of the goods produced by the industries of the OECD countries. In doing so, however, they acquired a tremendously high level of foreign indebtedness which, for the developing countries alone (that is, excluding Eastern Europe), had risen from less than $100 billion in 1973 to $640 billion in mid-1982. Debt became their main source of foreign capital during the years of crisis, as the annual flow of foreign direct investment rose slowly from $9 billion in 1973 to $14 billion in 1981 and official development assistance (both bilateral and multilateral) from all sources averaged less than $30 billion a year over the same period.

In 1980 and 1981, the only areas of the world that experienced any significant growth were again the developing countries. Their combined economies grew at an average of 3.1 per cent per annum while the real output of developed countries increased only 0.9 per cent per annum. In 1982, as the rate of growth of OECD countries plummeted to a meagre 0.2 per cent, the Third World expanded at a rate of 3.3 per cent, fuelled by continued borrowing from American, West European and Japanese bankers and provided industrialists in those countries with the only markets for their products which exhibited any growth prospects. In 1980, the developing countries accounted for over 28 per cent of all manufactured exports from the OECD countries. Preliminary figures for 1982 showed this proportion already exceeding 30 per cent of the total. For some countries such as the United States and France, the ratio exceeds 40 per cent.

The Third World's only hope of servicing their accumulated debts and continuing to increase their standard of living is through an expansion of their exports to the developed countries. The Eastern bloc countries do not have the capacity to provide the foreign exchange needed and South-South trade is suffering from the same restrictions that threaten to limit developing-country imports from the North: namely, economic recession and the lack of foreign exchange. But greater trade with the developing countries needs an improved capacity in the developed countries to manage the required adjustments at a minimum social cost. Both private and public agents need to understand more how the adjustment process works and what can be done to facilitate it. Unless this is done, the world is condemned to a reversal of the post-war experience of trade liberalisation and economic growth and risks the collapse of the international financial system. (Over 25 countries rescheduled their external debt in 1982.) As the first signs of economic recovery made their timid appearance in 1983, it became most urgent that discriminatory protectionism should not be allowed to divert governments or countries from the course of renewed growth and prosperity.

Lessons from the Clothing Industry

This essay examines the adjustment experience of eight developed countries in the clothing industry. Since this sector represents the most advanced thrust of the industrial competition offered by the developing countries, any lessons which can be drawn from an experience of over twenty years of decline and adjustment in the clothing industries in the largest OECD countries may have application for other sectors in the future.

Chapter 2 analyses the recent record of the clothing industry in the OECD countries in general, but with particular attention focussed on the employment, output, productivity and trade performance of eight countries in particular: Belgium, France, the Federal Republic of Germany, Italy, the Netherlands and the United Kingdom (representing the West European industry) and Japan and the United States. It concludes that, in spite of the various measures which have been applied to avoid facing the tough consequences of competition from lower-wage countries, a great deal of adjustment has taken and is taking place.

Chapters 3 and 4 examine the history of adjustment from a private and public perspective respectively. In the first instance, the various strategies employed by successful and unsuccessful companies are compared and some conclusions reached as to which seem to be more viable in the long term. Next, the record of public-sector intervention in the eight countries is analysed and related both to the classification scheme presented above in Table 1.1 and to the relative performance of each country's industry. Some generic public strategies for intervention emerge and are evaluated. The final chapter attempts a more prospective view and summarises the main conclusions of the analysis.

This essay complements Geoffrey Shepherd's study of adjustment in the textile industry of developed countries, also in the Thames Essay series, but the reader of both these studies will soon conclude that the two sectors are more dissimilar than similar. The study, therefore, excludes textiles and concentrates only on analysing survival and change — that is, inherent evolution — in what may still be the most 'Darwinesque' of all industries.

NOTES AND REFERENCES

1. *Policies for Adjustment: Some General Orientations* (Paris: OECD Secretariat, 1978).

2. For an analysis of these early attempts at international regulation of industrial adjustment policies and some suggestions for further work in this area, see A.J. Sarna, 'International Guidelines for Industrial Adjustment Policies', *Journal of World Trade Law*, London, November-December 1981, pp. 490-99.

3. For a thorough analysis of the adjustment policies undertaken by most OECD countries, see *Positive Adjustment Policies: Managing Structural Change* (Paris: OECD Secretariat, 1983).

4. A recent example being the ten-fold increase in tariffs on motorcycle imports announced by the Reagan Administration in April 1983.

5. Sarna, *loc cit.*, p. 498.

6. A report by the Sub-group on Transparency at the OECD discusses the practices used by eleven member governments (Australia, Belgium, Canada, France, West Germany, Italy, Japan, the Netherlands, Sweden, the United Kingdom and the United States) to improve the transparency of subsidy schemes. A summary report can be found in George Eads and Edward M. Graham, 'Transparency: a Prerequisite for Positive Adjustment', *OECD Observer*, Paris, November 1982, pp. 8-11.

7. See *Handbook of International Trade and Development Statistics 1979*, UNCTAD Secretariat, Geneva, for 1968 and 1974-75 figures. Current estimates are the author's.

8. Geoffrey Renshaw (ed.), *Employment, Trade and North-South Cooperation* (Geneva: International Labour Office, 1981) p. 40.

9. For a detailed discussion of the pros and cons of these and other arguments for protection with particular application to the textile and clothing sectors, see Gerard Curzon, José de la Torre, Juergen B. Donges, Alasdair I. MacBean, Jean Waelbroeck and Martin Wolf, *MFA Forever? Future of the Arrangement for Trade in Textiles*, International Issues No. 5 (London: Trade Policy Research Centre, 1981).

10. For the main results of these studies, see de la Torre, M.J. Jedel, Jeffrey S. Arpan *et al.*, *Corporate Responses to Import Competition in the US Apparel Industry*, Research Monograph No. 74 (Atlanta, Georgia: Georgia State University, 1978); de la Torre and Michel Bacchetta, 'The Uncommon Market: European Policies towards the Clothing Industry in the 1970s', *Journal of Common Market Studies*, Oxford, December 1980, pp. 95-122; de la Torre, 'Public Intervention Strategies in the European Clothing Industries', *Journal of World Trade Law*, March-April 1981, pp. 124-48; *Textile and Clothing Industries: Structural Problems and Policies in OECD Countries* (Paris: OECD Secretariat, 1983); and Arpan, de la Torre and Brian Toyne, *The US Apparel Industry: International Challenge — Domestic Response*, Research Monograph No. 88 (Atlanta, Georgia: Georgia State University, 1982).

CHAPTER TWO

Causes and Symptoms of Decline in the Clothing Industry

THE MOST commonly used measures of industrial performance — growth, employment, balance of trade, investment, price stability, profitability *et cetera* — when applied to the clothing sector of most OECD countries, invariably show a record of marked decline in recent years. This record is not uniform. It varies widely from country to country, among branches and firms and from period to period. Nevertheless, the aggregate measures are indeed sobering.

Between 1973 and 1980, the OECD countries suffered a loss of over 500,000 jobs in the clothing industry alone, in addition to losses of approximately one million in the various textile and fibre sectors. In some countries such losses represented nearly 1 per cent of the total civilian labour force. When compared with the rate of unemployment in the OECD countries during the same period, the loss of jobs in the textile and clothing industries taken together was equivalent to nearly 25 per cent of the net increase in unemployment in the region. Parallel to these developments, production declined or remained stagnant in most industrial countries. Whatever growth there was, was typically absorbed by higher levels of imports. As a result, the OECD's trade balance in clothing with the rest of the world deteriorated from a modest deficit of 900 million American dollars in 1970 to over $12.5 billion in 1979 and $15.1 billion in 1980.

These competitive pressures and the serious economic conditions prevailing during the last decade resulted in the net disappearance of over 2,500 clothing firms in the European Community and nearly 3,200 in the United States.

It is difficult to relate these events to each other in a tight causal chain, particularly as the level and extent of government intervention in the industry often prevented competitive forces from having their full impact on the market. This chapter first tries to isolate the main forces which have significantly altered the competitive environment for this industry during recent years. It then traces in more detail the evolution of production, employment and trade performance for the eight countries under study.

Pressures for Adjustment

Factors pressurising the clothing industries of the developed countries to adjust are many and varied. They range from the depressive effects of the low growth of demand to the dynamic stimulus of changes in materials, distribution and technology. They also include a factor which is both cause and consequence: the large increase in the proportion of the industry's activity that is subject to international competition among both developed and developing countries.

Low Growth of Demand

None of these factors had perhaps such a widespread influence on the industry as the stagnant demand conditions that have prevailed since the early 1970s. Changes in technology, input costs, import penetration and other factors have been exacerbated by the low level of growth in demand which made it difficult for firms in the industry to adjust to changing conditions. Unable to shift easily to expanding product sectors or to absorb increases in productivity through higher output, firms found their margins dwindling and were forced to shed labour as the only feasible short-term response open for survival.

There are several contributing factors to this low level of demand growth. First, the rate of increase in population in the major OECD countries has decreased considerably in the era since World War II. With the possible exception of the United States, still in the throes of the baby boom which began in the early 1950s, rates of population growth elsewhere in the industrialised world rarely exceeded 1 per cent per annum. Second, income elasticity of demand for clothing, considered to be a basic necessity, is normally estimated to be less than unity and, what is perhaps more important, it decreases with a rise in the absolute level of income. These two factors would support the argument that the rate of growth of consumption in the developing world, where population growth is much higher (two to three times that of the OECD area) and income levels lower, should exceed that of the industrialised countries and, *ceteris paribus*, result in a major shift of the share of worldwide production to the former areas. Finally, the cyclical economic conditions prevailing since 1974 have also had a major impact on disposable income and, therefore, on consumer expenditures on clothing.[1]

Table 2.1 provides data on the share of private consumption in each country that was spent on clothing and shoes. The weighted average for all eight countries dropped from 10.8 per cent in 1963 to 8.7 per cent in 1970 and to 8.1 per cent in 1980. The decline in relative expenditures for clothing was fairly general up to the end of 1973, after which it stabilised in most countries and increased slightly in Italy, the United Kingdom and the United States. It should be borne in mind that these figures are in constant prices (generally 1970 levels). Since the relative prices of clothing decreased considerably throughout the period, a similar comparison

TABLE 2.1

Consumers' Expenditure on Clothing[a] as a Percentage of Total Private Consumption (1970 prices)

	Belgium	France	West Germany[b]	Italy	Netherlands[b]	United Kingdom	United States	Japan
1963[c]	9.7	12.1	12.4	9.8	15.4	9.7	9.0	13.2
1970	7.4	10.0	11.3	9.2	10.5	8.7	8.1	10.2
1973	7.6	na	11.0	9.1	9.8	8.6	7.8	9.4
1974	7.7	8.2	10.9	9.2	9.1	8.9	8.1	9.0
1975	7.8	8.0	10.8	8.5	9.0	9.1	8.2	9.1
1976	7.5	7.4	na	8.9	8.9	8.6	8.1	9.1
1977	6.9	7.3	9.6	9.1	8.7	8.4	8.1	7.9
1978	6.6	7.1	9.4	9.0	8.7	8.6	8.3	7.7
1979	6.7	6.9	9.1	9.2	8.6	8.7	8.5	7.4
1980	6.8	6.6	9.1	9.5	na	8.9	na	7.2
Index of total consumption								
1970/1963[c]	119	127	137	139	132	118	170	151
1980/1970	144	117	119	132	106	134	148	137

SOURCES: *Textile Industry in OECD Countries*, OECD Secretariat, Paris, various issues; and *National Accounts of OECD Countries*, OECD Secretariat, Paris, various issues.

NOTE: In the table 'na' signifies 'not available'.

[a]Includes shoes. [b]Includes household textile products. [c]Based on 1963 price levels.

of patterns of consumption based on current prices would show a much greater drop in the average share of the household budget allocated to clothing. The last two rows of the table show the growth in total consumption for the two periods immediately preceding and following 1970. Only in the cases of Belgium and the United Kingdom was there a faster rate of growth of consumption in the 1970s than in the 1960s. Consumption growth dropped to nearly 1 per cent per annum after 1973 in the European Community as a whole, although it recovered slightly after 1979 to a more sustained pace of nearly 2 per cent per annum. The United States and Japan, however, while exhibiting annual growth rates of consumption in the 1970s which were half of those seen in the 1960s (4.0 per cent and 3.2 per cent, respectively, versus 7.9 per cent and 6.1 per cent), are still ahead of most West European countries in this respect.

Growth of Synthetic Materials

Changes in materials and in relative material prices also had a considerable effect on the industry. The growth and popularity of synthetic and other man-made fibres during the 1960s gave the clothing industries of developed countries a period of competitive advantage. This is not surprising, as most production of synthetic fibre and fabrics was centred in these countries and provided clothing manufacturers with easier access to fashion-oriented and competitive materials. By the early 1970s, however, as the fibre industry matured and spread worldwide in pursuit of fast-growing markets elsewhere, this advantage had disappeared.

Man-made fibres had captured over 50 per cent of the world's consumption of textile fibres by 1979, with synthetic fibre accounting for nearly three quarters of this. Clothing manufacturers, who represent approximately half of the fibre consumption in the OECD, also benefited from the considerable drop in the relative prices of man-made fibres induced by the high level of innovation in production and processing which was characteristic of the chemical industry during the 1960s and early 1970s. Polyester prices, for example, were lower in absolute terms in 1978 than they were in 1968. Price and income effects on demand were thus significant during this period.

The shift of the clothing industry to synthetic fibres had other direct and often contradictory effects on competitiveness. Lower material prices, for example, emphasised the role of other inputs in the total cost structure. Thus, differentials in the cost of labour would appear to gain in importance as a component of competitiveness. In addition, process innovations, particularly in knitting, increased the capital intensity and productivity of sectors of the industry to the point where the labour content was reduced to a very small part of the costs of production. On this basis, for example, the American industry made massive investments in the production of double-knit polyester in the early 1970s and hailed it as *the* response to the threat of foreign competition. Consumer resistance limited the success of such a strategy, however, and as synthetic fibres approached commodity status, any temporary advantages thus gained tended to diminish.

Composition of Demand and Distribution

The industry was also affected by a significant shift in the composition of demand for clothing. The remarkable growth of casual wear at the expense of traditional suits and dresses has imposed diverse requirements on the industry. The increase in market segmentation which resulted had implications for manufacturing flexibility, distribution, product range *et cetera*, all of which facilitated the survival of specialised small firms. On the other hand, the explosion of demand for denims and corduroy fabrics and the return to popularity of natural fibres in recent years have reversed some of these trends. It is interesting to note that simpler and more casual garments require less construction time and, therefore, lower labour input per unit. The resulting lower unit costs, as compared with traditional garments, have contributed both to the drop in relative prices and to the large increases in productivity shown by certain countries.

Changing fashion and consumer tastes in clothing also influenced a process, already under way in several countries since the 1950s, which helped to accelerate international competition in the industry. The importance of large chain and discount stores, with centralised buying departments that have the capability to scan the world for the best products and prices, rose significantly first in the United States and then in Western Europe. By the mid-1970s, national or regional stores accounted for 63 per cent of clothing retail sales in the United States. Similarly, the six largest retail organisations in the Netherlands controlled 52 per cent of clothing sales in that country in 1974. In the United Kingdom (where the influence of Marks & Spencer on behalf of the industry has been widely noted) and in the Federal Republic of Germany, similar levels of concentration have developed. As the trend spread elsewhere, the relative bargaining power of clothing manufacturers, caught between large suppliers and retailers, diminished significantly. The impact of this phenomenon, however, has to be differentiated according to product groups. For example, while chain and discount stores handled 34 and 17 per cent, respectively, of boy's clothing sales in the United States in 1977 (versus 19 per cent and 12 per cent for all clothing sales), small speciality stores were responsible for 35 per cent of women's and 37 per cent of men's clothing sales (versus 27 per cent overall). Again, the scope for segmentation and differentiated service strategies varied enormously between product groups, according to these trends. The growth of branded ('designer') clothing and 'boutique' chains has shaped the industry's structure significantly.

Potential for Technological Advance

Technology, of course, has also been of great importance in shaping potential response strategies. While technological progress has been slow in the textile industry relative to other sectors of a modern economy, the scope for innovation and improvements in the processing of clothing is limited. Production processes in the industry consist essentially of grading and cutting cloth, assembly, sewing the finished garment and pressing. Significant progress has been made in computerised marker and grading systems and in automated cutters, but total investment (see Chapter 3) in these machines is relatively high for the average clothing manufacturer. The sewing machine itself has also been improved considerably over the last twenty years, but, given that the average operator spends no more than 15-20 per cent of his or her time in actual machine operations, the actual impact of machine improvements on labour costs is small. Handling time has been, of course, the subject of countless studies and breakthroughs, such as the automated pocket-maker, have occasionally resulted. Currently, substantial effort is being spent, particularly by Japanese textile machinery companies, to devise flexible manufacturing systems for the industry based on existing robot technology plus advanced pattern-recognition systems. If they succeed — and the expectation is that these developments will take at least ten more years to bear fruit — a major revolution may once more alter the nature of the industry.

The advantage of such systems for the high-wage countries of the OECD lies mainly in their potential for reducing labour-cost disparities between the developed and the developing world. Yet, changes in wages and exchange rates have also had a major impact on labour costs per unit among OECD countries. Table 2.2 provides a comparison of labour costs per unit for the eight countries in the study and three others for the period 1970-80. (Specific comparisons for the clothing

TABLE 2.2

Changes in Labour Compensation, Productivity and Unit Labour Costs for All Manufacturing, 1970-80
(1970 = 100)

	Hourly compensation in local currency	*Output per man-hour*	*Exchange rate (versus $)*	*Unit labour costs (US$)*	
				Index	*Annual change (%)*
Belgium	357	193	170	314	12.1
Canada	276	132	89	187	6.5
Denmark	377	176	133	286	11.1
France	397	159	131	326	12.6
West Germany	280	160	201	352	13.4
Italy	625	162	73	283	10.9
Japan	357	202	159	281	10.9
Netherlands	324	184	182	321	12.4
Sweden	346	138	123	307	11.9
United Kingdom	532	133	97	388	14.5
United States	228	128	100	178	5.9

SOURCE: Bureau of Labor Statistics, United States Department of Labor, Washington.

industry are given in the next chapter.) Since labour costs represent between 25 and 30 per cent of factory prices for most countries,[2] sustained differences in wage rates and labour costs per unit can be absorbed only by significant losses of market share or profitability.

Table 2.3 presents selected data on average manufacturing wage rates for various countries, both developed and developing. Since inter-industry wage rates are subject to less variation nationally than

TABLE 2.3

Average Levels of Hourly Compensation in Manufacturing Industry (US$)

	1975	*1977*	*1980*
Western Europe			
Belgium	6.34	8.40	13.18
Sweden	7.14	8.82	12.60
Netherlands	6.49	8.21	12.18
West Germany	6.10	7.73	11.94
Switzerland	6.07	na	11.09
Norway	6.78	na	10.85
France	4.45	5.40	9.46
Italy	4.67	5.47	9.01
Finland	4.70	na	8.25
Austria	4.33	na	7.90
United Kingdom	2.88	3.34	7.07
Ireland	2.65	na	6.38
Spain	2.33	2.62	5.96
Greece	1.39	1.90	3.12
Portugal	1.46	1.60	1.68
Turkey	0.70	na	na
Other industrial countries			
United States	6.18	7.60	9.92
Canada	6.05	7.43	8.53
Japan	3.23	3.97	5.88
Developing countries			*1979*
Mexico	2.02	1.82	2.31
Brazil	1.14	1.40	1.80
Hong Kong	0.74	1.05	1.25
Singapore	0.77	0.85	1.23
South Korea	0.37	0.64	1.14
Taiwan	0.55	0.75	1.01
Egypt	na	0.37	na
Sri Lanka	na	0.12	0.15

SOURCE: Bureau of Labor Statistics, United States Department of Labor, Washington.
NOTE: In the table 'na' signifies 'not available'.

international productivity rates, it becomes clear that any industrial sector in the North must maintain a ratio of productivity advantage to its Southern competitor which approaches the inverse of the wage-ratio disadvantage. In plain language, the North, to remain cost-competitive, must produce the same amount of clothing as the South using considerably fewer workers. It is obvious that while such an advantage in output per man-hour is readily obtainable in technology-intensive and/or capital-intensive industries, it is much more difficult to achieve in sectors characterised by standardised, readily available technology, where unsophisticated labour skills account for a considerable proportion of input costs. The persistent wage escalation in the developed countries, occurring simultaneously with the loss of relative productivity advantages in industries such as textiles and clothing, is one of the major causes of the adjustment problem.[3]

Growth of International Trade

The last major force for change — in itself both a contributing factor as well as the result of the other variables discussed above — has been the significant growth in the volume and geographic diversity of trade in textiles and clothing products since the early 1960s. There are a number of aspects of this phenomenon that deserve special attention.

The rate of growth of trade in textile products has outpaced the growth in world production. Table 2.4 shows that, since 1963, the volume of world trade in textiles and clothing has increased by nearly 300 per cent while worldwide production has risen by only 79 per cent. An interesting comparison is offered by the ratio of the two indices. The relative trade intensity (the ratio of the export to total production indices as shown by X/P in Table 2.4) of all manufactures is now one and a half times what it was in 1963, the result of the rapid internationalisation of economic activity which characterised this period. For textiles and clothing, however, this ratio has more than doubled since 1963, to the point where they represent 8.9 per cent (10.8 per cent if fibres are included) of world manufactured exports in 1979. For clothing alone, the progression has been even faster: from 1.6 per cent of world manufactured exports in 1955 to 2.7 per cent in 1963 and 3.7 per cent in 1979. This rapid increase in the proportion of world

TABLE 2.4

World Production and Trade in Textiles and Clothing[a]
(1963 = 100)

	1970	*1973*	*1979*
All manufactures			
Production (P)	159	197	250
Exports (X)	204	280	387
X/P	1.28	1.42	1.55
Textiles and clothing			
Production (P)	133	155	179
Exports (X)	200	280	398
X/P	1.50	1.81	2.22

SOURCE: *Textile and Clothing Industries: Structural Problems and Policies in OECD Countries* (Paris: OECD Secretariat, 1983) Table 17.

[a]All figures are in volume; that is, current dollar values deflated by price/unit value indices.

textile markets open to international competition has accelerated the adjustment required of firms in all countries and segments of the industry.

A more detailed view of these trade flows can be seen in Table 2.5. While the overall acceleration in the rate of growth shown in the last line is partly due to the rise in prices over the period,[4] a great deal of variation exists among the growth rates that characterised trade flows in different product classes and among different groups

TABLE 2.5

Major Export Flows in Textile Products, 1955-70

Products and areas[a]	Total trade (US$ billion)				Annual rate of growth (%)		
	1955	*1963*	*1970*	*1979*	*1955-63*	*1963-70*	*1970-79*
Fibres (SITC 26)							
Industrial to industrial	1.23	1.54	1.46	5.15	-2.9	-0.8	15.0
Industrial to developing	0.17	0.33	0.50	2.00	8.6	6.1	16.6
Developing to industrial	1.59	1.49	1.25	2.80	-0.8	-2.5	9.4
World	5.27	6.11	6.08	17.90	1.9	-0.1	12.8
Textiles (SITC 65)							
Industrial to industrial	1.77	3.47	6.67	25.50	8.8	9.8	16.1
Industrial to ETA	0.05	0.11	0.39	1.70	10.4	19.8	17.8
Industrial to developing	1.50	1.33	2.00	7.80	-1.5	6.0	16.3

Developing to industrial	0.21	0.53	0.82	4.30	12.3	6.4	20.2
Developing to developing	0.38	0.43	0.76	3.85	1.6	8.5	19.8
Developing to ETA	0.01	0.07	0.22	0.50	27.5	17.8	9.6
World	4.70	7.03	12.43	48.80	5.1	8.5	16.4
Clothing (SITC 84)							
Industrial to industrial	0.37	1.18	3.40	15.40	15.6	16.3	18.3
Industrial to developing	0.16	0.27	0.36	1.60	6.8	4.2	18.0
Developing to industrial	0.04	0.21	1.13	10.90	23.0	27.2	28.6
Developing to developing	0.04	0.08	0.18	1.45	9.1	12.3	26.1
ETA to ETA	0.14	0.35	0.64	2.30	12.1	9.0	14.7
World	0.80	2.21	6.22	34.90	13.5	15.9	21.1
World total	10.79	15.35	24.73	101.60	4.5	7.1	17.0

SOURCE: *Textile and Clothing Industries: Structural Problems and Policies in OECD Countries* (Paris: OECD Secretariat, 1983) Table 18.

[a]Areas are defined as follows: 'industrial' includes all OECD member countries except Australia and New Zealand; 'ETA' is the Eastern trading area, including all centrally-planned economies except Yugoslavia; and 'developing' accounts for all other countries except South Africa. World totals, however, include these three countries.

of countries. For example, trade flows in fibres have generally lagged behind those of textiles and clothing, particularly prior to 1970. In textiles, developed-country exports as a whole grew at a rapid pace, although mainly directed to each other. Since 1970, however, after fifteen years of stagnation, textile exports from developed to developing countries accelerated dramatically. In the clothing sector, developed-country exports to each other maintained a fairly rapid rate of growth for the twenty five year period (1955-79 inclusively) and still accounted for nearly 45 per cent of total exports in 1979. The fastest growth, however, had been that of developing-country sales to industrial markets, which grew from practically nothing in 1955 to nearly 11 billion American dollars (one third of world trade in clothing) by 1979.

The results of these dramatic changes in the sources and commodity composition of international trade in textile and clothing products can be judged from the figures in Table 2.6. For the OECD countries as a whole, net trade in clothing passed from a balanced position in 1963 to a small deficit in 1970. From this point, a rapid loss of competitiveness — particularly related to non-OECD producers — caused the balance to deteriorate at a rate in excess of 20 per cent per annum, reaching a level of $15.1 billion in 1980. The situation in other textile products (fibres and textiles), on the other hand, improved during this period. Starting from a small deficit of $0.5 billion in 1963, the balance-of-trade deficit had been practically eliminated by 1970 and the balance of trade continued to improve until the end of 1980. Altogether, however, the surplus in textiles and fibres did not cover more than a quarter of the deficit in clothing in 1980 and this proportion had been even lower in previous years. When compared with a total value added in both textiles and clothing of $140 billion for all OECD countries, though, the 1980 trade

Table 2.6

OECD Trade in Clothing and Other Textile Products,[a] 1963-80 (US$ billion and per cent)

	Clothing (SITC 84)						*Other textile products (SITC 26 and 65)*					
	Total trade			*Trade with non-OECD countries*			*Total trade*			*Trade with non-OECD countries*		
	Exp.	*Imp.*	*Bal.*	*Exp.*	*Imp.*	*Bal.*	*Exp.*	*Imp.*	*Bal.*	*Exp.*	*Imp.*	*Bal.*
1963	1.4	1.4	0.0	0.3	0.3	0.0	8.7	9.1	-0.5	2.3	2.6	-0.4
1970	3.9	4.8	-0.9	0.6	1.4	-0.8	11.7	11.8	-0.1	3.8	3.8	0.0
1973	6.8	10.3	-3.5	0.8	4.2	-3.4	21.5	22.6	1.1	6.1	5.8	0.3
1975	8.8	14.2	-5.4	1.1	6.3	-5.2	25.0	23.3	1.7	7.9	5.7	2.2
1977	11.7	20.0	-8.3	1.6	9.6	-8.0	32.1	30.0	2.1	10.2	8.2	2.0
1979	17.2	31.0	-12.8	2.0	15.1	-13.1	45.2	43.9	1.3	13.0	11.5	1.5
1980	19.6	34.7	-15.1	2.7	17.0	-14.3	50.3	46.2	4.2	16.6	12.2	4.4
Annual rate of change (%)												
1963-70	15.8	19.2	...	10.4	24.6	...	4.3	3.8	...	7.4	5.6	...
1970-80	17.5	21.8	...	16.2	28.4	...	15.7	14.6	...	15.8	12.4	...

Source: *Statistics of Foreign Trade: Series C, Trade by Commodities*, OECD Secretariat, Paris, various issues.

Note: In the table '...' signifies 'not significant'.

[a]Discrepancies in this and other trade tables arise from the usual practice of accounting for exports on a f.o.b. basis and imports on a c.i.f. basis.

deficit of $11 billion appears a more moderate proportion.

This general picture is somewhat misleading since the actual trade profile varies enormously among the OECD countries. Seven countries — Austria, Canada, Denmark, Ireland, Norway, Sweden and the United Kingdom — run large deficits in both clothing and textile products. Belgium, the Federal Republic of Germany, Japan, the Netherlands, Switzerland and the United States appear to be closer to the OECD mean, since they partially offset large deficits in clothing with a positive if smaller trade balance in fibres and textiles. Finland has a positive balance in its clothing trade but is negative in textiles, while France nearly has a balanced position overall. New Zealand and Australia have strong surpluses in fibres but a negative trade balance in other products. Finally, Greece, Italy, Portugal, Spain and Turkey show positive balances in both clothing and textile products. In fact, West Germany, Italy and France are three of the world's largest exporters of textiles and clothing, Italy being the world's largest *net* exporter with a surplus in 1980 of $5.7 billion versus $4.2 billion for South Korea, the second largest (see Table 2.7). On the other hand, the deficit in clothing of the United States and West Germany alone amounted to $11.2 billion in 1980.

In summary, the major trends that can be discerned from the analysis of trade figures over the last decade are

(a) a very rapid rate of internationalisation of production in textile products, but particularly in clothing;

(b) a continuing, if lessening, dominance of trade among developed countries over that among developing countries across all product categories;

(c) a recent and rapid increase in clothing imports and textile exports with respect to the developing countries;

TABLE 2.7

Largest World Exporters of Textiles and Clothing, 1979
(US$ billion)

Rank	*Textiles and clothing*				*Clothing*			
	Total gross exports		*Net exports*		*Gross exports*		*Net exports*	
1	West Germany	8.6	Italy	5.4	Italy	4.4	Italy	3.8
2	Italy	8.5	South Korea	4.2	Hong Kong	4.2	Hong Kong	3.8
3	Hong Kong	5.5	Taiwan	3.3	South Korea	2.9	South Korea	2.9
4	France	5.2	Hong Kong	2.8	West Germany	2.6	Taiwan	2.0
5	South Korea	4.7	India	1.2	France	2.0	Portugal	0.5
6	United Kingdom	4.4	Portugal	0.8	Taiwan	2.0	India	0.4
7	Japan	4.4	Brazil	0.6	United Kingdom	1.6	Finland	0.4
8	United States	4.2	Pakistan	0.6	United States	1.0	Macao	0.3
9	Belgium/Luxembourg	4.1	Spain	0.5	Belgium/Luxembourg	0.9	Yugoslavia	0.3
10	Taiwan	3.5	Japan	0.4	Netherlands	0.8	Singapore	0.3
11	Netherlands	3.0	Greece	0.4	Finland	0.6	Greece	0.3
12	Switzerland	1.7	Thailand	0.4	Austria	0.5	Spain	0.2
13	Austria	1.5	Belgium/Luxembourg	0.4	Portugal	0.5	Philippines	0.2
14	India	1.2	Turkey	0.4	Singapore	0.4	Tunisia	0.2
15	Portugal	1.0	Egypt	0.2	Japan	0.3	Thailand	0.2

SOURCE: Martin Wolf, Hans Hinrich Glismann, Joseph Pelzman and Dean Spinanger, *Costs of Protecting Jobs in Textiles and Clothing*, Thames Essay No. 37 (London: Trade Policy Research Centre, 1984) Tables 3.9 and 3.10.

(d) a large rise in the overall trade deficit in clothing for the whole of the OECD; and

(e) a very mixed picture in terms of the relative position each developed country has achieved in this period of growing international specialisation.

Decline and Adjustment

The economic and competitive forces affecting the industry have been virtually identical in all developed countries. Yet their impact on each country's industry has differed to varying degrees. This section discusses the record of decline and adjustment for all eight countries in the survey. It covers output, employment and trade performance for their respective clothing sectors and deals with the issue of relative cost competitiveness. Finally, an attempt is made to ascribe approximate shares of employment losses to each of the major forces discussed below.

Shifting Patterns of International Output

With the sole exception of the Netherlands, the countries under study experienced modest growth in clothing production up to the end of 1973. In certain countries — notably Belgium, Italy and Japan — the rate of growth was substantial during this period, as shown in Table 2.8. The French, American, West German and British industries also exhibited some growth prior to 1973, although, in the last two cases, annual increases in production were insufficient to maintain a significant level of growth in employment. In all countries, the 1973-74 crisis hit the clothing industry very hard, highlighting weaknesses and accelerating the tendency towards contraction or consolidation already evident in most countries since the early 1970s.

Output actually declined in real terms in all countries in the post-1973 period, except in Italy and the United

States. The Netherlands suffered the most dramatic contraction of any clothing industry in the European Community. Real output dropped 33 per cent in only four years, which brought the industry to a level of activity which was less than half that of 1963. Elsewhere, the Belgian, West German and Japanese industries also experienced a decline of nearly 10 per cent in the first three years after 1974, while the French, Italian and American industries, for different reasons discussed below, appeared to have been relatively more successful in retaining the level of domestic output they had achieved by 1973. In general terms, the 1973-80 period saw the level of annual production of clothing in the European Community fall by nearly 10 per cent by 1980. By contrast, production in North America increased by about 7 per cent in the same period, while dropping 15 per cent in Japan. Preliminary figures for 1980-82 showed a continuation, even a deterioration, of these trends.

While most of the industrialised world reeled from the effects of world recession, production in the centrally-planned economies of Eastern Europe and in the developing countries continued to advance, albeit at a slower pace, during this period. As Table 2.9 shows, the Eastern bloc countries exhibited a rate of growth in clothing production of 5.2 per cent per annum for 1973-80, while the developing countries — particularly in East Asia — saw their output of clothing rise at over 3.5 per cent annually. As a result, the share of world production of the industrial nations dropped from 70 per cent in 1963 to 52 per cent in 1980.

Employment: the Politically Visible Factor

Employment, however, was the real issue behind public interest in the industry after 1973. Table 2.10 summarises the evolution of employment in the clothing industry for the eight countries from 1963 to 1980. Before 1973, the

Table 2.8

Production Indices for Clothing and All Manufacturing in Selected Countries, 1963-82

	1963	1970	1973	1975	1977	1979	1980	1981	1982	Annual growth rate (%) 1963-73	1973-80	1980-82[a]
Belgium												
Clothing	51	180	100	103	93	93	90	87	91[a]	7.0	-1.5	0.6
All manufacturing	59	85	100	94	102	111	108	106	106[a]	5.4	1.1	-0.9
France												
Clothing	74	95	100	101	104	98	95	91	na	3.1	-0.7	na
All manufacturing	56	83	100	94	105	112	111	107	105	6.0	1.5	-2.7
West Germany												
Clothing	79	100	100	94	90	87	83	77	70	2.4	-2.6	-8.2
All manufacturing	60	89	100	92	103	109	109	107	104	5.2	1.2	-2.3
Italy												
Clothing	56[b]	93	100	107	112	111	110	102	100[a]	8.6[b]	1.4	-4.7
All manufacturing	59	88	100	85	107	116	122	119	118	5.4	2.9	-1.7

Netherlands												
Clothing	136	122	100	87	67	66	65	57	55[a]	-3.0	-6.0	-8.0
All manufacturing	56	88	100	97	104	111	113	112	111	6.0	1.8	-0.9
United Kingdom												
Clothing	87	88	100	99	102	109	95	86	84	1.4	-0.7	-6.0
All manufacturing	72	91	100	93	95	96	88	82	82	3.3	-1.8	-3.5
United States												
Clothing	78	86	100	91	106	111	107	102	na	2.5	1.0	na
All manufacturing	58	82	100	89	107	118	113	115	106	5.6	1.8	-3.1
Japan												
Clothing	51	88	100	86	93	92	86	85	84[a]	7.0	-2.1	-1.2
All manufacturing	31	78	100	85	98	113	121	125	127	12.4	2.8	2.4

SOURCES: Wilhelm Kurth, 'Textiles and Clothing: a National and International Issue', paper presented at the International Symposium on Industrial Policies for the Eighties, organised by the Spanish Ministry of Industry and Energy and the OECD, in Madrid, 5-9 May 1980; Indicators of Industrial Activity, OECD Secretariat, Paris, various issues; José de la Torre, 'Public Intervention Strategies in the European Clothing Industries', *Journal of World Trade Law*, March-April 1981; and national sources.

NOTE: In the table 'na' signifies 'not available'.

[a]Figures correspond to an average for the first three quarters of the year.

[b]1966 and 1966-73.

TABLE 2.9

Worldwide Production[a] and Employment in the Clothing Industry, 1963-78/80
(per cent)

	Annual growth rate				Share in world					
	Production		Employment		Production		Employment		Population	
	1963-73	*1973-80*	*1963-73*	*1973-78*	*1963*	*1980*	*1963*	*1978*	*1963*	*1978*
Developed market-oriented economies[b]	2.1	0.0	1.1	−1.2	70.2	52.3	50.8	40.7	28.9	25.5
OECD Europe	2.2	−0.6	1.1	−1.4	24.7	17.9	24.6	19.8	15.0	12.9
European Community	1.6	−1.4	0.0	−3.1	22.1	14.4	21.3	13.6	9.8	8.1
North America	1.6	0.9	0.3	−2.3	42.6	31.8	21.3	14.8	8.5	7.5
Japan	6.9	−1.3	3.7	1.4	2.1	2.6	3.5	2.8	3.9	3.6

Centrally-planned economies[c]	6.7	5.2	2.9	0.8	24.7	41.0	37.7	39.5	13.3	11.5
Developing countries	5.8	3.5	4.4	8.4	5.1	6.7	11.5	19.8	57.8	63.0
Asia	4.8	3.9	4.2	9.8	2.1	2.8	4.9	9.9	36.9	39.6
World total	4.0	2.2	2.9	3.1	100.0	100.0	100.0	100.0	100.0	100.0
Textiles	4.9	1.6	1.4	0.7						
All manufacturing	7.2	3.3	1.9	2.0						

SOURCE: *Textiles and Clothing Industries: Structural Problems and Policies in OECD Countries* (Paris: OECD Secretariat, 1983) Tables 1-4.

[a]Production is measured as value added in constant prices. Annual growth rates include the footwear and leather industry. World share figures exclude China, for which data were not available.

[b]OECD countries plus South Africa and Israel.

[c]Eastern Europe and the Soviet Union.

TABLE 2.10

Total Employment in the Clothing Industry for Selected Countries, 1963-80[a]
(thousands)

	Belgium	France	West Germany	Italy	Netherlands	United Kingdom	European Community (9)	United States	Japan
1963	53.0	289		145[b]		443	—	1,131	275
1970	60.5	322	381	207	58.5	377	1,442	1,164	326
1973	66.3	323	356	213	40.8	326	1,360	1,213	398
1974	63.7	306	305	210	35.9	322	1,273	1,155	394
1975	59.5	287	286	212	27.1	306	1,206	1,065	427
1976	55.0	288	279	206	26.1	306	1,187	1,117	439
1977	48.7	278	265	196	22.8	305	1,145	1,106	436
1978	46.1	271	260	181	21.3	288	1,096	1,139	416
1979	42.3	273	257	177	20.1	291	1,088	1,118	396
1980	39.5	251	249	171	18.1	257	1,012	1,075	392

Net change (%)									
1963-73	25.1	11.8	- 6.8	46.9[b]	- 40.6	- 26.4	—	2.9	44.7
1973-80	- 40.4	- 22.3	- 30.1	- 19.7	- 55.6	- 21.2	- 25.6	- 11.4	- 1.5

SOURCES: Wilhelm Kurth, 'Textiles and Clothing: a National and International Issue', paper presented at the International Symposium on Industrial Policies for the Eighties, organised by the Spanish Ministry of Industry and Energy and the OECD, in Madrid, 5-9 May 1980; *Indicators of Industrial Activity*, OECD Secretariat, Paris, various issues; and José de la Torre, 'Public Intervention Strategies in the European Clothing Industries', *Journal of World Trade Law*, London, March-April 1981.

NOTE: In the table '—' signifies 'not applicable'.

[a]Most data represent annual averages except for France and Japan (December figures), West Germany (September) and the United Kingdom (June for 1963-70 and then October).

[b]1966 and 1966-73.

relatively fast growth rates of output in Belgium, Italy and Japan were well ahead of any productivity gains, thus expanding employment opportunities in the industry. In two of these cases, a major contributing cause to the rapid expansion of the sector was foreign investment by clothing firms with headquarters in the Netherlands and West Germany, which sought lower-cost manufacturing locations within the European Community. Attracted by lower wage rates and substantial regional incentives, plus the existence of cultural and linguistic affinity in the case of Dutch investments in Flanders, Dutch and West German manufacturers responded to the tight labour markets at home in the 1960s by redeploying a portion of their manufacturing operations 'southwards'. This explains in part the rapid decline of employment in West Germany and the Netherlands in the early period and the resulting large increase in productivity which accompanied the process of rationalisation under way in both countries' industries since the mid-1960s. This southward deployment also occurred within the United States where the share of industry employment in the north-eastern and mid-Atlantic states declined from over 60 per cent in the early 1960s to 42 per cent by 1976.

In the United Kingdom, however, no such displacement through investment in manufacture abroad took place. The low growth of domestic demand and relatively high productivity gains, together with significant increases in import penetration, contributed to the British clothing industry losing 26 per cent of its jobs in the decade between 1963 and 1973.

After 1973, the situation in all countries took a dramatic turn for the worse. Employment in Belgium, the Federal Republic of Germany and the Netherlands — the three countries most seriously affected — dropped by 157,000 workers, or just over a third of their combined 1973 employment level. The impact on people and, therefore, on the political system, however, was not comparable. In the Netherlands, these losses came at the end of a long process of winding down the clothing industry which had its roots in the rapid industrialisation of the country throughout the 1950s and 1960s. The capital-intensive or high-technology sectors, which were responsible for this transformation, had provoked large wage increases since 1964 to which labour-intensive industries such as clothing and textiles had had difficulty in adjusting.

Those that survived, whether by moving production to lower-cost areas or by shifting to less price-sensitive product lines, were soon to face additional challenges. Some of the large textile firms, led by Nijverdal ten Cate, grew rapidly through internal growth and mergers so that, by 1974, the four largest firms accounted for approximately 75 per cent of Dutch textile production. 'Downstream' (that is, further along the manufacturing and trading process) retailers also experienced a rush of mergers. By 1974, the six largest (four central buying organisations and two specialised chain stores) controlled 52 per cent of the retail clothing market. These large retailers triggered an internationalisation of price competition between their suppliers which turned out to be disastrous for the Dutch clothing industry. Squeezed between these powerful oligopolies, the fragmented clothing manufacturers had difficulty in adapting rapidly to the new competitive conditions and lost a third of their employees within three years, from 1970 to 1973. On the eve of the world recession of 1973-74, the Dutch clothing industry was already weak and ailing. The stagnation that followed was the last straw and, during the next three years (1973-76), the industry lost a further 34 per cent of its employees. Fortunately, throughout most of this period, alternative jobs existed for female workers in the still-growing electronics and chemical industries. Employment in these sectors appeared considerably more secure; the clothing industry was so discredited that, 'even in regions with a high unemployment rate, the Dutch clothing industry has been forced to attract foreign workers'.[5]

The clothing and textile industries in West Germany also suffered a major contraction after 1973 which greatly surpassed in intensity the gradual process under way since 1963. For the period 1973-76, however, the number of workers registered as unemployed from these two sectors remained relatively low, rising from 13,000 in 1973 to 31,000 by 1976. This increase of 18,000 in the number of registered unemployed amounted to only 10.5 per cent of the number of jobs actually lost in both sectors — 79,000 jobs in clothing and 93,000 in textiles — during the same period. Later figures showed that, from August 1976 to August 1978, registered unemployment in these two sectors remained stable at about 28,500, while an additional 43,000 jobs had disappeared in both industries.[6] Failing a generalised reluctance by textile and clothing workers to register and collect their rightful unemployment benefits, it would seem that the West German economy had been able to absorb a large number of these redundant workers into other activities during the past years, thus reinforcing whatever ideological bias the Federal authorities had for not intervening on behalf of troubled industries.[7]

By contrast, the situation in Belgium was somewhat different over the same period. From 1973 to 1977, employment in the Belgian clothing industry decreased by 36,000, but the number of clothing workers registered as unemployed jumped from 4,550 to 22,800, an increase representing more than half the total job-loss figure. The Belgian economy did not appear to have been as successful in absorbing the displaced workers. This fact, together with the high regional concentration of clothing and textile industries in the Flemish provinces (see Table 2.11), intensified the pressure on the government for direct intervention in the Belgian industry.

France, Italy and the United Kingdom fared somewhat better during the post-1973 period. The losses due to lower output coincided with a drop in the growth rate of productivity in both France and Britain after 1974.

TABLE 2.11

Regional Concentration of Textile and Clothing Employment in the European Community, 1978

Region	*No. of jobs in textiles and clothing (thousands)*	*% of total jobs in manufacturing*
Tuscany (I)	120.0	21.7
East Flanders (B)	42.3	19.9
Abruzzi-Molise (I)	26.7	19.5
Oberfranken (D)	45.0	18.4
West Flanders (B)	31.0	18.1
Northern Ireland (UK)	37.5	18.0
East Midlands (UK)	129.4	17.7
Nord-pas-de-Calais (F)	112.3	17.5
Tübingen (D)	55.7	17.2
Veneto (I)	111.3	16.3
Basilicata (I)	6.8	15.8
Umbria (I)	16.7	14.5
Lombardy (I)	263.0	14.4
Piedmont (I)	120.0	13.6
Apulia (I)	39.4	13.2
Yorkshire-Humberside (UK)	127.8	12.8
Manche (F)	27.6	12.1
North-west (UK)	156.1	12.0

SOURCE: Commission of the European Community, taken from *European Trends*, EIU Report No. 68 (London: Economist Intelligence Unit, 1981).
NOTE: The average for the European Community in 1978 was 8.7 per cent of employment in manufacturing.

France was able to withstand this drop in competitiveness partly through the relative lack of price sensitivity in her more differentiated product range. The United Kingdom, though, had to take refuge in a rapidly devaluing pound in order to hold the line against international competition. Nevertheless, by 1980, when the pound rose as a result of the oil-price increase of that year, the competitiveness of the British clothing industry had already deteriorated considerably. The Italian industry's ability to sustain employment in spite of rapid increases in productivity was due both to its success in the market place and, in large part, to the extensive intervention of the state aimed directly at the safeguarding of jobs, a subject which shall be covered in Chapter 4.

Any such analysis, however, is somewhat suspect given certain peculiarities of the Italian labour market. Social security and other indirect charges on the Italian clothing industry amounted to more than 110 per cent of direct labour costs so that the latter accounted for less than 45 per cent of total compensation. By contrast to the United Kingdom, where 87 per cent of the total labour bill was direct labour costs and where personal income tax rates were high, social welfare programmes in Italy were financed by heavy employment taxes. This situation encouraged the creation of a large pool of part-time non-reported workers whose output was estimated to range from as low as 10 per cent to as high as 30 per cent of total production in the clothing industry.[8] Their existence also put great pressure on industrialists to remain small and thereby avoid unionisation and its resulting higher wage rates. Over 70 per cent of the 'official' workforce in Italy's clothing industry belonged to one of the three affiliates of the largest national unions. Many firms survived labour-union and cost pressures by sub-contracting part of their needs either to non-union shops or directly to groups of more or less organised 'home workers' working for less than 40 per cent of the full-cost union-negotiated rate.

In general, the pace of growth of government intervention in the industry accelerated dramatically after 1975. The negotiation of a much tighter set of import quotas in the 1977 renewal of the Multi-fibre Arrangement (MFA), the arrangement governing trade in textile products between developed and developing countries, together with a series of domestic measures aimed at protecting employment, had a major effect in safeguarding jobs in most countries. As can be seen in Table 2.10, the pace of contraction of employment in clothing slowed down considerably between 1976 and 1979 in most countries in the European Community, only subsequently to pick up again.

It is quite evident that a major shift of employment away from the textile and clothing industries — both nationally (inter-industry) and internationally (intra-industry) — has been under way since the 1960s and that this process has been moving considerably faster since the 1974-75 crisis. On the first point, Figure 2.1 illustrates clearly the massive shift of employment from the textile and clothing industries among most OECD countries. Only Greece and Spain (figures for Portugal and Turkey are not given) exhibited a relative strengthening of their textile and clothing sectors during this period. For all other countries, the decline has been sustained, particularly in the case of the smaller and relatively more open economies such as those of Belgium, the Netherlands, Switzerland and the Scandinavian countries. To the extent that other sectors in the economy were expanding and able to absorb these labour resources, the process of adjustment could take place at a relatively smooth pace. But, if this were not the case — as occurred after 1974 — the pressures mounted to accord protection or other forms of relief to the industry in order to shield it from whichever source of competition appeared most threatening.

The trend towards greater geographic dispersion for the clothing industry is confirmed by Table 2.9. After employment in the developed countries expanded at an average of 1.1 per cent per annum up to the end of 1973,

FIGURE 2.1

Share of Textiles, Clothing and Leather in Total Manufacturing Employment

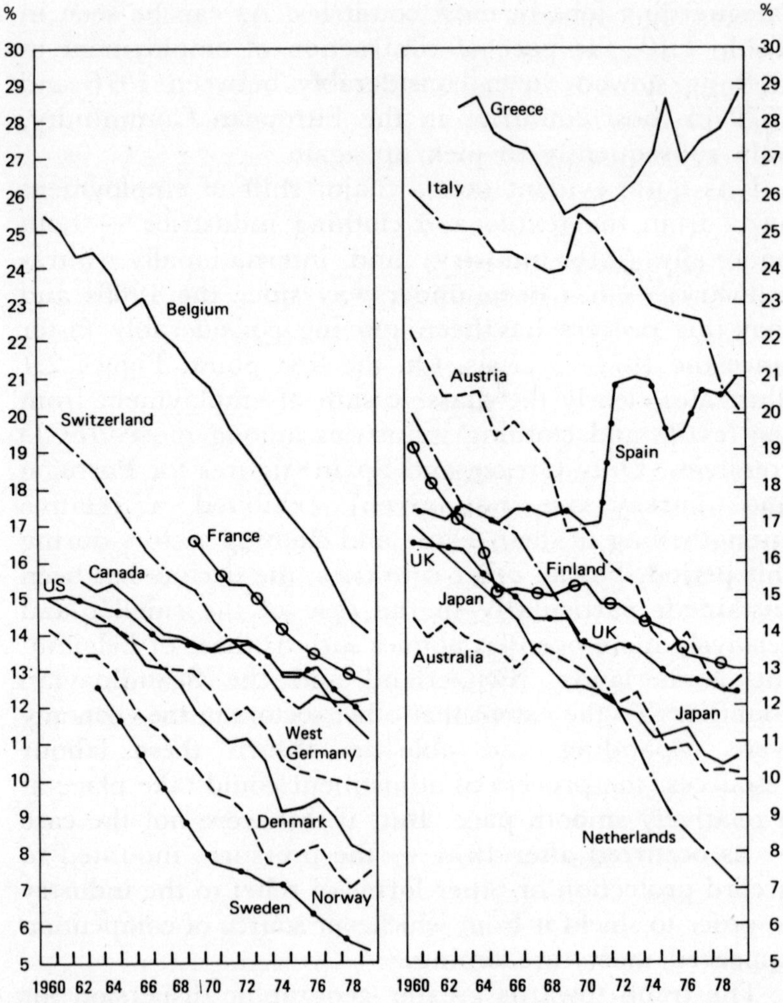

SOURCE: *Textile and Clothing Industries: Structural Problems and Policies in* OECD Countries (Paris: OECD Secretariat, 1983) Chart VIII.

it dropped precipitously for the next five years, especially in the European Community and North America.[9] The result was that the developed countries' share of world employment in the clothing industry dropped from 51 per cent in 1963 to just over 40 per cent in 1978. Some interesting contrasts can be drawn by comparing the world share of production and employment held by different groups of countries. Thus, the United States and Canada in 1978 accounted for nearly 32 per cent of world production with only 15 per cent of world employment in the industry (and barely 7.5 per cent of the world's population). The developing countries of East Asia, on the other hand, increased employment at a very rapid pace throughout the 1970s. Their share of world industry employment in 1978 (nearly 10 per cent) is out of proportion, however, to either their share of world production (2.8 per cent) or world population (40 per cent).[10]

In a way, these figures highlight the choices faced by the developed countries in this industry. If inter-industry adjustments prove difficult or slow in absorbing the large number of unemployed in the textile and clothing sectors, there appears to be plenty of room for international adjustment through specialisation. While the total number of jobs to be saved via this route may be small, they will be likely to involve a higher level of value added per worker, a situation in keeping with the relatively high wages prevailing in developed countries.

General Decline in Trade Performance

Perhaps the most pertinent measure of an industry's performance, and the most readily comparable, is the evolution of its net trade position through time. Trade was anything but fair in the clothing industry, although the six countries in the European Community were operating under similar rules for most of the period under consideration, and certainly since 1973. These rules were not significantly different from those being applied by the United States in the context of the MFA and theoretically available to Japan as well. The extent to which differences in the degree of enforcement of these shared trade rules or in export subsidies and assistance could have affected overall performance is examined in Chapter 4.[11]

Table 2.12 summarises the trade history of the eight countries since 1963. In keeping with the evidence on production and employment, the data show an early start in balance-of-trade deficits for the Federal Republic of Germany, the Netherlands and the United States. After almost twenty years of uninterrupted decline, the combined trade deficits of these countries in 1980 represented nearly 90 per cent of the total deficit for the OECD area. Belgium, the United Kingdom and Japan, which had maintained relatively balanced trade throughout the 1960s, had joined the ranks of the net importers by 1973. Thereafter, import growth vastly exceeded any improvements on their export accounts. France managed to maintain a fairly strong positive trade balance through the mid-1970s, but a relative slow-down of export growth after 1975 eroded the country's international position and deficits appeared in 1979 and 1980. Only Italy was able to improve her trade balance during the last decade; by 1980, her surplus of nearly $4 billion in clothing was the world's largest.

As the figures show, the explosion of imports for most of these countries was also accompanied by a rapid increase in their export activities. Table 2.13 measures the degree of trade specialisation achieved by the six largest countries in the sample. In all cases, except for the United States, a rise in the import penetration of clothing products was partially offset by large increases in export production. The case is the most extreme in the Federal Republic of Germany, with imports providing 55 per cent of domestic consumption in 1979 and exports rising from a mere 3 per cent of production in 1962 to 19 per cent by the end of the period. It appears, therefore, that any appropriate measure of trade performance must take into account not only the rising level of import penetration, but also the relative success of the country's firms in shifting resources to those lines of clothing where they enjoy some international competitive advantage.

Lastly, there is also the question of inter-industry shifts discussed briefly above. Although not the main concern of this study, some countries have succeeded in responding to the challenge of international competition in the clothing industry (where labour content and, therefore, wage differentials have the greatest impact) by shifting resources up the textile chain. Figure 2.2 illustrates some of these shifts for the period 1970-80. While the United States improved its trade balance in fibres and textiles during the 1970s, the Federal Republic of Germany and Japan also added a strong rising surplus in textile machinery to their overall balance in related sectors. Italy, on the other hand, has continued to rely on its strength in the clothing sector. For the remaining four countries, the picture is one of a deteriorating clothing balance, but with little else occurring within the textile system to compensate for this decline.

To compare the trade performance of the eight countries on an equal basis, the measure that appears to be most appropriate is the ratio of the countries' net trade in clothing to their level of (apparent) domestic consumption. There are difficult methodological problems, though, with this and other measures of import penetration that affect their comparability over time and among countries.[12] Table 2.14 presents the best available data on net trade performance according to various methods and sources. The data highlight the very rapid deterioration of the competitive position of the Dutch, West German and Belgian industries over this period. In the Netherlands and West Germany, the negative

TABLE 2.12

Clothing Exports, Imports and Net Trade, 1963-80
(US$ million)

	Belgium			*France*			*West Germany*			*Italy*		
	Exp.	*Imp.*	*Bal.*	*Exp.*	*Imp.*	*Bal.*	*Exp.*	*Imp.*	*Bal.*	*Exp.*	*Imp.*	*Bal.*
1963	103	66	37	203	70	133	146	256	– 110	338	26	312
1970	279	221	58	435	261	174	430	1,030	– 600	865	98	767
1973	570	556	14	1,029	587	442	909	2,544	– 1,635	1,305	195	1,110
1974	658	684	– 26	1,161	682	479	975	3,078	– 2,103	1,534	257	1,277
1975	674	829	– 155	1,338	897	441	1,142	3,664	– 2,522	1,844	221	1,623
1976	685	961	– 276	1,252	1,119	133	1,439	4,161	– 2,722	2,106	261	1,845
1977	743	1,141	– 398	1,488	1,297	191	1,748	4,740	– 2,992	2,585	337	2,248
1978	806	1,337	– 531	1,714	1,474	240	2,103	5,913	– 3,810	3,309	354	2,955
1979	906	1,596	– 690	2,007	2,182	– 175	2,589	7,307	– 4,718	4,353	535	3,818
1980	999	1,823	– 824	2,294	2,637	– 343	2,882	8,326	– 5,444	4,584	797	3,787

	Netherlands			United Kingdom			United States			Japan		
	Exp.	*Imp.*	*Bal.*	*Exp.*	*Imp.*	*Bal.*	*Exp.*	*Imp.*	*Bal.*	*Exp.*	*Imp.*	*Bal.*
1963	65	146	– 81	111	181	– 70	93	392	-299	211	8	203
1970	208	465	– 257	295	311	– 15	227	1,269	– 1,068	462	91	371
1973	406	848	– 442	440	818	– 378	287	2,168	– 1,881	368	571	– 203
1974	471	1,116	– 645	538	942	– 404	418	2,323	– 1,905	329	826	– 497
1975	523	1,329	– 806	588	1,120	– 532	421	2,551	– 2,130	332	540	– 208
1976	532	1,617	– 1,085	740	1,226	– 486	561	3,613	– 3,052	416	788	– 372
1977	530	1,788	– 1,258	1,044	1,338	– 294	670	4,123	-3,453	463	868	– 405
1978	618	2,212	– 1,594	1,286	1,767	– 481	719	6,124	– 5,405	479	1,233	– 754
1979	777	2,707	– 1,930	1,597	2,538	– 941	958	6,355	– 5,397	344	1,800	– 1,456
1980	875	2,875	– 2,000	1,878	2,858	– 980	1,219	6,943	– 5,724	488	1,537	– 1,049

SOURCE: *Statistics of Foreign Trade: Series C, Trade by Commodities*, OECD Secretariat, Paris, various issues.

Table 2.13

Trade Specialisation in Clothing 1962, 1969 and 1979 (per cent based on weight)

		1962	*1969*	*1979*
France				
P/C		106	97	85
M/C	Total	2	9	27
	(extra-Community)	(1)	(1)	(16)
X/P	Total	8	6	14
	(extra-Community)	(7)	(2)	(5)
West Germany				
P/C		96	87	56
M/C	Total	7	19	55
	(extra-Community)	(4)	(11)	(40)
X/P	Total	3	6	19
	(extra-Community)	(2)	(3)	(8)
Italy				
P/C		111	123	139
M/C	Total	1	2	9
	(extra-Community)	...	(1)	(7)
X/P	Total	11	20	35
	(extra-Community)	(6)	(5)	(8)
United Kingdom				
P/C		95	95	82
M/C	Total	9	13	29
	(extra-Community)	—	—	(24)
X/P	Total	4	8	13
	(extra-Community)	—	—	(6)
United States				
P/C		98	96	90
M/C		3	6	13
X/P		3	1	2

Japan	*1965*	*1970*	*1975*	*1980*[a]	*1985*[b]
All textile products					
M/C	0.6	4.3	10.0	18.0	17.6
Outer garments					
M/C	na	7.5	16.9	20.8	25.0
X/P	na	26.1	16.3	14.2	12.4
Underwear					
M/C	na	1.1	8.4	11.9	20.0
X/P	na	2.6	10.2	10.4	13.1

trade balance of the early 1960s expanded rapidly relative to the total domestic market to the point where, by 1980, net imports exceeded 70 and 30 per cent, respectively, of domestic consumption. The deterioration of the Belgian industry's trade position is perhaps more dramatic, having started from a position of surplus which has since been transformed into a headlong decline. Japan, the United Kingdom and the United States also exhibited a significant decline in their net trade position, but in none of these cases was the situation as dramatic, and the British position has in fact improved since 1973. France has also lost its net exporter status of the 1970s, even more recently than Belgium, but not to the same extent. The performance of Italy is indeed remarkable. The figures shown in the table are obviously exaggerated due to the fact that trade flows can be measured much more reliably than production figures.[13] Nonetheless, the continued and overwhelming improvement in performance of the Italian clothing industry is of crucial importance to all developed countries since it constitutes the main example of successful adjustment.

The degree of specialisation of each country's foreign trade was closely linked to its performance. Belgium and

---

SOURCES: Geoffrey Shepherd, 'Public and Private Strategies for Survival in the Textile and Clothing Industries of Western Europe and the United States', Sussex European Research Centre, University of Sussex, mimeograph, September 1980, Tables 6 and 7. Figures for Ministry of International Trade and Industry's (MITI) Long Range Vision on Industry Structure for 1979, as reported in Ippei Yomazawa, 'Adjustment of the Japanese Textile Industry to the Advanced Developing Countries', Hitotsubashi University, Tokyo, working paper, September 1980.

NOTE: Figures in parentheses exclude trade among the six initial member countries of the European Community for 1962 and 1969 and among the nine member countries for 1979. In the table '—' signifies 'not applicable' while '...' signifies 'not significant' and 'na' signifies 'not available'.

P/C = ratio of production to consumption x 100

M/C = ratio of imports to consumption x 100

X/P = ratio of exports to production x 100

[a]Estimated figures except for 'all textile products' which is the actual 1979 level.

[b]Projected figures.

FIGURE 2.2
Trade Balances in Fibre, Textiles, Clothing and Textile Machinery, 1970 and 1980
(US$ billion)

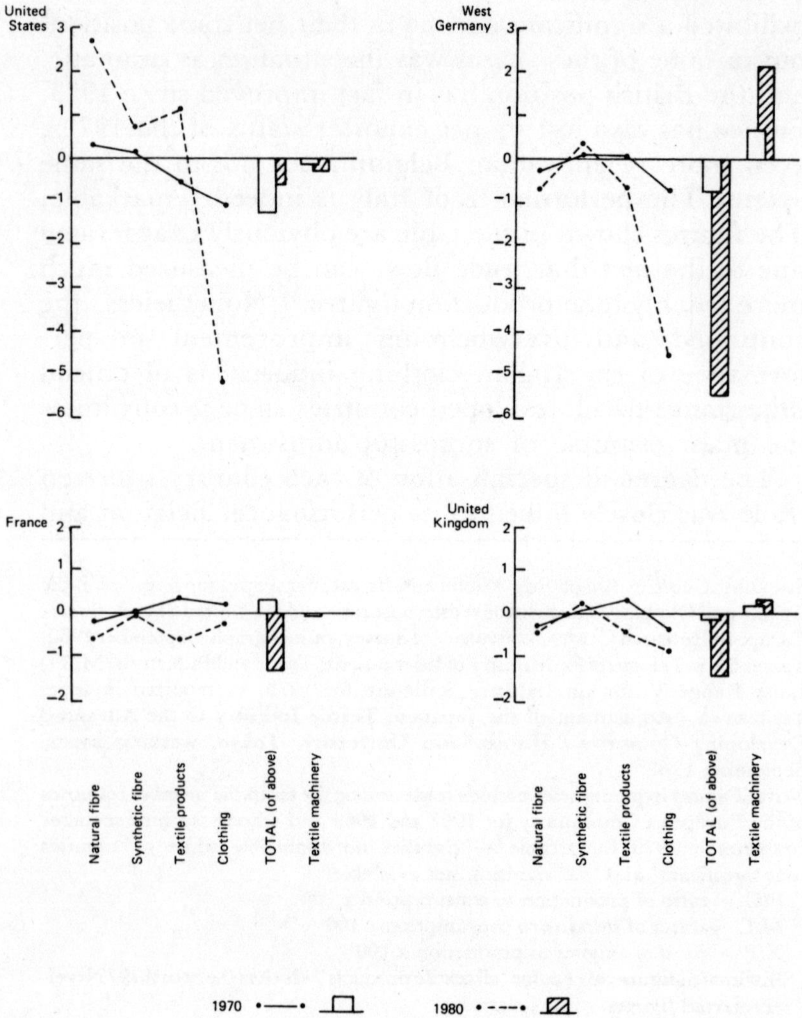

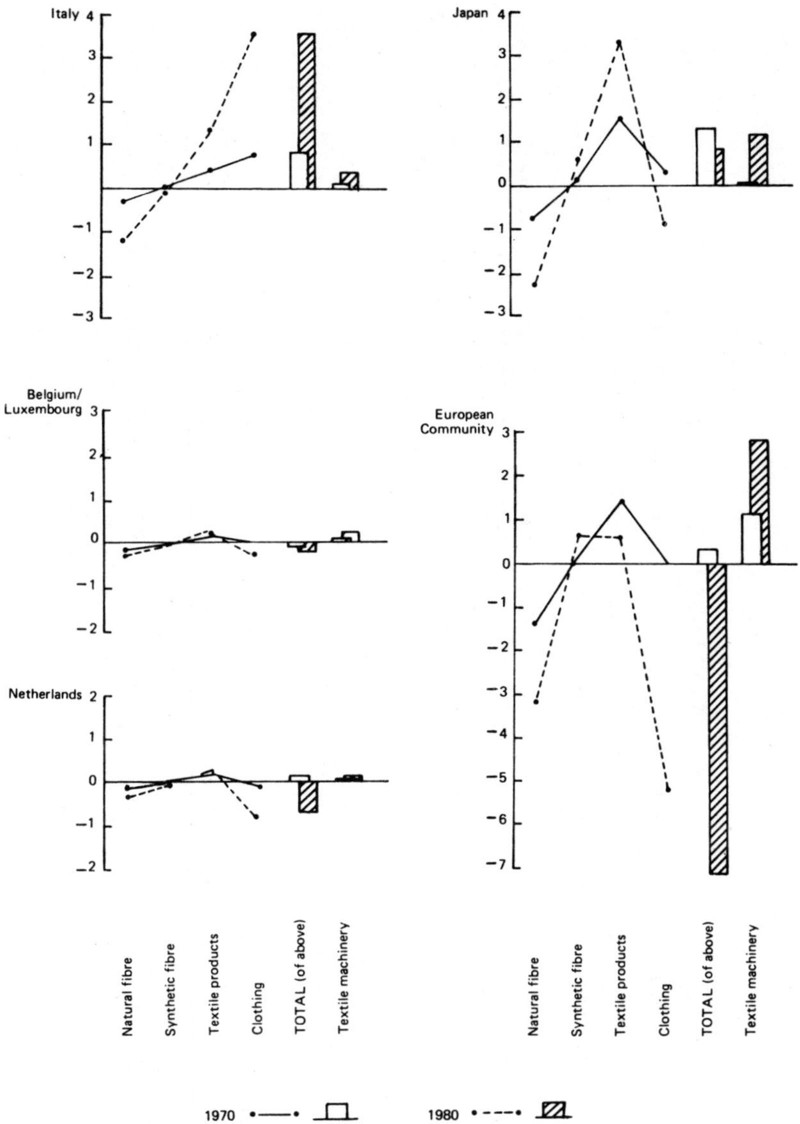

SOURCE: *Statistics of Foreign Trade: Series C, Trade by Commodities*, OECD Secretariat, Paris, various issues.

Table 2.14

Trade Performance in the Clothing Industry, 1963-80
(net trade as a percentage of domestic apparent consumption, in value)

	Belgium	*France*	*West Germany*	*Italy*[a]	*Netherlands*	*United Kingdom*	*United States*	*Japan*
1963	15.8	7.3	4.2	30.5[b]	- 18.0	- 3.7	- 1.6	7.8
1970	13.3	6.7	- 13.5	28.0	- 39.5	- 0.7	- 4.3	7.2
1973	1.6	11.1	- 21.4	28.0	- 47.5	- 11.3	- 5.9	- 2.1
1977	- 24.3	3.4	- 27.5	37.3	- 71.6	- 6.1	- 8.2	- 3.0
1978	- 27.5	4.0	- 29.9	56.8	- 72.9	- 7.8	- 10.8	- 4.3
1979	- 30.6	- 2.4	- 31.5	53.9	- 75.6	- 11.6	- 9.9	- 8.1
1980	- 33.7	- 4.3	- 34.0	43.0	- 74.8	- 10.9	- 9.4	- 5.6
Change in the ratio								
1963 – 73	- 14.2	3.8	- 17.2	- 2.5[b]	- 29.5	- 7.6	- 4.3	- 9.9
1973 – 80	- 35.3	- 15.4	- 12.6	15.0	- 27.3	0.4	- 3.5	- 3.5

SOURCE: Calculated from Tables 2.8 and 2.12 and José de la Torre and Michel Bacchetta, *Decline and Adjustment: European Policies Towards their Clothing Industries* (Fontainebleau: Institut Européen d'Administration des Affaires [INSEAD], 1979).

[a]It includes an estimate of 'undeclared legal production' as defined in footnote 8.

[b]Data refer to 1966 and 1966-73.

the Netherlands, for example, while both maintaining relatively open trading economies, traded mainly with other developed countries. Nearly 90 per cent of Dutch clothing exports and 65 per cent of its imports went to and came from, respectively, other countries within the European Community in 1980; the equivalent figures for Belgium were 92 and 82 per cent. Table 2.15 shows the degree of geographic specialisation characteristic of each of the eight countries studied. The United States, Japan and the United Kingdom, for both historical and geographical reasons, rely considerably on developing-country suppliers. Belgium, Italy, France and the Netherlands do so to a much smaller extent. Equally, American exports are heavily oriented towards developing countries, where the popularity of American casual wear (for example, denim) has been a major competitive force.

By gradually moving out of low value-added products, which can be imported at significantly lower prices from the developing countries, and concentrating domestic resources on higher value-added items, a country's terms of trade in clothing ought to improve considerably. Detailed computations by the GATT Secretariat on price and unit-value indices for all manufactures as well as for textiles and clothing, showed that (using an index 1963 = 100) export prices of manufactures had risen to 159 by 1973 and to 304 by 1979.[14] The same index for textiles and clothing was 138 in 1973 and 226 in 1979. By taking the ratio of the two series, it can be concluded that countries which export mainly manufactures and import textiles and clothing have seen their relative terms of trade improve by 15 per cent between 1963 and 1973 and by an additional 17 per cent during the 1973-79 period.

Within the clothing sector, specialisation should yield similar beneficial results. The more disaggregated data in Table 2.16 reveal wide differences between the countries listed and show the importance of specific

Table 2.15

OECD Trade in Clothing with non-OECD Countries, 1970 and 1980
(per cent of value)

	Imports from				Exports to			
	Centrally-planned economies		*Developing countries*		*Centrally-planned economies*		*Developing countries*	
Trading area	*1970*	*1980*	*1970*	*1980*	*1970*	*1980*	*1970*	*1980*
OECD total	2.8	6.0	27.7	43.0	3.5	2.0	11.1	11.7
Japan	12.1	17.2	58.2	55.4	8.0	6.6	19.3	31.9
United States	0.2	5.6	53.8	84.3	0.5	0.3	64.6	57.7
European Community (9)[a]	12.0	11.2	53.2	62.5	8.0	3.6	18.8	28.4
Belgium/Luxembourg	0.9	0.9	1.8	11.2	1.4	0.2	1.4	2.8
France	2.3	6.0	7.3	29.0	1.7	1.3	15.5	14.9
West Germany	4.8	8.3	21.1	38.5	2.9	1.7	5.7	6.7
Italy	1.1	12.7	4.3	28.3	3.0	0.6	4.3	7.6
Netherlands	3.3	4.7	7.0	20.0	3.4	3.2	1.0	5.4
United Kingdom	2.9	2.6	44.2	52.2	5.6	1.4	13.6	16.9

Source: *Statistics of Foreign Trade: Series C, Trade by Commodities*, OECD Secretariat, Paris, 1970 and 1980.

[a]Excludes intra-Community trade.

trading partners. Thus Japan's clothing trade with other OECD countries has always been in terms of exchanging low value-added for high value-added goods and this relationship deteriorated during the 1970s. Japan's trade with China (her main partner in the category of centrally-planned economies) and with neighbouring developing countries, however, appears to have been increasingly advantageous to Japan. As a result, and given the geographical composition of the Japanese clothing trade which relies increasingly on these latter countries, Japan's overall terms of trade in clothing improved by 34 per cent during the decade.

Italy, which has succeeded splendidly in upgrading her clothing industry to higher value-added product lines through a heavy reliance on OECD (that is, wealthier) markets, has matched Japan's record and also considerably improved her terms of trade during the decade. At the other end of the spectrum, Belgium and the Netherlands, with their heavy reliance on developed-country suppliers, have seen their own terms of trade either stagnate or deteriorate.

Unit Labour Costs as a Measure of Performance

An area of performance that must be considered against this background of declining trade balances is the rise in unit labour costs in the industry over the period. Table 2.17 summarises the estimates based on the best data available.[15] All six European countries listed experienced large increases in wage costs over the period, averaging about 15 per cent annually. Once adjusted for productivity increases, West Germany, the Netherlands and Belgium had the lowest increases in labour costs per unit, while Italy had by far the highest. Only after changes in the exchange rate during the period are taken into account, however, can the real competitive impact of changes in labour costs be appreciated. The United

TABLE 2.16
Relative Changes in the Terms of Trade[a] for Clothing, 1970 Compared with 1980

Trading area	*Terms of trade*		*% change*
	1970	*1980*	*1980/1970*
Japan			
Total	0.74	0.99	+34
OECD	0.28	0.23	
Centrally-planned economies	1.36	2.00	
Developing countries	0.83	1.06	
European Community			
Total[b]	2.34	1.98	−15
OECD	1.77	1.86	
Centrally-planned economies	2.09	1.45	
Developing countries	2.42	1.68	
Belgium/Luxembourg			
Total	0.89	0.82	−8
OECD	0.87	0.75	
Centrally-planned economies	2.32	0.85	
Developing countries	1.89	1.15	
France			
Total	1.68	2.01	+20
OECD	1.52	1.63	
Centrally-planned economies	3.33	1.47	
Developing countries	2.70	2.70	
West Germany			
Total	1.56	1.81	+16
OECD	1.25	1.54	
Centrally-planned economies	2.48	1.52	
Developing countries	1.64	1.09	
Italy			
Total	1.02	1.38	+35
OECD	0.91	1.10	
Centrally-planned economies	3.53	1.33	
Developing countries	2.38	1.52	
Netherlands			
Total	0.91	0.92	+1
OECD	0.84	0.78	
Centrally-planned economies	1.86	2.07	
Developing countries	0.67	0.80	

Trading area	Terms of trade 1970	Terms of trade 1980	% change 1980/1970
United Kingdom			
Total	na	1.78	na
OECD	na	1.33	na
Centrally-planned economies	na	1.44	na
Developing countries	na	2.16	na

SOURCE: *Statistics of Foreign Trade: Series C, Trade by Commodities*, OECD Secretariat, Paris, 1970 and 1980.
NOTE: In the table 'na' signifies 'not available'.

[a]Defined here as the ratio of unit export prices to unit import prices, both measured in US$ per kg, for SITC 842 through to 847 (all clothing articles made of textile materials), normalised by weight per category.

[b]Six countries in 1970 as against nine in 1980. Excludes intra-Community trade in both cases.

Kingdom emerges clearly as the best performer on the strength of reasonable productivity increases and a devalued pound, although a drop in the ratio of value added to output during the period from 49.5 to 40.2 per cent raises some questions about the comparability of British figures. Yet the improvement in British trade performance in 1977 was surely due partly to this relative gain in unit labour costs, just as its deterioration after 1978 is related to the strengthening of the pound in that period. Italy also recuperated in part her competitive edge in labour costs through the fall in the value of the lira, while others suffered from the strength of their respective currencies.

In general, the relative cost competitiveness of the principal West European producers did not deviate much at any time from a central rising trend. The American performance on this score, nevertheless, is quite remarkable. Because wages in the clothing industry rose at a much lower rate than both average manufacturing wages in the United States and industry wages in Western Europe, American clothing firms gained a large theoretical cost advantage over their West European competitors.

Estimates by one American manufacturer, shown in Table 2.18, confirm this large cost advantage, yet American clothing companies did little during this period to exploit the situation. By 1981, the rising dollar had wiped out much of this differential.

Employment, output, trade and unit costs are not, of course, the only performance measures that can be considered. Style, product differentiation, design, quality

TABLE 2.17

Changes in Labour Compensation, Productivity and Unit Labour Costs in the Clothing Industry, 1970-76 (1970 = 100)

	Hourly compensation in local currency	*Output per worker*	*Exchange rate (versus $)*	*Unit labour costs ($)*	
				Index	*Annual change (%)*
Belgium	216.9	131.7	128.5	111.5	13.3
France	232.6	119.5	116.1	226.0	14.6
West Germany	175.3	123.2	144.8	206.7	12.9
Italy	313.3	120.9	75.4	195.3	11.8
Netherlands	216.7	145.9	137.1	203.6	12.6
United Kingdom	236.2	124.5	75.4	143.1	6.2
United States	141.0	125.8	100.0	112.1	1.9

SOURCES: José de la Torre, 'Public Intervention Strategies in the European Clothing Industries', *Journal of World Trade Law*, London, March-April 1981; and national accounts.

of workmanship *et cetera* are also important, particularly as the industry in all developed countries tends to seek refuge from low-priced import competition in the higher-priced quality segments of the market. No systematic comparisons have been attempted here as they would be extremely difficult — if not impossible — to ascertain in an objective manner. The individual country analyses, however, point to a few major changes in these factors, such as Italy's push in the high-fashion women's ready-to-wear market, the loss of certain American markets to more stylish products from the European Community and the Belgian industry's attempt to establish greater product identity. Some of these issues will be discussed in the next chapter. Other relevant comparisons, such as concentration ratios (that is, the percentage of domestic supply accounted for by the four or ten largest manufacturers) and the extent of multi-plant operations (companies operating more than one manufacturing or

TABLE 2.18

Effective Labour Costs in the Clothing Industry, 1978

	Wage and benefits ($/hour)	*Productivity rating (US = 100)*	*Effective labour costs ($/hour)*	*Effective labour costs (US = 100)*
United States	4.50	100	4.50	100
West Germany	5.50	95	5.79	129
Japan	3.75	70	5.36	119
Hong Kong	1.10	90	1.22	27
Taiwan	0.77	80	0.96	21
Singapore	0.80	70	1.14	25
South Korea	0.60	80	0.75	17
Dominican Republic	0.60	60	1.00	22

SOURCE: Private corporate records based on one company's experience in these countries.

assembly facility), were not possible due to the incompatibility of existing data. A more detailed and rigorous study would be necessary to establish comparable information in most other areas of economic performance.[16]

Determinants of Employment Losses

There is no satisfactory way of relating the number of jobs lost in the West European, Japanese and American clothing industries to any specific set of causes.

TABLE 2.19

Impact of Changes in Demand, Productivity and Trade on Employment in the Clothing Industry, 1970-80

	Belgium	France	West Germany	Italy[a]	Netherlands	United Kingdom	United States	Japan	Total
Total employment (thousands)									
1970	60.5	322	381	207	58.5	377	1,164	326	2,896
1980	39.5	251	249	171	18.1	257	1,075	392	2,453
Change	− 21.0	− 71	− 132	− 36	− 40.4	− 120	− 89	+ 66	− 443
% change	− 34.7	− 22.0	− 34.6	− 17.4	− 69.1	− 31.8	− 7.6	+ 20.2	− 15.3
Effect on employment (% of 1970 employment) of changes in:[b]									
Domestic demand	+ 82.1	+ 6.7	+ 10.7	− 1.6	+ 46.5	+ 20.5	+ 32.8	+ 10.2	+ 21.7
Productivity	− 77.1	− 20.1	− 23.9	− 29.3	− 61.4	− 44.4	− 34.2	+ 25.4	− 27.0
Net imports	− 39.9	− 8.6	− 21.4	+ 13.5	− 54.2	− 7.9	− 6.3	− 15.4	− 10.0

SOURCE: Calculated from data in the preceding tables.

[a]Italian figures have been adjusted to account for 'undeclared legal production' as defined in footnote 8.

[b]Additions appear to be incorrect due to rounding of figures. See footnote 16 for details.

Yet there are two underlying assumptions in most national programmes to protect and reconstruct the industry: first, that the major cause of job losses is the deterioration in international competitiveness (by which is really meant disruptive import competition) and, second, that the essential remedy for this situation is to obtain increases in productivity through higher investment in plant and equipment. Table 2.19 is the result of an attempt to draw a rough causal link between the number of jobs lost in each of the countries studied and three major trends occurring during the period 1970-80. These three trends were: (i) changes in the total level of demand (apparent consumption) for clothing; (ii) increases in labour productivity (measured in terms of output per man-year); and (iii) changes in the net import penetration of the respective domestic markets.[17]

On average, productivity increases in the eight countries for the period 1970-80 had a negative impact on employment which was nearly three times greater than that of increases in net trade penetration. It follows that, even in the absence of any further deterioration of the net import situation after 1970, the clothing industry in these countries would have experienced a cumulative loss of 5.3 per cent of its workforce (a total of 153,000 jobs) through increases in labour productivity that were only partially offset by increases in the level of demand.

These numbers are, of course, only approximate.[18] They do not consider explicitly, for example, the fact that a large proportion of the increase in productivity experienced during the period must have been induced by the heightened competitive pressures resulting from imports. Nor are they totally accurate in that changes in the level of inventories have not been incorporated into the analysis for lack of comparable data. Also, the evolution of total demand varies widely from country to country and better insights are needed into the causes of these variations (for example, the reduction of foreign workers in West Germany) before broad generalisations can be made with confidence. Two things remain clear, even from this rough approximation.

First, only in the cases of West Germany and the Netherlands has net import penetration been a significant direct cause of job losses among the various West European industries, the United States or Japan.[19] While imports rose in some cases both absolutely and relatively, some countries expanded their exports as fast or faster in the context of a strategy of product specialisation; others reacted by significant improvements in their productivity which had a much more serious impact on employment than had the increased imports.

Second, the often prescribed remedy for all declining sectors — that they must achieve higher productivity through investment — may in fact enhance the industry's international competitiveness, but it will not add to the employment rolls in mature industries, especially those characterised by low income elasticity of demand. The solution to the employment problem must lie elsewhere in the economy or in other industries.

NOTES AND REFERENCES

1. For a more detailed discussion of some of these issues, see *Textile and Clothing Industries: Structural Problems and Policies in OECD Countries* (Paris: OECD Secretariat, 1983).

2. Recent figures for seven countries in the study are:

	1970 (%)	*1976* (%)
Belgium	28.6	28.9
France	25.3	26.6
West Germany	24.6	24.8
Italy	28.3	36.7
Netherlands	29.3	26.4
United Kingdom	28.8	25.4
United States	na	23.0

In the table 'na' signifies 'not available'.

See de la Torre and Bacchetta, 'Decline and Adjustment: European Policies towards their Clothing Industries', working paper, for the Institut Européen d'Administration des Affaires (INSEAD), Fontainebleau, June 1979, Appendix A.

3. For a more detailed discussion of this issue, see Deepak Lal, *Resurrection of the Pauper-labour Argument*, Thames Essay No. 28 (London: Trade Policy Research Centre, 1981).

4. Textile and clothing export prices rose by 126 per cent between 1970 and 1979; that is, at an annual rate of about 9.5 per cent.

5. In any event, foreign workers represented less than 5 per cent of the industry's workforce in the mid-1970s. See 'Industrial Adjustment in the Netherlands', Development Research Institute, Tilburg University, mimeograph, 1975.

6. Statistical data from the Bundesministerium für Wirtschaft. See, also, 'Die Bekleidungsindustrie in der Bundesrepublik Deutschland im Jahre 1977', Bundesverband Bekleidungsindustrie, Cologne, mimeograph, 1978.

7. There are no apparent reasons why clothing and textile workers would behave differently from other West German workers with regard to unemployment compensation. While women constituted 82 per cent of the clothing industry workforce and 55 per cent of the textile industry workforce (versus 29 per cent for all manufacturing), they were entitled to the same benefits as any other worker as long as they actively remained in the job market. One would have to assume a large propensity for dropping out of the labour market or a disproportionate number of part-time or temporary employees among these workers in order to justify the figures above. Equally, foreign workers accounted for 12 per cent and 19 per cent of the clothing and textile industries' workforces respectively, which did not compare unfavourably with a figure of 15 per cent for all manufacturing, thus eliminating another possible explanation for the discrepancy between actual job losses and registered unemployed. See Axel D. Neu, 'Protection of the German Textile Industry', in W.M. Corden and Gerhard Fels (eds), *Public Assistance to Industry: Protection and Subsidies in Britain and Germany* (London: Macmillan, for the Trade Policy Research Centre, 1976) pp. 170-71.

8. The 1971 Census of Manufacturers reported a total of 350,000 employees in the clothing industry. This is approximately 65 per cent higher than that reported by the Labour Ministry which covers all firms with more than fifty workers and some of those units employing between ten and fifty workers. Actual employment is probably much higher. If all non-reported and irregular workers are added to the census figures, plus artisan tailors and other cottage industries, the total number employed may be as high as 500,000. In 1978, the Italian Central Statistical Office (ISTAT) revised the gross national product accounts to include estimates of the level of 'undeclared legal production'. Accordingly, the GNP was revised upwards by 9-10 per cent and industrial output by 14-15 per cent for 1975-77. Critics have argued that these revisions were insufficient and that industrial output should be adjusted by an additional 21-30 per cent. For more details on these figures, see Derek Blades, 'The Hidden Economy and National Accounts', Occasional Studies, *OECD Economic Outlook*, Paris, June 1982.

9. While the figures shown in Table 2.9 for Japan are positive, they correspond to the peak of Japanese employment in the industry. From 1977 to 1980, Japanese clothing jobs dropped by 10 per cent (see Table 2.10).

10. By comparison, employment in 1979 in some of the major clothing producers among the developing countries was (in thousands): Hong Kong 251, South Korea 205, Singapore 27, India 38, Sri Lanka 6 and Mexico 46. The low levels of production (value added) relative to employment also reflect the higher proportion of external inputs as well as the relative simplicity of domestic garments in many of these countries.

11. The issue of restraints on trade in clothing and textiles is not discussed here other than in the context of public adjustment policies (Chapter 4). For a detailed discussion of these issues, see Donald B. Keesing and Wolf, *Textile Quotas against Developing Countries*, Thames Essay No. 23 (London: Trade Policy Research Centre, 1980); and Curzon *et al.*, *op. cit.*

12. These include, among others, choosing the right level of aggregation, accounting for cyclical changes in inventories and demand, incorporating the price and volume effects of trade restrictions and balancing the distortions deriving from differences in import-product and export-product unit values. Since developing-country exports, for example, have increased in terms of their unit values, calculations based on physical units, *ceteris paribus*, will tend to overstate early penetration levels and underestimate import growth. The reverse is of course true if import penetration were calculated in value terms. For more details, see Keesing and Wolf, *op. cit.*, pp. 208-9; and *Textile and Clothing Industries: Structural Problems and Policies in OECD Countries*, *op. cit.*, pp. 53-57.

13. See footnote 8 above.

14. Reported in *Textile and Clothing Industries: Structural Problems and Policies in OECD Countries*, *op. cit.*, p. 44.

15. These estimates are based on aggregate data and suffer from all the shortcomings typical of such calculations. They are presented here only to illustrate the order of magnitude of the figures and not their exact value. Whenever data were available, the possibilities of changes in the product mix and in the ratio of value added to output were analysed with no significant effects found in either case, except where noted in the text.

16. The best data available on some of these issues are presented in *Textile and Clothing Industries: Structural Problems and Policies in OECD Countries*, *op. cit.*

17. In attempting to relate lost employment to changes in each industry's environment and competitiveness, the sequential process was as follows. First, the effects of changes in demand were estimated by calculating the jobs that would have been created due to a given increase in apparent consumption over the period if there had been no changes in net import levels or in worker productivity, all in real terms. Thus

$$\triangle Wd = (D_t - D_o)(1/P_o)$$

where $\triangle Wd$ = change in employment due to demand factors;
D = apparent consumption at time t; and
P = output per worker at time t.

Next, an allowance was made for changes in the level of worker productivity and a measure was made of what the job impact of the actual increase in output per worker would be under the assumption that net imports remained constant. Thus

$$\triangle Wp = (D_t - I_o)(1/P_t - 1/P_o)$$

where $\triangle Wp$ = change in employment due to productivity increases;
I = net imports (imports less exports) at time t; and
$(D_t - I_o)$ = the necessary level of domestic production in order to satisfy domestic demand at time t given that net imports have been held constant.

Finally, changes in net imports were allowed to reflect actual values and their impact on employment measured as

$$\triangle Wi = (I_o - I_t)(1/P_t).$$

18. For a discussion of the methodological problems associated with any attempt to ascribe probable causes to employment losses, see Keesing and Wolf, *op. cit.*, pp. 115-18; and *Textile and Clothing Industries: Structural Problems and Policies in OECD Countries*, *op. cit.*, pp. 91-96. For a more technical discussion, see John P. Martin and John M. Evans, 'Notes on Measuring the Employment Displacement Effects of Trade by the Accounting Procedure', *Oxford Economic Papers*, Oxford, March 1981, pp. 154-64.

19. The data for Japan show a negative growth in productivity during the 1970-80 period which is clearly erroneous. They are reported here in a manner which is consistent with the figures for the other seven countries, but they should not be given much weight.

CHAPTER THREE

Adjustment Strategies for Sustained Competitiveness

THE TRENDS discussed in the previous chapter are evidence of a major transformation under way in the international structure of the clothing industry. Declining rates of growth in consumption, stagnant employment levels and an increase in the share of the domestic market captured by foreign suppliers were the early symptoms. They were first observed in either the smaller, open economies of Northern Europe or in the wealthy, larger economies of the United States, the United Kingdom and West Germany, where alternative job opportunities in the high-growth era of the 1960s were able to divert possible social unrest and blunt the political consequences. Over time, the conditions fostering this decline spread sequentially to other countries: France in the early 1970s began to show the same symptoms, as did Japan towards the end of the decade. Only Italy, of all the countries studied, managed to endure this period of nearly twenty years of intense competition and emerge with a strong and viable industry.

Dramatic changes in employment, production and trade have, of necessity, required major adjustments in the economies of the developed countries. Both labour and capital have either shifted to new activities or areas within the industry, or have abandoned it altogether and sought opportunities in other sectors or, in the case of labour, swollen the unemployment figures. The results of these massive transfers of resources can be derived from the data set out in Chapter 2: rising specialisation in trade, inter-industry shifts within the textile chain, locational changes both nationally and internationally, rising productivity *et cetera*.[1] They stem from a series of decisions taken by firms and workers as they sought to fight or accommodate to changing competitive conditions. This chapter attempts to look at the major strategies that clothing companies in the developed countries can adopt in response to the challenge posed by the new competition.

Elements of an Adjustment Strategy

There are many responses open to any clothing firm facing international competitive pressures. This first section will look in detail at six major sets of possible actions concerning technology and investment, size and concentration, wage policies, market segmentation, manufacturing abroad for the domestic market and foreign direct investment. One possible and highly rewarding strategy not considered here is in the non-economic field. Pressing governments for higher levels of protection and for public assistance to facilitate adjustment in the industry has been a preferred and successful option for many national industries. Government policies shall be dealt with in the next chapter and the focus here shall be only on private economic responses to the competitive crisis facing the industry since 1963.

Limits to Technical Development

The clothing industry typically has one of the lowest ratios of capital to output or capital per worker of any manufacturing industry. It also has a very low level of human capital per worker; that is, the average worker has a low standard of education when compared with other industrial sectors, and the industry spends less than

0.05 per cent of sales revenue on research-and-development activities (United States data). As a result, there is a school of thought in the industry and among many government officials that claims the only feasible way to redress the industry's problems is drastically to increase its level of investment in plant and equipment. By significantly automating manufacturing processes, the theory goes, developed countries can close the gap that separates them from low-cost producers.

Two recent studies have compared the levels of physical (that is, actual machinery) and human capital per worker for the Federal Republic of Germany and the United States in a number of sectors subject to competition from developing countries (see Table 3.1). The first measure represents the more classical interpretation of capital intensity; the second is an attempt to quantify the skill composition of the industry's workforce relative to other sectors. It is evident from the data that the clothing industry lags in both measures and in the case of West Germany, where long-term comparisons are available, the situation does not appear to have improved since 1962.[2]

This does not mean, however, that productivity growth has been stagnant in the clothing industry. On the contrary — aided no doubt by the closing of many marginal firms with lower levels of cost competitiveness — the industry's rise in productivity outpaced the average for all manufacturing industry both in the United States and in five out of the six sample West European countries used in this study for the period 1973-78. In some instances — the Netherlands in particular — the annual rate of growth of productivity was much above that of manufacturing (6 per cent as against 4 per cent). The exceptions were the Federal Republic of Germany and Japan, where very rapid increases in output and investment in all manufacturing, with the resulting lead that these two countries gained over the other major developed countries in industrial productivity growth since the mid-1960s, made productivity improvement in the clothing industry unexceptional.

The advocates of a technological solution are not calling for the acceleration of the process of gradual technological improvement, but, rather, a radical

Table 3.1

Physical and Human Capital per Worker in Clothing and Other Industries in West Germany and the United States

	Physical capital			Human capital		
West Germany	*1962*	*1969*	*1977*	*1962*	*1969*	*1977*
Clothing						
(DM)	9,249	13,655	22,962	5,043.	7,982	17,239
(index)	100	100	100	100	100	100
Textiles (index)	299	315	336	121	125	125
All manufacturing (index)	355	360	335	147	158	162
United States		*1978*			*1978*	
Clothing						
(US$)		2,370			11,000	
(index)		100			100	
Textiles (index)		422			151	
Motor vehicles (index)		544			231	
Chemicals (index)		902			232	
Household appliances (index)		350			355	
Iron and steel (index)		1,169			256	

SOURCES: Gerhard Fels and Klaus-Dieter Schmidt, *Die deutsche Wirtschaft im Strukturwandel*, Kieler Studien No. 166 (Tübingen: J.C.B. Mohr, for the Institut für Weltwirtschaft an der Universität Kiel, 1981); and Bela Balassa, *Structural Change in Trade and Manufactured Goods between Industrial and Developing Countries*, World Bank Staff Working Paper No. 396 (Washington: World Bank, 1980).

transformation of the industry through massive investment in new technology. Some of the preconditions necessary for this transformation are already in place. For the last decade, the United States has been the centre of new developments in automated equipment for the clothing industry. Using their experience in electronics and automation processes, industrial machinery companies with no relation to the textile or clothing industries, such as CAMSCO, Hughes Aircraft and Gerber Scientific, have led the field in innovations of this sort.

CAMSCO, which manufactures an automatic grader and marker with a value per unit of nearly $250,000, sold about $40 million worth of this type of equipment during 1980. Its clothing industry business has been growing at a rate of 80 per cent per annum. Gerber's computerised cutters (approximately $500,000 per unit) achieved sales worth nearly $25 million in 1980. One company alone — Cluett-Peabody, the fourth largest firm in the American clothing industry — spent $4 million over two years in automating their cutting operations with CAMSCO-Gerber systems. Such investments (over $1 million per system including software and personnel training) are, however, only available to large firms. While savings on labour costs and fabric yields can be significant (up to 20 per cent of raw material costs alone), the need to cover amortisation on the investment limits its attractiveness to firms with a sales volume of over $20 million a year; that is, less than 10-20 per cent of the firms in the industry.[3] But not all improvements need to be capital-intensive. A French research centre working on problems specific to the industry estimated that 90 per cent of any productivity gains would be the result of improved methods, with only 10 per cent attributable to investments in plant.[4] Equally, a proposal by some engineering experts in the United States identified nine projects requiring a total budget of $2.5 million per annum (the whole industry spent $16 million on research and development in 1978) that could double the rate of productivity increases in the industry, without requiring major capital investments by the firms adopting the technologies.[5]

One major issue that deserves attention is the tremendous variability in capital/output ratios among sectors of the industry (for example, underwear versus ladies' dresses) and between processes (for example, cutting and assembly). The implications of this variable capital/output ratio are two-fold. First, research resources could be applied to those areas and problems which are both significant bottlenecks in production and amenable to automation. Second, however, it also implies that, to the extent that various processes are discrete, firms could choose between automation and relocation (to low-wage areas) for every step in the manufacturing process according to the economics in question. To the degree that this latter alternative is viable, innovations in automation will have to be justified not only on how many highly-paid developed-country workers they replace, but on a similar comparison based on the option to execute that particular process using cheaper labour abroad. Furthermore, the fact that most new technology is immediately available to producers in the developing countries (witness the high degree of automation of Hong Kong's industry) reduces the advantages to be gained by following such a strategy.

The future for technological change is thus clouded by uncertainty. Japanese machinery companies, spurred on by the Ministry of International Trade and Industry (MITI) as discussed below, are committing large amounts of research-and-development resources to automate clothing manufacturing at all stages through the use of flexible manufacturing systems. Others are experimenting with three-dimensional forming and bonding techniques that may drastically alter the way garments are made. A recent study for the Commission of the European Community by the industrial consultants, Kurt Salmon Associates,[6] analysed the potential impact of these new technologies on the operations of a 'typical apparel manufacturer'. They assumed three levels of investment: hardware per worker would increase three times (medium technology), seven times (high technology) and twenty times (super technology) from current levels of about $2,500. Their assessment assumed reductions in labour content of production of 25 per cent, 50 per cent and 70 per cent, respectively, accompanied by increases in average hourly earnings due to higher levels of skill and the need to pay for the indirect labour necessary to programme and maintain the equipment. The optimal investment level appeared to be in the order of ten to twelve times current levels. On this basis, if current production in the European Community, the United States and Japan were to be modernised to this level, it would entail the loss of 1.2-1.5 million operator jobs and an investment in the order of $25 billion.

Size and Scale of Individual Companies

In spite of whatever pressures technology has imposed on the minimum corporate size required for survival, the evidence to date shows very little increase in the levels of industry concentration or average size of firms. Vertical integration (that is, control of production processes from raw material stage to finished product) is also a rare phenomenon in the clothing industry, with a few notable exceptions such as Courtaulds in the United Kingdom and Prouvost in France. In this, the most fragmented of all industries (over 50,000 firms operate in the eight countries under study), the disadvantages of scale appear to have prevailed.

The analysis of value added per manufacturing man-hour in the American industry in the late 1960s and early 1970s[7] showed that large plant size could have a negative effect on economic efficiency. In fact, some segments of the industry appeared to experience significant diseconomies of scale in factories with more than 250 employees. Firms which operated a number of manufacturing plants, however, could benefit from the advantages of scale inherent in centralised administrative, design, cutting and information systems without incurring the penalties associated with large size. By organising production in a series of small manufacturing establishments, each with no more than 250-300 employees, in rural areas located in a circle around a centralised warehouse and distribution centre, the firm could organise its various functions in terms of their respective sensitivity to effects of scale. In this 'spokes-and-wheel' system, the manufacturing facilities would remain manageable and perform those processes (essentially assembly) not amenable to automation.

A similar more recent analysis of the clothing industry in Italy shows that the relationship between size and efficiency is the same there.[8] Significant economies of cost were possible by transferring sewing and pressing operations to specialised plants. Unit costs were found to drop by 5 per cent as volume increased from 100,000 to 500,000 units per annum, but by less than 1 per cent if volume increased to 1,500,000 units. The analysis established that 24 firms operating 72 plants of the minimum efficient scale (600,000 units) would be sufficient to supply in an optimal fashion the total Italian market. Instead, Italy had 470 companies engaged in this one sector, an indication of the potential gains in efficiency which could be obtained from a more rational industry structure with fewer firms operating several plants. Of course, issues such as flexibility, independence, avoiding labour-union pressures and diversified production may account for the continued resistance of the industry to the benfits that could be derived from rationalisation.[9]

In the United Kingdom, the 100 largest clothing firms accounted for barely 9 per cent of output in 1973 versus 40 per cent in all manufacturing. In the Federal Republic of Germany, the three largest firms did not reach 5 per cent of clothing sales in 1975 by contrast to 25 per cent of all industrial activity. In Japan, the five largest clothing manufacturers represented less than 20 per cent of production in 1970 as opposed to 50 per cent for all industry. In the United States, the eight largest companies in the industry did not exceed 15 per cent of clothing sales in 1976, half the manufacturing average.[10] Yet, at the sub-sector level, the degree of concentration can be higher. For example, at the four-digit level of the International Standard Industrial Classification (ISIC) in two sub-sectors (work-clothing and brassières), the American industry showed eight firm concentration ratios of about 50 per cent in 1972; however, these firms are the exception.

These are extraordinarily low levels. When combined with high specialisation ratios (many firms have often in excess of 90 per cent of production in the same four-digit ISIC product category), the degree of vulnerability is high. An industry populated by many small firms operating in a narrow product range is bound to exhibit a high mortality rate in the best of circumstances. In Kurt Salmon Associates' annual performance profile of apparel companies in the United States, it is always the 'diversified' companies (with many product categories, for example, men's and women's wear, sportswear and formal wear *et cetera*) that perform the best. In 1978, they showed a net income-to-sales ratio of 5.6 per cent versus about 2 per cent for single-product-line companies. Since the diversified firms are also the largest, though, it is not easy to distinguish both effects. Nevertheless, single-product firms with aggressive acquisition strategies aimed at dominance in a product market have also performed well. This has been the strategy of a company such as Kindy in France, which sought dominance through acquisitions in the sock business throughout the mid-1970s.

In summary, there would appear to be plenty of scope for rationalisation and concentration across all product groups and all countries. The cost of inefficient industry structures is borne by both consumers and society in general, as it aggravates the vulnerability of the industry to foreign competition and, therefore, its propensity to call for greater protection. Size alone is clearly not a solution to the competitive problems the industry is facing, but the state of the industry's structure in all the countries studied[11] did not allow for even the most basic investments either in technology or in product design and administrative support systems for the vast majority of firms in each country. Unfortunately, the family-owned nature of most firms and the fierce sense of independence that characterises most of their management are major obstacles to concentration in the industry.

Wage Adjustment

A preferred and time-honoured response of textile and clothing companies to cost competition has been to seek the lowest wage possible. They have attempted this by avoiding highly industrialised areas where alternative employment opportunities would push up wage costs, by employing large proportions of low-cost labour such as women, immigrants or low-skilled workers and by fighting labour unions with every means available.

In most OECD countries, the clothing labour force has absorbed a large proportion of the adjustment burden, not only by having to seek jobs elsewhere as part of the industry's contraction, but also by reducing their relative earning power. The weighted-average wage in the clothing industry declined from 73 per cent of the average manufacturing wage in 1967 in the countries listed in Table 3.2, to 68.5 per cent in 1978. Exceptions to this general rule were countries where the level of contraction in the industry had been the highest (for example, in Switzerland, the Netherlands and Sweden) or where it was expanding the fastest (for example, in Italy). The textile industry, on the other hand, seems to have fared better in these terms since, as shown above, it has succeeded in greatly enhancing its competitiveness through investment and modernisation.

One major means of achieving wage reduction has been domestic migration. The experience of the British

TABLE 3.2

Relative Hourly Earnings[a] in the Textile and Clothing Industries, 1967 and 1978
(average for manufacturing each year = 100)

	Textiles		*Clothing*	
	1967	*1978*	*1967*	*1978*
Austria	80.1[b]	74.9	75.9	64.4
Belgium	86.4	81.4	73.6	68.7
Canada	74.2	72.7	67.1	70.1
Denmark	82.5	89.2	82.5	85.5
Finland	79.0	77.5	74.3	72.1
France	80.6	84.5	84.0	76.9
West Germany	84.6	83.2	78.3	74.7
Italy	82.5	89.6[c]	74.6	82.1[c]
Netherlands	94.5	92.9	68.9	73.6
Norway	81.7	80.9	78.9	75.8
Sweden	82.6	88.5	78.0	83.8
Switzerland	80.1	82.7	71.8	73.1
United Kingdom[d]	82.0	85.4	67.4	64.0
United States	73.0	69.6	72.0	63.9

SOURCE: *Textile and Clothing Industries: Structural Problems and Policies in OECD Countries* (Paris: OECD Secretariat, 1983) Table 37.

[a]Wages for time worked including time rates, piece rates, shift supplements, overtime supplements and regularly paid bonuses and premiums.

[b]Figure refers to 1969.

[c]Figure refers to 1977.

[d]Figures refer to England, Scotland and Wales.

clothing industry with respect to domestic locational shifts during the first half of this century[12] was later duplicated by its American and West European counterparts.

Hence, the concentration of clothing-industry employment in the northern states of the United States dropped from nearly 80 per cent immediately after World War II to 51 per cent in 1970 and 42 per cent in 1976. There were two main reasons for this. First, a trained cutter — cutting being one of the most skilled roles on the shop floor — earned in 1977 between $4.36 and $5.33 an hour in any of the northern states. The same worker in the south-eastern or south-central states earned between $3.71 and $4.63 an hour; that is, 80-85 per cent of the equivalent northern wage. Second, while the clothing industry was 90 per cent unionised in the north, the proportion of union workers in the south and west was 33 and 44 per cent respectively. A similar situation prevailed in other countries where the Dutch industry moved to Belgium in the 1960s in search of lower wages, Italian companies moved to the south and West German firms moved both within the Federal Republic and to countries in southern and Eastern Europe.

The evidence from some countries is also fairly clear in terms of the employment of lower-wage workers in the industry. The high proportion of women, immigrants, older and poorly-educated workers allowed the industry to keep its average wage at a fraction of the overall manufacturing wage in the country and to widen this gap over the years. The price of these actions was high employment turnover and resistance to change. As the industry contracts further and begins to require higher skills in keeping with the progressive modernisation of its manufacturing processes, a key social and corporate problem will be one of training.[13] The specific characteristics of low-skilled workers in the industry make their absorption into other sectors of the economy considerably more difficult. When aggravated by the regional concentration of the industry (see Table 2.11) and by the fact that much of the displaced workers' income goes to supplement already meagre family incomes, the social consequences of change in the industry are rendered more dramatic.

Probably one of the more ambitious studies of what happens to labour made redundant in this industry was carried out in the 1977-78 Canadian Labour Force Tracking Project.[14] Clothing and textile workers represented 47 per cent of the total sample of 9,626 workers separated from their jobs in 154 establishments and included in the survey. Among the clothing workers, 25 per cent left the labour force following separation, particularly if they were female, married to an employed spouse or over 55 years old, where the ratio was close to 60 per cent. Of those remaining in the workforce, 51 per cent had found employment within four months and an additional 30 per cent within the next eight months. Age, sex, marital status and experience all affected the speed of re-employment as might be expected. An interesting fact is that most clothing workers (37 per cent) found their next job in the same industry, while the average for the sample was only 16 per cent. They also tended to improve their wage earnings (55 per cent) in their next job more readily than workers in other sectors. These two points confirm the lack of mobility and low earnings of most clothing workers that compounds the inter-industry adjustment problem.

Product and Market Shifts

One of the most successful adjustment strategies utilised by developed-country producers is to move 'up market' and incorporate better product design, higher quality, more elaborate materials and accessories, or — perhaps more important than all others — to improve the distribution network and services provided to retailers. The philosophy behind such moves stems from a conviction that there is little the clothing manufacturer in a high-wage country can do to meet the price competition of developing-country producers. Given the wage-rate differentials, no amount of investment and automation can close the gap in the short-to-medium term. Thus the solution lies in shifting the competitive struggle to non-price factors where, so this theory goes, advanced-country producers have a comparative advantage.

The most widely used stratagem in this area is to develop and actively promote a brand name to consumers and retailers. This implies, obviously, certain support activities such as quick re-ordering turn-around, advertising support and frequent model changes that add value to the product line and margins to both the producer and retailer. There are plenty of examples of successful differentiation strategies in all of the countries under study. Levi Strauss uses its popular brand name in jeans to promote other products and supports them with an advertising budget which amounted to $59 million in 1979. Blue Bell, the second largest jeans company, followed this diversification strategy and managed to reduce its dependency on jeans from 75 per cent to just over 50 per cent of sales during the 1970s. The objective is not only to profit from the goodwill inherent in the brands but also to have the capability to shift resources rapidly from one product area to another in response to fashion and competitive trends. Accordingly, when the jeans market dropped by 7 per cent in 1978, Levi Strauss was able to increase sales volume by nearly 8 per cent and net income by 11.6 per cent. Other jeans companies which were less diversified at the time fared less well.[15]

Throughout Western Europe many companies have used the same concepts of brand image and careful segmentation. A well-known success story is that of the Italian sportswear manufacturer, Benetton, which promotes brand awareness for its limited line of products and uses colour as its distinctive competitive tool. It has also developed a unique franchising system throughout the world and now has more than 2,500 exclusive outlets. The company, however, goes beyond acting only on its marketing strategy by organising production processes in ten plants and hundreds of sub-contractors in such a way that its unit costs are about 28 per cent lower than its West European competitors.[16] A number of French companies have also 'upgraded' their products and image in recent years or invested heavily in maintaining their distinctiveness from cheap competitors. Lacoste and Timewear have succeeded in sportswear, as have Absorba Poron in children's wear and Petit Bateau in infants' and toddlers' wear.[17]

One variation on this theme, which has taken off significantly in the last decade, has been to buy or license the signature of a prominent designer or couturier and attach it to products made in large quantities. French and Italian companies have led the field with their ready-to-wear lines supported by the big design houses of both countries. Starting with limited and exclusive distribution in the late 1960s, they have now progressed to a system akin to franchising and 'designer boutiques' are sprouting up throughout the OECD markets. In spite of this crowding phenomenon, which may eventually render the strategy useless, it continues undaunted. One of the more dramatic success stories consists of Puritan Fashions' agreement to launch a line of jeans under the signature of Calvin Klein with massive advertising support. Palm Beach, an old and staid men's suit company, began to emphasise innovation and designer products in the early 1970s. Among its early successes it signed on the Evan Picone name for a line specifically designed for working women which happened to hit the market when more and more women were demanding specially tailored office wear. The company's sales doubled to $230 million in 1973-78, its earnings increased six times and its return on equity at 25 per cent was over three times the industry average.[18] Japanese designers, after spending an apprenticeship in French and Italian houses, have also begun to make a major impact on the ready-to-wear markets. The collections of Kenzo, Kansai Yamamoto, Hanae Mori and others have made major inroads into West European and American markets. Renown, the largest clothing company in Japan, conversely, licenses many Western designer labels and styles and has been a major force in pioneering international styles within the Japanese market.

In general, an international market appears to be rapidly developing for well-designed high-quality clothes, which are relatively high-priced and are sold in exclusive and high-quality department stores and in significant volume. Not all of the OECD's clothing industry can gain access to this market, but those who succeed are guaranteed relative immunity from developing-country competition. It remains to be seen whether production of these lines will remain in the developed countries or whether the successful international houses that pioneered them will also move abroad for their labour-intensive processes.

Evidence of the effects of these strategies can be gleaned from the continued importance of clothing exports from most developed countries. Table 2.16 (above) reveals from the divisible nature of the clothing manufacturing the major improvements in clothing terms of trade for Italy, Japan, France and the Federal Republic of Germany: four countries that have invested heavily in product differentiation. An obstacle to this international specialisation, however, is the continued protection given by most developing countries to their own domestic industry. Except for two notable cases, Hong Kong and Singapore, most major producers of clothing in developing countries are also heavily involved in protecting and supporting their native firms. While perhaps justifiable in terms of the level of economic development and their need to conserve foreign exchange, this attitude hands over to would-be protectionists in the developed countries one of their most formidable political arguments to resist further liberalisation in their own markets.[19]

Foreign Assembly and Sub-contracting

Foreign assembly (known as 'offshore manufacturing' in the United States and 'outward processing' in West European economic jargon) is the practice followed by many manufacturers in high-wage countries whereby home-designed and home-cut pieces of clothing are sent to foreign (low-wage) locations for assembly and then re-imported into the home country. In most, but not all, cases and with subtle variations in their application, most governments of the originating country will exempt the domestic content from import duties and tax only the foreign value added at the appropriate rate. The interest in such a system derives from the divisible nature of the clothing manufacturing process which allows for different operations to be performed independently from one another. As discussed earlier, the operations that can benefit from economies of scale in processing and design are thus maintained 'at home' and the cut pieces are shipped to the foreign affiliate for assembly. Since this last process is less amenable to automation, is the most labour-intensive and requires relatively low skills, the developing countries are ideally suited for carrying it out. In fact, the Commission of the European Community, in a statement on the industry's international difficulties, has said that 'outward processing should be considered as a particularly well suited instrument of industrial cooperation... This type of operation can contribute to maintain production levels in the Community's industry and to protect employment.'[20]

The United States has been operating such a system since the early 1960s and American clothing manufacturers have increasingly made use of its '807' provisions (as the American foreign value-added system is called) in order to reduce their overall unit costs in manufacturing. As shown in Table 3.3, 7-10 per cent of all clothing imported into the United States in recent years has come under the value-added regime. Given that only 35 per cent of the value of the imported product represents foreign content, this arrangement allows the country to retain a significant share of economic activity that might otherwise be lost to foreign competitors.[21] In the American case the major beneficiaries are Caribbean countries, which in 1980 accounted for 72 per cent of all clothing imports under item 807, with Mexico alone representing nearly 40 per cent of the total. Yet, in spite of the fast growth of this activity since 1970, it accounted for slightly less than 1 per cent of total sales of clothing products in the United States in 1980.[22]

The number of American companies involved in 807 imports are many and their experiences are often mixed. Manhattan Industries and Philips-Van Heusen, two large shirt makers, and Warnaco and Kellwood, all among the largest fifteen clothing manufacturers in the United States, reportedly import about 30 per cent of their total requirements each from either offshore assembly or sub-contracting operations abroad. In many cases they do not own these facilities, but simply supply the cut fabric and some technical assistance. Oxford Industries, for example (1978 sales of $234 million), concluded a five-year agreement with a group of Chinese manufacturers to license them several proprietary machine designs and processes in exchange for shirts that would be made in China for re-export to the United States, using Oxford's specifications.[23] Beaumont International, a diversified producer whose sales grew from $2.5 million in 1950 to $160 million in 1974, has followed a similar aggressive policy of sub-contracting abroad without acquiring ownership. Beginning with Portugal in 1965, the company later expanded its '807' business to Brazil,

TABLE 3.3

Imports of Clothing and all Products under Item 807 of the US Tariff Schedules, 1970-81 (US$ million and per cent)

	Total imports (A)	*Total imports (B)*	*Item 807 imports (C)*	*C/A (%)*	*C/B (%)*	*American content on 807 imports (%)*	*American content on Item 807 imports (%)*	*Item 807 clothing imports from Mexico (% of C)*
1970	1,257	2,007	36.8	2.9	1.8	21.6	na	na
1971	1,510	2,569	49.5	3.3	1.9	20.9	na	na
1972	1,875	3,093	66.5	3.5	2.2	22.0	na	na
1973	2,154	3,784	96.4	4.5	2.5	20.1	na	na
1974	2,323	4,828	231.6	10.0	4.8	20.9	na	na
1975	2,551	4,710	222.3	8.7	4.7	21.3	na	na
1976	3,590	5,248	272.5	7.6	5.2	24.2	na	na
1977	4,123	6,723	311.6	7.6	4.6	25.3	64.6	na
1978	6,124	9,337	409.7	6.7	4.4	25.1	61.7	na
1979	6,355	11,559	457.2	7.2	4.0	26.7	63.3	na
1980	6,943	13,762	515.6	7.4	3.7	26.0	64.2	38.7
1981	na	15,924	565.7	na	3.6	26.8	62.0	35.0
Annual change (%)								
1970-80	18.6	21.2	30.2	—	—	—	—	—

SOURCES: Jeffrey S. Arpan, José de la Torre and Brian Toyne, *The US Apparel Industry: International Challenge, Domestic Response*, Research Monograph No. 88 (Atlanta: Georgia State University, 1982) p. 70; and *Tariff Items 807.00 and 806.30: US Imports for Consumption* (Washington: International Trade Commission, 1981).

NOTE: C/A and C/B refers to ratio of columns 3:1 and 3:2. In the table 'na' signifies 'not available' and '—' signifies 'not applicable'.

Barbados and Trinidad, and supplemented it with subcontracting agreements in Taiwan and South Korea, all of which represented 20 per cent of its volume in 1973.[24]

But not all is rosy in this business; many companies attempting to set up assembly operations abroad have run into problems caused by low productivity, high employee turnover, over-zealous government bureaucrats, delivery delays and bad quality control. Casualwear Inc., an American company with a $40 million turnover manufacturing women's wear, invested in a joint venture in Haiti in the mid-1960s to supply part of its needs. After a year it discovered that the extremely low wages ($1 per day) were not enough to compensate for the low productivity and high turnover problems that developed. As the cost per Haitian unit produced and shipped to the United States came to 90 per cent of its American costs, the company decided to look elsewhere. Eventually, it settled for a twin-plant arrangement straddling the Mexico-United States border with very satisfactory results.[25] By sewing and assembling 20-30 per cent of its requirements in Mexico, Casualwear was able to lower its average costs while maintaining better marketing services than a foreign exporter. Yet not all products were amenable to such a system. The data in Table 3.4 quantify the value of foreign assembly for nine product categories. Only in men's shirts and slacks are the advantages evident.

West Germany and the Netherlands are the two West European countries that have made the widest use of outward-processing provisions in their customs regulations. Table 3.5 reproduces some historical data showing that roughly 12-15 per cent of clothing imports into the Federal Republic of Germany benefit from special value-added duty provisions and that foreign value added is roughly similar to that in the American case.

The total, however, represents about 5 per cent of West German clothing consumption versus 1 per cent in the United States. Although no breakdown is available for country of origin, various estimates are that, in 1972, 59 per cent came from Eastern Europe and Yugoslavia, and 28 per cent from Mediterranean countries.[26] Similarly, it has been estimated that 68 per cent of all East European clothing exports to West Germany and

TABLE 3.4
Comparison of Per-unit Retail Price between Articles of Apparel Made in the United States and those Made in the United States with Item 807 Assembly

	Made in the United States ($)	*United States with Item 807 assembly ($)*	*Advantage (%)*
Sweaters	17.21	18.28	−6.2
Women's knitted blouses	9.41	9.18	2.4
Men's dress shirts	10.32	9.11	11.7
Women's slacks	8.74	8.77	−0.3
Men's knitted sports shirts	8.20	7.56	7.8
Men's casual slacks	11.83	10.64	10.1
Men's jeans	11.20	11.02	1.6
Women's skirts	9.07	9.47	−4.4
Men's briefs	2.04	2.20	−7.8

SOURCE: *Marketing Strategies for US Apparel Producers to Compete More Effectively with Imports* (Atlanta: Georgia Institute of Technology, 1980).

90 per cent of those from Yugoslavia consist of outward-processing activities conducted by West German firms. In fact, West German manufacturers, through their foreign assembly, sub-contracting and direct investment activity are supposedly responsible for 40 per cent of all West German clothing imports.[27]

Dutch companies have also been known to be active in processing activities abroad. In 1972, for example, 6.4

million pieces of men's outer-wear were processed to some extent abroad, compared with 11.2 million pieces produced entirely in the Netherlands. Three years later, while the figure for foreign processing of men's outer-wear remained at roughly 6.5 million pieces, national

TABLE 3.5

West German Imports of Clothing under Value-added Duties
(million marks and per cent)

	Value	*% of total clothing imports*	*% of all imports under value-added duties*	*Domestic content in offshore assembly of clothing (%)*
1961	17	2.6	23.9	79.6
1962	55	6.6	29.8	77.2
1963	102	10.1	29.4	73.1
1964	158	13.0	25.4	75.1
1965	290	17.0	27.0	78.6
1966	343	16.7	24.0	71.8
1967	280	16.3	22.6	70.8
1968	293	13.9	34.1	69.6
1969	268	6.8	46.4	75.7
1970	331	9.3	41.7	72.3
1971	532	11.9	48.5	78.8
1972	786	13.7	56.1	70.0
1973	917	14.9	54.5	69.6
1974	1,108	15.7	54.3	70.5
1975	1,062	13.3	46.4	75.9
1976	1,282	13.5	52.1	63.5
1977	1,261	12.7	55.3	65.0
1978	1,327	12.5	60.9	65.2

SOURCE: *Textile and Clothing Industries: Structural Problems and Policies in OECD Countries* (Paris: OECD Secretariat, 1983) Table 27.

production had dropped to 6.1 million.[28] Although data are not specifically reported for outward-processing activities, Dutch companies have been estimated to rely almost entirely on East European countries (about 95 per cent of the total) for such processing. It is also estimated that the domestic clothing industry accounts for about 40 per cent of total imports subject to value-added duty.[29] Thus outward processing has also played a major defensive role for the industry in the Netherlands. As Figure 3.1 indicates, this activity represented a major share in the market for medium-price clothing in such items as men's suits and trousers. While low-wage developing countries dominated the lower-price sectors, outward processing complemented domestic production in the middle sectors, allowing domestic companies to compete with imports from other countries in the European Community. This was not the case for the higher-price sectors where other producers in the European Community held the majority of the Dutch market.

The French industry began to use processing abroad more recently, in the teeth of French official opposition to a liberal foreign-assembly policy.[30] Some preliminary estimates claim that imports under outward-processing arrangements, mainly involving Morocco, Tunisia and Portugal, have risen from 5 to 7 per cent of all imports of ladies' clothing within the two years 1977-79.[31] Gaston Jaunet, for example, one of Baron Bich's companies with 600 employees and 1980 sales of 140 million French francs, derives 20-25 per cent of its volume from assembly facilities in North Africa and Eastern Europe. Management claims it is two or two-and-a-half times cheaper in spite of high overhead costs, the duties paid on East European production and the inevitable delays in clearing customs by having to demonstrate the French content in fabrics.[32]

The perils of processing abroad can also be seen in the experience of a French shirt manufacturer, Sunay-Fortier, a company that had sales in 1977 of FF109 million and employed 1000 people. The company used

FIGURE 3.1

Netherlands: Market Share by Price Segment and Product Origin, Men's Suits and Trousers, 1975

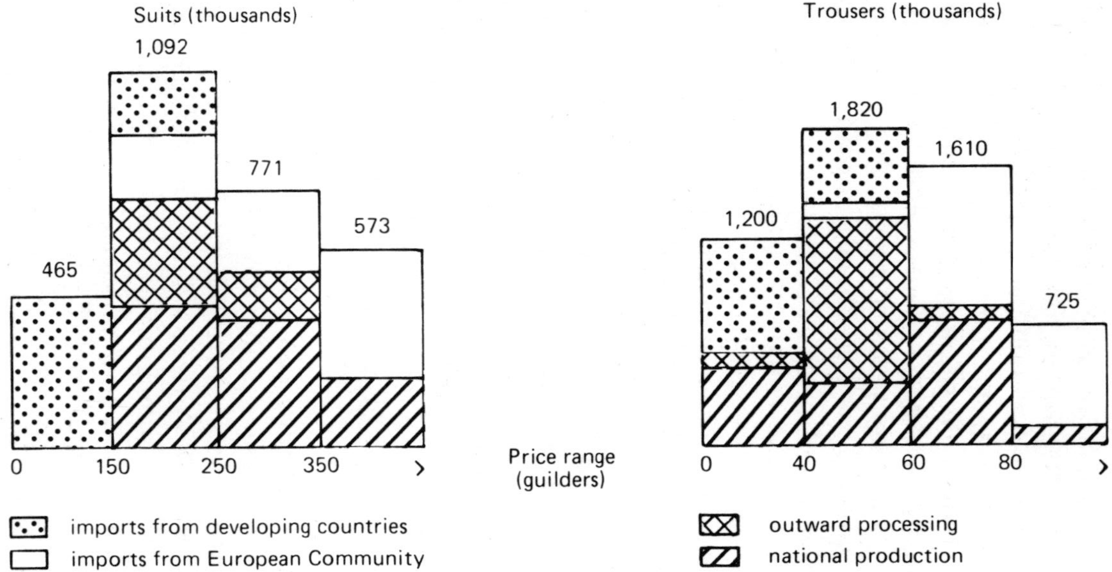

SOURCE: *Herstructurering Nederlandse Confectie-Industrie: deel 1 Herenbovenkleding-Industrie* ('s-Hertogenbosch: Nederlandse Herstructureringsmaatschappij [NEHEM], 1977).

to produce low-cost shirts for large department stores. From 1973, when it began to feel the impact of low-cost competition from East Asia, it took three steps. First, it moved its entire production 'up market' to '*fantaisie*' shirts and sportswear. Second, it restructured its four plants into two (without shedding labour) and introduced modern automated equipment designed to increase productivity. Third, it began to import, through both outward-processing activities and sub-contracting, the lower end of its product range. By 1977, one third of its volume was produced abroad. Following the renegotiation of the MFA and France's tough new policy on imports, the company found itself cut off from this source of low-cost supplies. After scrambling unsuccessfully for eight months to replace the lost sources, the company had to close its doors.[33]

For the rest of the OECD countries, foreign processing arrangements are practically non-existent. Switzerland, the United Kingdom and Japan have rather strict eligibility rules and the Italian industry does not appear interested. They can find their own low-wage suppliers either in the labour black market or in the Mezzogiorno. This results in interesting conflicts within the European Community as to how to deal with outward-processing activities.

The developing countries, on the other hand, can see major advantages in this direction. As a measure of their interest, nine countries had eleven export-processing zones in 1970. A decade later, the list had expanded to 34 countries managing a total of 96 export-processing zones. The potential impact on jobs for some of these countries is significant. Table 3.6 shows some recent data for the major countries promoting these zones. In South Korea, for example, 14.7 per cent of all enterprises and 7.4 per cent of all the investment in the country's export-processing zones are in the textile and clothing industries.

For Sri Lanka, the proportions are 42 per cent and 29 per cent respectively. In Egypt, 1,655 jobs in its export-processing zones, or 54 per cent of total manufacturing employment in the zones, are in clothing and textiles. These and other similar countries are trying to attract foreign investors to set up processing facilities in these

TABLE 3.6

Employment in Export-processing Zones (EPZs)
(data range from 1978-80)

	Industrial jobs within EPZs[a]	*Total industrial employment*	*EPZ/Total (%)*
Mauritius	20,151	73,500	27.4
Dominican Republic	20,500	192,000	10.7
Malaysia	80,920	962,600	8.4
Taiwan	80,166	1,701,000	4.7
Mexico	119,500	4,150,000	2.9
Sri Lanka	13,200	812,000	1.6
Philippines	24,974	2,463,900	1.0
Brazil	46,500	6,820,000	0.7
South Korea	30,642	4,310,000	0.7
Senegal	600	159,300	0.4
Egypt	3,061	2,496,000	0.1
India	6,000	28,710,000	...

SOURCE: Antoine Basile and Dimitri Germidis, *Politiques d'attractions des investissements étrangers orientés vers l'exportation: le rôle de zones franches industrielles d'exportation* (Paris: OECD Development Centre, 1982) Table 12.2.
NOTE: In the table '...' signifies 'not significant'.
[a]Includes both companies located within export-processing zones and those benefiting from similar privileges but located elsewhere — for example, the *maquiladoras* in Mexico.

zones which will then export assembled goods to the investors' home countries.[34] Their success, however, depends not only on how well they can perform but also on whether they will be allowed to try.[35]

Regulating foreign processing by the clothing industry has been a hot political issue within the European Community for some time. Given that most countries providing foreign processing to the Community benefit from preferential access to its markets (they are either associated members or belong to one or another preferential agreement), the Community has no legal right or power to control this traffic. In order to do so, the Community had to offer the Mediterranean countries reasonably generous outward-processing quotas in addition to those of general applicability, which had been previously negotiated through a series of 'voluntary' export-restraint agreements with most of these countries. The United Kingdom refused to accept these additional volumes and with French support asked for the drafting of a regulation.[36] The drafting process took nearly three years until the Council of Ministers approved a final version in February 1982. The Regulation reserves outward-processing quotas for clothing manufacturers and imposes severe limitations on the use of materials not of Community origin. But the issue as to whether such quotas would be in addition to or part of other quantitative restrictions (MFA or VER quotas) has not been resolved to the satisfaction of France and the United Kingdom, which are together taking the lead in promoting the narrowest interpretation possible.[37]

Foreign Direct Investment

Whether in support of their foreign processing activities or as a way to enter and aggressively exploit market opportunities worldwide, foreign direct investment by clothing manufacturers could provide another dimension to the adjustment process. The reality is that the level of investment in foreign subsidiaries is extremely low in general for all countries, particularly when compared with the size of the industry and the average propensity to invest abroad of most OECD countries.

Japan is probably the major exception and for some very peculiar reasons. According to a recent study on the subject,[38] Japanese fibre and textile companies observed the import-substitution strategies of their neighbouring countries and, beginning in the early 1960s, committed large amounts of resources to build fairly integrated

TABLE 3.7.

Japanese Direct Investments in the Asian-Pacific Textile System, 1980 (number of projects)

	Man-made fibres	*Spinning, weaving, knitting and dyeing*	*Clothing*	*Total*
Taiwan	3	20 (22)	22	45
Hong Kong	0	12	4 (6)	16
South Korea	5	8 (9)	33	46
Sub-total (East Asia)	8	40 (43)	59 (61)	107
Thailand	2	21	7 (9)	30
Indonesia	4	19 (20)	3 (4)	26
Philippines	4	3	6	13
Malaysia	1	10	3	14
Singapore	0	5	3 (4)	8
Sub-total (ASEAN)	11	58 (59)	22 (26)	91
TOTAL	19	98 (102)	81 (87)	198

SOURCES: Jeffrey S. Arpan, Mary Barry and Tran Van Tho, 'The Textile Complex in the Pacific Basin: the Patterns and Textures of Competition and the Shape of Things to Come', University of South Carolina, mimeograph, undated, Table 6; and Van Tho, 'Industrial Policy and the Textile Industry: the Japanese Experience', *Journal of Contemporary Business*, Seattle, Vol. 11, No. 1, 1982, Table 2.

NOTE: The figures in parentheses include projects already counted in an upstream activity, but which incorporate more than one stage of production.

complexes in each of these countries. Taiwan and Thailand were the first markets to which this policy was applied. South Korea and Indonesia soon followed, after which operations were extended to Malaysia and the Philippines. Table 3.7 summarises the available data. By the end of 1980, Japanese companies owned 198 subsidiaries in these countries, almost half of which were in clothing manufacturing. Of the 198, 66 were controlled by seven large fibre firms, 27 by nine large spinning companies and 91 by Japan's trading companies.[39] But the key role was played by the fibre companies as they followed the initial steps taken by 'mid-stream' producers (those manufacturing yarn and textile fabrics) and consolidated Japan's control over the vertical chain; that is, all production processes from fibre to clothing in many of these markets.

A case in point is Toray Industries, Japan's largest producer of textile fibre, whose initial strategy consisted of establishing vertically-integrated complexes in each country with the help of other Japanese mid-stream or later-stage producers. In the early 1970s, it reached an agreement with Textile Alliance, a Hong Kong-based international concern with clothing subsidiaries in Taiwan, Hong Kong and Thailand, and excellent marketing support in Australia and the United States. The link-up was most successful and Toray is now firmly entrenched in all of these markets as well as its own.

The impact of Japanese investment in some of these countries has been substantial and, moreover, has greatly contributed to continued export strength for Japanese producers of fibres and fabrics. In 1980, Japan controlled about 70 per cent of foreign textile investment in Taiwan and 60 per cent in Thailand. Elsewhere, Japan controlled all synthetic fibre production in Indonesia and Malaysia, 80 per cent in the Philippines and Thailand and 60 per cent in South Korea (the figure had been 100 per cent until Japan was forced to sell some of her investments to local interests in the late 1970s). In keeping with the shift from trade to investment, the share of Japanese-manufactured exports in textile products traded worldwide dropped from 18.7 per cent in 1965 to 4.9 per cent in 1980.

Investment by the Federal Republic of Germany in foreign production of clothing is mainly confined to foreign processing of clothes for the West German market. One estimate is that employment in foreign subsidiaries of West German clothing manufacturers (expressed as a percentage of domestic employment) rose from 3.7 per cent in 1966 to nearly 10 per cent in 1974.[40] But the total volume is tiny. Another author estimates that West German total outward and inward foreign investments in 1979 for the clothing industry amounted to DM251 million and DM667 million respectively. This represents 0.4 per cent and 1.2 per cent of total West German outward and inward foreign investment.[41]

As for the French, investment abroad met both local production and re-import objectives, but in different markets. Companies such as Prouvost set up a facility to assemble its Rodier brand products in Tunisia; Bidermann invested in several facilities in North Africa and Colombia;[42] Cacharel in Japan; and Thivy Sivem and Lejaby in Tunisia. All these have committed resources to manufacture in these countries primarily for the French and West European markets.[43] In addition to making defensive investments in low-wage countries, Bidermann now produces 40 per cent of its total output in the United States to satisfy the American market. Others such as La Lanire de Roubaix (woollens), Diroco (tights) and Eminence (men's underwear) are also investing abroad with the conviction that in order to succeed there, they must be locally implanted.[44]

The Dutch industry's investment in foreign supply facilities also seems to be made mainly with a view to re-importing to the home market and only partially as a way of gaining access to foreign markets. By 1980, it was estimated that the production capacity of foreign affiliates of Dutch clothing companies was equivalent to 15,000 jobs. Of these, 50 per cent were in Belgium, 20 per cent in Portugal and 15 per cent in Tunisia. By comparison, total clothing-industry employment in the Netherlands was less than 20,000.[45]

Other countries have much less in the form of foreign investments. American jeans manufacturing companies have set up facilities in Western Europe and East Asia, but, other than a few assembly plants sprinkled around the Caribbean, there is no evidence of the significant use of foreign direct investment as a means of entering foreign markets. Nor are the West Europeans, other than those discussed above, very active in this sense. As the upper end of the market becomes more of a global business, investment abroad in key markets will become an essential requirement for survival in that product group.

Exit and Diversification

When all else fails and there is little chance left of adjusting to new competitive conditions, then the market may reassign the resources thus released to other more profitable activities. The French industry has lost an estimated 25,000 jobs per year since 1973 in both clothing and textiles and saw a yearly average of nearly a hundred companies disappear. In 1981-82, the American industry was shrinking at a rate of two to three hundred companies per annum. Some were relatively large companies with well-known brand names. Bobbie Brooks, for example, the twenty sixth largest in the industry with sales of $200 million in 1981, was forced into bankruptcy the following year. In some cases, an option remains to apply the same technology to other markets. Thus one troubled French clothing manufacturer realised the difficulties that awaited him in the future and is now making seat belts for cars and other industrial textile products, areas where competitive storms are somewhat less turbulent.

Integrated Approach to Survival and Prosperity

All of the responses outlined above are in themselves important elements in the process of adjustment, but none can guarantee by itself that prosperity or even survival will follow. Henri Scalabre, President of Scalabre-Belliteste, a medium-size men's shirt manufacturer in France, described *his* approach to the business. His product policy had consisted of occupying the upper-middle level of the price range for shirts — to this end, he acquired exclusive distribution rights for Arrow shirts in France — and thus avoided the fight at 'the 25-franc shirt level'. He manufactured 15 per cent — 'but not more' — of his shirts in low-wage countries, which allowed him to obtain lower overall costs when foreign wage costs were averaged with those of his local high-cost production. But he also expanded both in France and in other West European countries by acquiring existing firms that could be salvaged in a short time and whose existing products or facilities fitted his strategy. Finally, he invested FF30 million in automatic processes and production robots in order to maximise output per worker and improve profitability sufficiently to gain access to the stock market for further expansion.[46] There are elements in this brief case history to illustrate all the points made above. It is managing the total business that matters and doing so in a consistent manner.

Judging Strategies by Performance

In a detailed study of ten clothing manufacturers, which was carried out in the United States between 1972 and 1975, an effort was made to judge the effectiveness of different corporate strategies for facing foreign competition in domestic markets.[47] Since many strategic adjustment options were open to each firm, a classification scheme was devised to facilitate analysis. The following elements were identified separately in each case studied:

(a) adjustments in marketing policy, including revisions in product mix, customer mix, pricing and payment terms, distribution and promotion and selling policies;

(b) adjustments in production policy, encompassing variations in (i) raw-material utilisation and supplies mix, (ii) production processes in terms of capital/labour ratios, scale of operations, degree of production integration and efforts at value engineering and process innovation and (iii) production scheduling, planning and quality control;

(c) adjustments in location policy, consisting of changes in location of production facilities — national and international — and in intra-company logistics and handling of materials;

(d) adjustments in managerial and organisational policy ranging from changes in the number of specific roles of management staff to revisions of organisational structure, ownership and labour-management relations;

(e) adjustments in financial policy, such as modification in capital structure, working-capital management and financial control practices; and

(f) adjustments in external relations with industry or trade associations, government and other external agencies.

The ten firms selected for detailed case analyses ranged in size, measured by 1972 sales, from less than $1 million to more than $140 million. They included both privately-held and publicly-owned companies and were located in a variety of urban and rural settings. All but one had their headquarters in the south-eastern United States. In addition to data on strategic choices, a wide range of performance data was collected on the various firms.

According to most performance characteristics — growth, earnings, employment and value added — the sample firms fell into three distinct groups. The first group consisted of 'growth' companies, singularly successful during the period under analysis. The second group of firms was composed of those whose existence had been a constant struggle until such time as they either made adjustments to their strategies which enabled them to effect significant improvements in their performance or else inevitably collapsed. A third group, which in terms of performance lies between the other two, consisted of those firms that managed to survive more or less comfortably. Although sales performance basically remained constant, the 'comfortably surviving' firms managed to maintain high profitability and were at no time in serious danger. Almost all firms within a given performance group shared a common set of strategies which differentiated them from those in other groups. A series of propositions can therefore be offered linking strategies to performance.

'Growth' Firms

Five of the companies in the sample fit the 'growth' category: Arpog, Beaumont, Casualwear, Shapiro and Y&L.[48] Measured in terms of sales value, Beaumont expanded more than fifty-fold during the period 1950-73 from $2.5 million to just over $140 million. Casualwear experienced a growth in sales from less than $1 million in the mid-1950s to almost $25 million by the early 1970s and Y&L increased its sales volume in 1973 to five times that of 1955 (from $4.5 to $22.3 million). The remaining two companies recorded more modest growth: during the fifteen-year period the sales of Shapiro and Arpog doubled from base figures of $9 million and $25 million, respectively.

While all the firms studied paid considerable attention to the management of production, the growth-oriented firms excelled at it, devoting significant engineering resources to it and promoting innovative ideas in the organisation of production so as to minimise total costs. Their concern for production costs led these firms to search for optimum balances between labour, handling and inventory costs, on the one hand, and economies of scale, on the other. The production and distribution facilities of these companies were the result of these balancing concepts and were arranged geographically in terms of the 'spokes-and-wheel' concept. A relatively large distribution warehouse and the firm's administrative headquarters were located at the centre of this imaginary wheel. Piece goods, ordered and stocked centrally, were sent to the decentralised production units for cutting and assembly. These were then transported back to the centralised facility for processing, warehousing and shipping to the firm's customers. While the central administrative unit was typically in an urban location, the production facilities were almost always located in rural settings where semi-skilled labour was relatively abundant and inexpensive. Beaumont employed the same strategy on a divisional basis involving a total of more than twenty plants in rural locations.

The use of foreign suppliers and outward processing were other distinguishing characteristics of the 'growth' firms. These companies experimented with a number of such production arrangements and found them relatively effective for the manufacture of stable standardised lines which had long production lead times, low demand uncertainty, large volume and a transferable production learning curve.

Perhaps the most distinguishing characteristic of the 'growth' companies, however, was their deep involvement in managing the external dimension of their businesses. These firms placed considerable emphasis on and applied substantial managerial resources to matters dealing with distributors and customers, style, outlets and fashion. For example, all considered a close tie-in to New York City to be an essential aspect of their business. 'Growth' firms also shared a similar method of handling contract business with large retail houses or chains. This type of customer provided a margin of insurance against the more profitable but somewhat less reliable direct-sales business, but the 'growth' companies aggressively monitored their sales to the chain stores in order to guard against excessive dependence on any single customer.

These firms also emphasised the more design-intensive, higher-margin sectors of the trade in which more finishing work was required, lead times were shorter, quicker reactions were necessary and delivery was often more crucial than price; in other words, those sectors least likely to suffer from import competition. They also managed their finances aggressively, employing both public and private equity sources, incurring debt as necessary and showing a tendency to re-invest rather than distribute earnings as dividends each year.

'Struggling' Firms

A different set of strategic activities characterised the four firms that comprised the 'struggling' group: Brooks, Rosenbaum, Shaydon and Sullivan. Three of them had a volume of sales in the early 1950s comparable with that of some of the 'growth' firms — that is, between $1 and $2 million per year (the fourth firm in the category was not created until 1960). But, whereas the 'growth' firms increased their sales volume several times during the 1960s, not one of the four struggling firms' sales had exceeded a value of $2 million by 1971 and one of them had gone bankrupt.

The most significant differentiating characteristic of this 'struggling' group of companies was their almost total lack of involvement in the management of the 'external' dimension of the business. Instead, management concentrated on the internal (production) operations of the firm and relied largely on outside agents to perform all external functions. They relied heavily on contract business, for example, typically to large chain stores and mail-order houses. Sales to one or a few contract accounts often represented 100 per cent of their total sales. The most diversified had contract sales of 40 per cent and this was divided among six buyers.

Another distinction between this group and the 'growth' companies concerned production strategy. The struggling firms were typically one-plant operations with little opportunity or inclination to implement a 'multi-plant' strategy. Moreover, limited financial resources and low profitability made it difficult to adopt the sort of modernisation programmes required to increase labour productivity. Finally, these four companies were active in segments of the clothing market which experienced the highest incidence of import competition: men's dress shirts, ladies' blouses, certain standard items in ladies' slacks and sportswear and children's pyjamas.

By the late 1960s, competitive conditions had deteriorated to the point where swift and drastic measures were required. All four companies experienced significantly reduced earnings and/or losses during the 1967-70 period. Faced with this situation, the firms reacted in different ways. Rosenbaum adhered to a no-change strategy and collapsed within two years. Brooks limited its adjustment to a few changes in its product line, including an attempt to improve the style content of some articles, and dropped highly-competitive and import-sensitive items such as ladies' blouses. The company barely weathered the crunch of the import crisis in 1968-70, returned to a profitable level of operations after the general upswing of the clothing market in 1971-73 and succumbed in the 1974-75 recession. The other two firms in this 'struggling' group took a series of measures designed to correct the situation drastically. The strategic behaviour and performance of these two firms, together with that of the one remaining firm in the sample, Stuart Manufacturing, place them in a discrete category.

'Comfortably Surviving' Firms

A number of major characteristics distinguish the 'comfortably surviving' firms from the struggling firms. All three had established direct access to the market and had reduced contract work considerably. Shaydon, for example, had completely severed its dependence on its sole contract buyer (who initially owned half the firm) and increased direct marketing activities, both through a New York subsidiary and directly to retail outlets, thereby aiming to reduce its total contract business to less than one third of sales by 1975. Sullivan ran down its sales force and left the children's clothing business completely. Its shift to the higher-style and higher-margin sector of ladies' sportswear, accomplished with the assistance of two independent New York-based agents, resulted in a doubling of sales to more than $4 million by 1973. Unlike the two newcomers to this category, Stuart Manufacturing could be classified as having been 'comfortable' since the early 1950s. The company distributed over half its volume of good-quality medium-price men's suits and coats through its own sales organisation, with the other half being handled by three jobbers in Los Angeles, Boston and Chicago.

One element common to these three firms was their renewed commitment to style. The level of resources and effort they devoted to styling and market information appeared to be comparable to that of the growth companies. Shaydon and Sullivan had made drastic changes to their product lines as a result of their associations with their respective New York partners.

Stuart had employed a full-time designer and staff since its inception and allocated a significant amount of money to the design staff for salaries and travel. Another salient characteristic of the 'comfortable' companies was the incipient adoption of the 'spokes-and-wheel' concept. They were cognisant of the labour-market conditions that had forced the larger firms to decentralise production and were taking steps to follow suit. These plans, however, did not include the use of processing facilities abroad, rejected by the firms as 'too complicated'.

There was also a number of differentiating features between a 'comfortably surviving' strategy and a 'growth' strategy. Stuart, for instance, had followed a strategy clearly designed to maintain a volume of activity at some 'manageable' level. Sullivan also appeared to adhere to this principle, even after a change of product and market strategy significantly altered its ability to embark on a growth strategy should it have chosen to do so. Such an approach, while typically controlling growth, had as its objective a high rate of profitability and was often successful in obtaining it. For example, after-tax return on equity for Stuart — not counting salaries and other executive compensation perceived by the owner/managers — averaged 23 per cent in 1971 and 1972. By contrast to the financial policies of the growth firms, the comfortably surviving firms made little use of debt capital, withdrew sizeable after-tax profits each year in the form of dividends, had generous compensation schemes for their owner/managers and limited their capital investment to the acquisition of equipment designed to improve productivity and cut labour costs. This was partly due to the narrow base of ownership of these firms as compared with the growth companies. For all comfortably surviving firms, ownership was limited to one small family or one or two individuals. By contrast, two of the growth firms were publicly-owned and the three family-owned firms in that group had a much broader shareholder base.

Ability to Adjust

The foregoing analysis indicates that the industry's plight is not common to all its members. There are, and will continue to be, a number of firms that cannot cope with the intensive price competition that low-cost foreign producers can mount on a wide range of product lines. But these case studies show that domestic firms can adjust successfully to the challenge (or avert it altogether) by pursuing aggressive policies aimed at both the internal (productivity) and external (sales) sides of their business.

Manufacturing costs are a critical area for control regardless of a company's strategy on other fronts. The most successful firms in the sample devoted considerable resources and effort to keep costs down and productivity up. The 'spokes-and-wheel' concept, high capital/investment ratios, foreign processing facilities, large industrial engineering staffs and extensive efforts aimed at training and motivating personnel were found to be prevalent among these firms. Size was clearly important, not because it allowed for larger plants, but because it permitted the firm to centralise a number of production services that could, in turn, be provided to its various plants at significant savings. Nonetheless, the chances for survival appear to be severely limited, even when a successful cost-control programme is in effect, for firms that place high reliance on contract-manufacturing business.

A second condition necessary for success appears to be a product-marketing strategy aimed at the leading edge of the fashion market. By investing heavily in a product-differentiation strategy that includes a fashionable branded product line and dependable delivery schedules, a firm can compete successfully at premium prices. Even among discount stores (the major recipients of imported goods), the successful firms in the sample were able to maintain a competitive position through the pursuit of these policies.

In the final analysis, management remains the key to success. The small family-oriented firm pursuing unchanging policies in the midst of rapid environmental change is not likely to survive unscathed. But, if these firms were to incorporate external managerial resources attuned to the market place and capable of formulating and implementing rapid adjustments in corporate policies as competitive trends develop, their performance could be extremely successful. Unfortunately, the industry, partly through its own attitudes and traditions, partly because of the 'bad press' which has been directed at it on many occasions and partly due to the sheer limitations of small size and fragmentation, has never succeeded in attracting talented professional management to the extent necessary.

NOTES AND REFERENCES

1. On inter-industry adjustment within the textile system, see Geoffrey Shepherd, *Textile-industry Adjustment in Developed Countries*, Thames Essay No. 30 (London: Trade Policy Research Centre, 1981); and Arpan, Mary Barry and Van Tho, 'The Textile Complex in the Pacific Basin: the Patterns and Textures of Competition and the Shape of Things to Come', University of South Carolina, Columbia, South Carolina, mimeograph, undated.

2. Another measure of human capital is the percentage of the labour force in the industry with less than a ninth grade education. Data for the United States reveal the proportion to be 34 per cent for the clothing industry in 1975 versus 16 per cent for all manufacturing. See Arpan, de la Torre and Toyne, *The US Apparel Industry: International Challenge — Domestic Response*, Research Monograph No. 88 (Atlanta: Georgia State University, 1982) p. 11.

3. See 'L'industrie textile aux USA', Directorate for Science, Technology and Industry of the OECD, Paris, mimeograph, 1980, p. 62.

4. 'Guide de la formation continue dans l'industrie de l'habillement', Centre d'Etudes Techniques des Industries de l'Habillement (CETIH), Paris, mimeograph, 1972.

5. John Bragg, 'Assessment of New Technology', in *Domestic Apparel Program* (Washington: International Trade Administration, United States Department of Commerce, 1980).

6. *The 1980s: the Decade for Technology*, Report prepared for the Commission of the European Community (Washington: Kurt Salmon Associates, 1979).

7. de la Torre, Jedel, Arpan *et al.*, *op. cit.*, pp. 37-43.

8. Paolo Giuiuzza and Sergio Mariotti, *Economies of Scale and Multi-plant Operations in a Branch of the Italian Clothing Industry*, Working Paper 80-3 (Brussels: European Institute for Advanced Studies in Management, 1980).

9. It is a surprising fact, for example, that more independent suppliers of designing, marking and cutting services have not sprung up to meet the needs of small firms that cannot afford the investment on their own. Such arrangements or alternative cooperative agreements are extremely rare. The fiercely independent nature of owner/managers may account for part of this.

10. *Textile and Clothing Industries: Structural Problems and Policies in OECD Countries*, *op. cit.*, p. 25; and Arpan, de la Torre and Toyne, *op. cit.*, p. 38.

11. A 1976 comparison of all major developed countries conducted by the International Apparel Association in Amsterdam identified a total number of establishments in excess of 85,000 with average employment ranging from 14 workers per plant in Japan to 76 in West Germany. This average has increased slightly over recent years, there being, for example, an increase from 55 to 59 workers per plant in the United States over the 1967-76 period. Again one should be aware of vast differences among sub-sectors. For example, ISIC 237 (fur goods) averaged eight workers per plant, while ISIC 231 (men's suits and coats) had an average of 151 workers in 1976. See Arpan, de la Torre and Toyne, *op. cit.*, pp. 16 and 88.

12. See, for example, Caroline Miles, *Lancashire Textiles: a Case Study of Industrial Change* (Cambridge: Cambridge University Press, 1968).

13. For a detailed discussion of these characteristics of employment in the textile and clothing industries, see *Textile and Clothing Industries: Structural Problems and Policies in OECD Countries*, *op. cit.*, pp. 72-78.

14. *A Report on the Labour Force Tracking Project: Costs of Labour Adjustment Study* (Ottawa: Canadian Department of Industry, Trade and Commerce, 1980).

15. Another example of the greater aggressiveness of diversified clothing companies in the United States is their greater ratio of investment to sales. For the four-year period 1975-78, they invested on average 2.1 per cent of sales while the non-diversified (that is, those with over 80 per cent of sales in the same three-digit ISIC category and 50 per cent or more in one four-digit group) invested on average less than 1.6 per cent of sales. For other comparisons, see *Annual Performance Profile of Apparel Companies*, Kurt Salmon Associates, New York.

16. See 'Benetton Takes on the World', *Fortune*, New York, 13 June 1983, pp. 114-19.

17. For a description of these and other successful French strategies in the clothing industry, see *Le Nouvel Economiste*, Paris, 28 December 1981, pp. 38-43.

18. *Fortune*, 15 January 1979, pp. 104-7; and *Business Week*, New York, 14 May 1979, pp. 60-70.

19. For more on this, see Curzon *et al.*, *op. cit.*, pp. 24-25. The OECD in analysing this issue concluded: 'The trade and industrial policies followed by the vast majority of textile-exporting developing countries insulate them from outside competition and have contributed to worldwide over-capacity; furthermore, they will impede their adjustment process to comparative

advantages that are neither immutable nor homogeneously distributed among the developing world'. See *Textile and Clothing Industries: Structural Problems and Policies in OECD Countries, op. cit.*, p. 110.

20. *EEC Information*, Brussels, No. 44/81, April 1981, p. 13.

21. In a thorough analysis of the 807 and 806.30 provisions, the United States Tariff Commission, predecessors of the United States International Trade Commission, concluded that the net benefits of retaining them were significant and positive. See *Economic Factors Affecting the Use of Items 807.00 and 806.30 of the Tariff Schedules of the United States* (Washington: US Government Printing Office, for the International Tariff Commission, 1970).

22. In a recent study, Gerald K. Helleiner, of the University of Toronto, calculated that 'related-party' imports into the United States from developing countries were 7.8 per cent of total imports in textiles, 11.5 per cent in clothing and 4.4 per cent in shoes. By contrast, comparable figures for non-electrical and electrical machinery were 63.5 and 72.5 per cent, respectively. The relatively low levels of intra-firm imports in the first three industries explains in part their lack of an international commitment when it comes to trade and other foreign economic policy issues. See Helleiner, *Intra-firm Trade and the Developing Countries* (New York: St Martin's Press, 1981).

23. Arpan, Barry and Van Tho, *op. cit.*, p. 39.

24. de la Torre *et al.*, *op. cit.*

25. *Ibid.* For a discussion of Mexico's early experiences with *maquiladoras* (firms set up exclusively to process imported components for re-export) and their relative performance, see P.W. Bareersen, *The Border Industrialisation Program of Mexico* (Lexington, Mass.: D.C. Heath, 1971). He reports that productivity levels ranging from 80 to 140 per cent of those in the United States were common.

26. Keesing and Wolf, *op. cit.*, pp. 33-34.

27. Uwe Schwarting, 'Strategies for Survival: the Example of the Clothing Industry', *Intereconomics*, Hamburg, January-February 1979, pp. 15-19.

28. See *Herstructurering Nederlandse Confectie-Industrie: deel 1 Herenbovenkleding-Industrie*, 1977 and *deel 2 Damenbovenkleding-Industrie*, 1978 ('s-Hertogenbosch: Nederlandse Herstructureringsmaatschappij [NEHEM]).

29. Sanjaya Lall, 'Offshore Assembly in Developing Countries', *National Westminster Bank Quarterly Review*, London, August 1980, pp. 14-23. For an evaluation of the effects of these regulations on the American, Dutch and West German economies, see J.M. Finger, 'Trade and Domestic Effects of the Offshore Provision in the US Tariff', *American Economic Review*, Menasha, Wisconsin, September 1976, pp. 598-611; and Finger, 'Offshore Assembly Provisions in the West German and Netherlands Tariffs: Trade and Domestic Effects', *Weltwirtschaftliches Archiv*, Kiel, No. 2, Vol. 113, 1977, pp. 237-49.

30. E. Jahan, C. Jaedlicki, M. Lanzzarotti and J. Massini, *La stratgíe des investisseurs français face à la concurrence des pays à bas salaires* (Paris: Institut de l'Entreprise [IEDES], and the OECD Development Centre, 1980) concluded also that offshore assembly favoured net employment generation in France.

31. *Textile and Clothing Industries: Structural Problems and Policies in OECD Countries, op. cit.*, p. 61.

32. *Le Nouvel Economiste*, 28 December 1981, p. 42.

33. *Le Nouvel Economiste*, 2 January 1978, pp. 32-33. See, also, David Morawetz, *Why the Emperor's New Clothes are Not Made in Colombia*, World Bank Staff Working Paper No. 386 (Washington: World Bank, 1980) for the problems Colombia has had as a source country.

34. For more details on their scope and activities, see Antoine Basile and Dimitri Germidis, *Politiques d'attraction des investissements étrangers orientés vers l'exportation: le rôle de zones franches industrielles d'exportation* (Paris: OECD Development Centre, 1982).

35. O. Kreye, 'World Market Oriented Industrialization of Developing Countries: Free Production Zones and World Market Factories', in *The New International Division of Labour* (Starnberg: Max Planck Institut für Sozialwissenschaften, 1977) p. 336, claims that American and West German plant managers in Malaysia's export-processing zones were achieving productivity rates comparable to those at home in just a few months. P. Tandon, *The Case of India*, a report for the Free Trade Zone Project of the OECD's Development Centre, Paris, 1981, compares similar electronics companies both inside and outside of the St Cruz export-processing zone in India and found that those outside the zone achieved only 60 per cent of the productivity of those inside.

36. In the meantime, some countries in the European Community closed their markets to West German goods suspected of being processed in Eastern Europe. Using Article 115 of the Treaty of Rome, member countries could block goods originating from outside the Community (which are normally subject to quantitative restrictions) from reaching their markets. The table below shows the number of instances where Article 115 has been invoked in this sense, and by whom, for the years immediately preceding and following the 1977 renegotiation of the MFA:

	Benelux	*France*	*West Germany*	*Italy*	*Ireland*	*United Kingdom*	*Total*
1977	10	20	9	1	3	5	48
1978	42	57	2	9	32	15	157

37. Stephen Woolcock, 'Textiles and Clothing', in Louis Turner and Neil McMullen (eds), *The Newly Industrializing Countries: Trade and Adjustment* (London: Allen & Unwin, 1982) p. 37.

38. Arpan, Barry and Van Tho, *op. cit.*

39. By contrast, Japan owned only fifteen firms in the American textile industry versus 150 owned by West European firms.

40. A study by Fröbel *et al.*, cited in Shepherd, 'Public and Private Strategies for Survival in the Textile and Clothing Industries of Western Europe and the United States', European Research Centre, University of Sussex, mimeograph, September 1980, note 17 above.

41. Ernst-Jürgen Horn, *Management of Industrial Change in Germany*, Sussex European Paper No. 13 (Brighton: European Research Centre, University of Sussex, 1982).

42. Pierre Cardin, which had entered into an agreement with the Colombian company Everfit to manufacture under licence for the American market, was forced to terminate the deal because of problems of delivery and cost; see *Business Week*, 8 December 1975, p. 41.

43. Diana Green, *Managing Industrial Change? French Policies to Promote Industrial Adjustment* (London: Her Majesty's Stationery Office, for the Department of Industry, 1980) p. 11. She cites a report to the French Senate's Trade Committee claiming that over 2,000 jobs have been lost due to these foreign investments by French firms.

44. *Le Nouvel Economiste*, 28 December 1981, p. 43.

45. Ben Evers and Gerard de Groot, 'The Netherlands', in Shepherd (ed.), *Employment, Trade and North-South Cooperation* (Geneva: International Labour Organisation, 1981) p. 133.

46. *Le Nouvel Economiste*, 28 December 1981, p. 42.

47. The following sections are a summary of an analysis in de la Torre *et al.*, *op. cit.*, ch. 2.

48. All names have been disguised to protect the confidentiality of the firms.

CHAPTER FOUR

Government Strategies for Easing Adjustment

GOVERNMENT intervention in the textile and clothing industries is by no means a recent phenomenon. Control over trade and trade routes was always among the first prerogatives claimed by fledgling nation states. As production of manufactures (of which textiles was a major component) gained in importance, the mercantilist states of seventeenth-century Europe combined control over trade with domestic incentives to promote industry and enhance national welfare, then measured primarily by the size of the surplus in the balance of trade.

In a more modern setting, the textile and clothing industries of most developed countries have again been the focus of government attention. The justification this time, however, has been primarily that government intervention can help to sustain employment levels. As recently as 1963, both industries represented over 10 million jobs in the OECD countries or nearly 17 per cent of total manufacturing employment in the area. The steady decline chronicled in Chapter 2 and the more dramatic deterioration of employment in the post-1973 period brought about a marked increase in the level of intervention by government in both industries. This chapter aims to document the various dimensions of this process among the eight developed countries being covered in the study and to relate the observed patterns of public intervention to the relative success or failure of national adjustment strategies. The first section deals with trade policy, an instrument traditionally employed by governments to influence industrial structure, although with significant differences in its application. The second section examines the so-called industrial policies pursued by the eight selected countries during the 1970s for much the same purposes. Finally, the various national strategies are grouped by reference to their primary objectives and evaluated accordingly.

Trade Policy and Protection

Of the two instruments available to governments to protect home industries, namely tariffs and quantitative restrictions, the latter have assumed much greater weight in recent years. Below, the principal restrictive agreements negotiated since 1956 are first chronicled and evaluated and then the extent to which either tariffs or preferential agreements have affected resource allocation in the industry is discussed.

Quantitative Restrictions on Imports of Clothing and Textiles

The post-World War II history of international trade in clothing and textiles has been characterised by increasing quantitative controls on trade by the major importing countries. The trend began in the United States in the mid-1950s, as the American textile and clothing industries began to suffer from increased competitive pressures in cotton goods from Western Europe and, more particularly, Japan.[1] In 1956, President Eisenhower's Administration 'persuaded' Japan to exercise 'voluntary' restraints in their cotton textile exports to the United States. By 1960, the American authorities became convinced that a multilateral approach was necessary and sought to enlist the support of some key West European countries in convening a conference of both importing and exporting countries under the auspices of the GATT. Lengthy negotiations followed which culminated in the signing of a series of agreements restricting trade in textile goods in the interests of 'orderly' market growth and development.[2]

The first of these agreements — the Short Term Agreement (STA) — which covered a one-year period from October 1961, was intended to give the importing countries some breathing space until a long-term agreement regulating international trade in cotton textiles had been negotiated. This was accomplished with the signing of the Long Term Arrangement Regarding International Trade in Cotton Textiles (LTA) on 9 February 1962 covering a period of five years from the expiry of the STA. The preamble of the LTA stated that the agreement 'continued the attempt to balance the need for increased access to the national industrial markets for exports from the developing countries, in order to facilitate the latter's economic expansion and development, with the need to prevent market disruption in importing countries'. In 1962, the LTA was signed by nineteen governments. It is worth noting that the main target was cotton textile imports and not clothing or apparel. Total developing-country exports of clothing in 1962 amounted to only US$240 million in value; and of that, Hong Kong accounted for $202 million. Subsequently, the impact of the LTA was made specific through the signing of multiple bilateral agreements concluded directly between pairs of importing and exporting countries. The United States led the way by signing 22 such bilateral agreements. The LTA was renewed in 1967 and 1970 and, by 1973, 80 countries had signed the agreement.

The impact of the LTA was quickly felt throughout the importing countries as the rate of increase in imports of cotton textiles stabilised. Meanwhile, the exporting countries geared their production to man-made products, often incorporating fibre of American or West European origin. While the United States, for example, saw its imports of cotton textiles almost double from 1960 to 1970, imports of man-made fibre textiles increased tenfold during the same period. Faced with this situation, the United States again led the importing countries in restricting trade in man-made fibres by negotiating bilateral agreements in 1971 with five East Asian countries: Japan, Hong Kong, Taiwan, South Korea and Singapore. Shortly thereafter, negotiations started under the GATT to replace the now ineffective LTA with a broader arrangement covering all textile products.

By 1974, a new Multi-fibre Arrangement was signed by 50 countries whereby the exporting countries would avoid 'disrupting' the markets of the importing countries. 'Disruption' was defined as

> 'the existence of serious damage to domestic producers or actual threat thereof. Such damage must be demonstrably caused by ...
>
> (a) a sharp and substantial increase or imminent increase of imports of particular products from particular sources ...
>
> (b) products [which] are offered at prices which are substantially below those prevailing for similar goods of similar quality in the market of the importing country ...
>
> and not by factors such as technological change or changes in consumer preferences.'

The implication was clear: adjustment caused by 'domestic' forces was permissible and desirable but if it had its roots in competitive imports it must be controlled.

Import limitations were determined in the same way as under the LTA, yearly increases in imports of products under restraint being fixed at not less than 6 per cent other than in exceptional cases. The MFA covered cotton, wool and man-made fibre textiles and textile products; it was designed to legitimise and regulate all the bilateral agreements on trade in non-cotton textiles that countries had negotiated outside the LTA in the early 1970s and to consolidate all fibre trade into one agreement. The MFA allowed for gradual, but not negligible, increases in textile imports from developing countries at a time when, as it happened, consumption in the developed markets was stagnant and unemployment rising fast.

Deep divisions soon surfaced between the United States and the European Community (and within the Community itself) on the terms for renewing the MFA.[3] Following the 1973 accord, American negotiators speedily concluded comprehensive bilateral agreements with most large exporters. The European Community, however, was committed to a unified stance and had to seek internal agreement on such complex issues as 'burden sharing' — who will import how much? — within the Community prior to negotiating bilateral agreements. The resulting delays meant that, for the two years immediately following the implementation of the MFA (1974 and 1975), American imports of textiles and clothing grew by only 3 per cent, while Community imports increased by 41 per cent. European industry was dismayed at these results and political pressure in certain countries — the United Kingdom and France in particular — was running high in favour of a much more restrictive agreement. By 1977, the Community claimed it had lost 430,000 jobs in the textile and clothing industries due to import competition while the first MFA was in force.[4]

Under French and British leadership, a new and more comprehensive agreement was signed in December 1977. The new Arrangement and its accompanying set of regulations added up to a nearly unintelligible mass of restrictions whose impact, however, was not long delayed.[5] For the European Community, total textiles and clothing imports (in volume) increased at only 4 per cent per annum during the period from 1976 to 1980.[6] Imports from MFA countries subject to bilateral agreements grew at 2.3 per cent per annum (sensitive products at 0.8 per cent per annum); the big exporters (Hong Kong, South Korea, Brazil and India) were limited to 1.2 per cent growth per annum, while other small countries were able to increase their exports to the Community at a rate of 3.4 per cent per annum. The principal beneficiaries were the Mediterranean countries (whose exports to the Community grew at 7.4 per cent per annum) and the associated countries of Africa, the Caribbean and the Pacific, known as the ACP countries (8.2 per cent per annum), although the ACP's total share of Community imports was still less than 2 per cent. This shift away from traditional suppliers to those not covered by the MFA can be seen from the data in Table 4.1 at a lower level of aggregation. In general, the major Asian exporters, the other developing countries (that is, those not covered by preferential agreements) and the centrally-planned economies lost ground in the Community market relative to other industrial countries and the associated nations of southern Europe, the Mediterranean and the ACP region.

For the United States, the effect of a more restrictive quota system was equally effective in curtailing the growth of developing-country imports.[7] For the same period (1976-80), American clothing imports grew at 2.8 per cent per annum in volume, while textile imports actually declined by a total of 22 per cent. Exports from the Asian 'Big Three' (Hong Kong, South Korea and India) increased by less than 0.9 per cent per annum. Only Latin American countries and some small suppliers in the Far East managed to show annual growth rates in the vicinity of 4 per cent.

The effect of these shifts on total import penetration and employment in the developed countries was significant. Thus total exports of textiles and clothing from the developing countries attained a 27 per cent share of world exports in 1976 (up from 17.5 per cent in 1970), but did not exceed 26.5 per cent in any subsequent year up to the end of 1980. Equally, their share of total developed-country imports of textiles and clothing, which climbed from 15.6 per cent to 26.8 per cent between 1970 and 1976, hovered around 25 per cent between 1978 and 1980. The data cited earlier on output and employment in the eight countries under study reflect an easing of the pressure on developed-country producers for the first time since the early 1970s.

Scarcely two months after the heads of government of major developed and developing countries had met in Cancun, Mexico, and resolved to subordinate future North-South negotiations to the spirit and the letter of their joint *communiqué*, the third Multi-fibre Arrangement was concluded in Geneva on 22 December 1981.[8] The clothing industry in the developed countries set out to relate the growth of imports to the growth of domestic demand, to lengthen the Arrangement's duration and to obtain a reduction in the market share held by the largest Asian suppliers, namely Hong Kong, Taiwan and South Korea. The signatories, however, finally agreed only to recognise that the decline in the rate of growth of per-capita consumption in the importing countries increased the likelihood of 'market disruption'. It was also agreed that rapid surges in imports resulting from the filling of previously under-utilised quotas could justify emergency restrictions on otherwise legal imports, but that, in such an event, 'equitable and quantifiable compensation' should be provided to the exporting country. In general, most observers felt that the second renewal of the MFA, extending it for four years and seven months from 1 January 1982, represented no significant change in the situation subsequent to the first renewal in 1977.[9]

The following twelve months were a period of difficult and often strident negotiation of the bilateral agreements under the MFA. The European Community made it

Table 4.1
Shifts in the European Community's Import Shares in 1976-78, Selected Categories (tonnes and per cent)

	Knitted shirts			*Woven shirts*			*Woven blouses*		
Source of imports	*1976*	*1978*	*% change*	*1976*	*1978*	*% change*	*1976*	*1978*	*% change*
All countries	27,099	26,860	– 1	41,096	41,766	2	14,856	16,004	8
Industrial countries[a]	1,186	1,647	39	672	1,448	116	340	400	18
Southern Europe[b]	8,219	9,594	17	972	1,665	71	1,021	1,350	32
Yugoslavia	986	369	– 63	2,811	2,100	– 25	361	277	30
Asian 'Big Three'[c]	6,076	5,833	– 4	22,320	22,733	2	5,020	6,025	20
ACP countries[d]	186	321	73	281	227	– 19	133	134	1
Other developing countries	7,143	6,580	– 8	9,135	9,571	5	7,250	6,492	– 10
Centrally-planned economies[e]	3,313	2,509	– 24	4,907	3,993	– 19	1,172	1,247	6

	Knitted sweaters			*Men's and boys' trousers*		
	1976	*1978*	*% change*	*1976*	*1978*	*% change*
All countries	41,170	37,140	– 10	59,744	60,069	1
Industrial countries[a]	1,776	2,054	16	8,816	5,555	– 37
Southern Europe[b]	4,884	4,943	1	7,174	11,026	54
Yugoslavia	511	324	– 37	1,750	1,265	– 28
Asian 'Big Three'[c]	22,078	18,840	– 15	24,766	23,416	– 5
ACP countries[d]	989	1,864	88	631	387	– 39
Other developing countries	7,418	6,682	– 10	13,011	14,549	12
Centrally-planned economies[e]	3,506	2,440	– 30	3,594	3,147	– 12

SOURCE: *Analytical Tables of Foreign Trade*, Statistical Office of the European Community, Luxembourg, various issues.

[a]Australia, Austria, Canada, Finland, Iceland, Japan, New Zealand, Norway, South Africa, Sweden, Switzerland and the United States.

[b]Greece, Malta, Portugal, Spain and Turkey.

[c]Hong Kong, South Korea and Taiwan.

[d]Fifty one former colonies in Africa, the Caribbean and the Pacific with preferential access to the European Community's markets.

[e]Twelve countries among which Bulgaria, Hungary, Poland and Romania are MFA signatories.

clear from the start that it would take strong unilateral action unless it got its way by the autumn of 1982. It demanded cutbacks of 10-12 per cent in the volume of 'sensitive' imports from major producers and tough guarantees against 'surges'. It was not, in fact, until early December 1982, that a final deal was struck with the last three major suppliers, Hong Kong, South Korea and Macao. Taiwan, not being a signatory to the MFA, is subject to unilateral quotas. The dominant suppliers accepted cuts in volume of 6-8 per cent for some 'sensitive' products, a 'restrained level' of import growth in 34 categories and a maximum growth rate of 4 per cent for non-sensitive goods. The Arrangement was thus saved again.

Tariffs and Preferences

In addition to the comprehensive quota system established under the MFA, tariffs provided an important element of protection to national manufacturers, particularly in terms of competition from other developed-country suppliers. Table 4.2 provides some estimates of the average levels of tariff protection for the major importing countries, before and after the Tokyo Round negotiations were concluded. While these averages obviously encompass a great deal of variation among product categories and countries of origin, it is clear that textile products and clothing continued to enjoy among the highest levels of protection still remaining in force for manufactured goods (except in Japan). Effective rates of protection are even higher for the clothing industry, as indicated by the degree of tariff escalation associated with the final stages of the manufacturing process. Furthermore, Figure 4.1 shows how, in the case of both the Kennedy and Tokyo Rounds, textile and clothing products were subject to smaller proportional cuts. This aggravated the disparity between the levels of protection accorded industries where competition takes place, largely among developed-country producers, and those where the developing countries are major exporters.

TABLE 4.2

Average Import-weighted *ad valorem* Tariffs for Textile Products Before and After Completion of the Tokyo Round of Multilateral Trade Negotiations (per cent)

	All dutiable manufactures		*Textile mill products*		*Apparel and miscellaneous made-up products*	
	Actual	*% change*	*Actual*	*% change*	*Actual*	*% change*
United States						
All countries						
1976	8.1		17.0		25.9	
Final	5.6	- 30.8	11.4	- 32.9	21.1	- 18.5
Developing countries						
1976	na		12.0		26.7	
Final	na	na	8.2	- 31.7	22.0	- 17.6
European Community						
1976	10.0		11.7		16.0	
Final	7.1	- 29.0	8.6	- 26.5	12.1	- 24.4
Japan						
1976[a]	15.3		10.5		13.5	
Final	13.4	- 12.4	9.0	- 14.3	13.2	- 2.2
Canada						
1976	12.8		21.5		22.9	
Final	9.1	- 28.9	15.1	- 29.8	21.2	- 7.4

SOURCE: Donald B. Keesing and Martin Wolf, *Textile Quotas against Developing Countries*, Thames Essay No. 23 (London: Trade Policy Research Centre, 1980) Table 3.3.
NOTE: In the table 'na' signifies 'not available'.
[a]Actual rates which are smaller than required under previous GATT commitments.

The actual tariff level applied to imports of clothing by developed countries is also determined by the various

FIGURE 4.1

Percentage Tariff Cuts, Kennedy and Tokyo Rounds

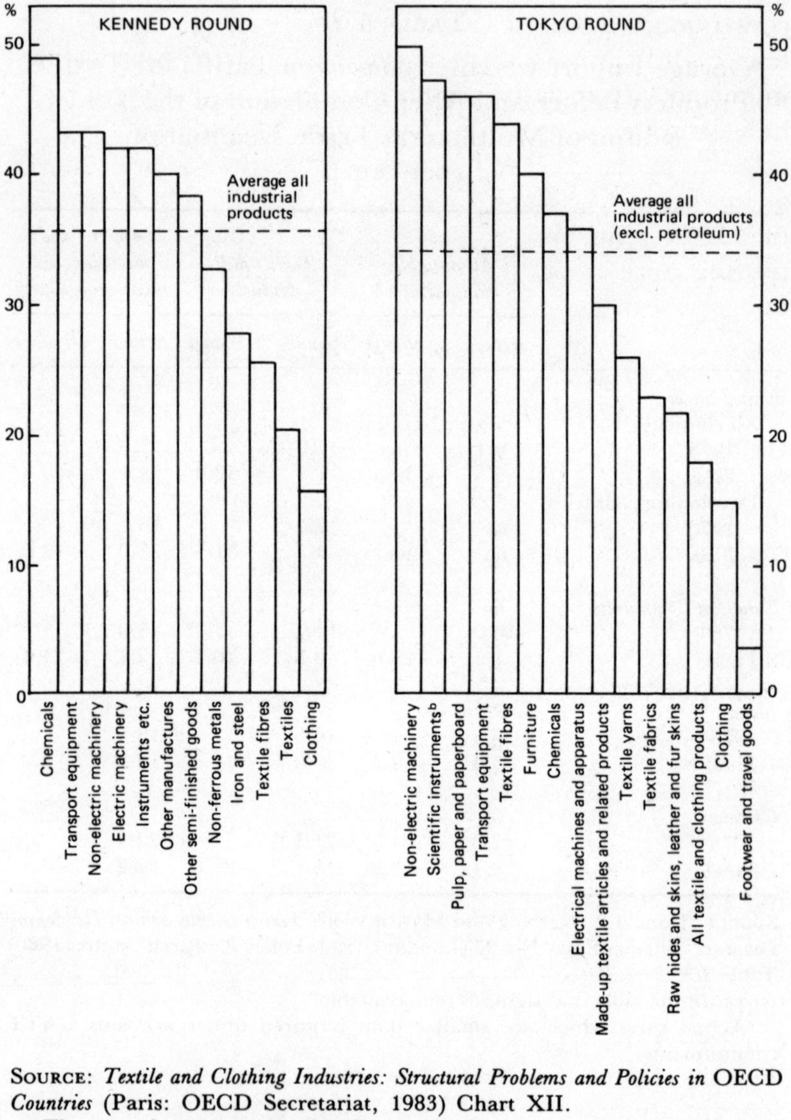

SOURCE: *Textile and Clothing Industries: Structural Problems and Policies in* OECD *Countries* (Paris: OECD Secretariat, 1983) Chart XII.

[a]The two charts are not directly comparable.

[b]This group denotes professional, scientific and controlling instruments, photographic apparatus, clocks and watches.

preferential agreements in effect between developed and developing countries. The broader system known as the generalised system of preferences (GSP) is of little consequence, as most OECD countries effectively exclude textile and clothing imports from GSP provisions. More important are regional agreements such as that concluded between the European Community and 46 former colonies in Africa, the Caribbean and the Pacific (known as the Lomé Convention) or those reached with a number of Mediterranean countries for reciprocal preferential trading agreements covering a wide spectrum of goods and services.[10]

Role of Protection

In general, the relatively high tariff levels applying to clothing imports in most developed countries provide a considerable measure of protection from the competition of producers in other similar countries. Thus, the three major trading areas — the United States, Western Europe and Japan — remained relatively isolated from each other, while trade within the European Community and trade with the developing countries advanced dramatically in the 1960s and early 1970s.

The widespread shift in trade patterns which followed the conclusion of the 1977 MFA seems to have heightened the impact of tariffs. Not only has trade in clothing among developed countries increased relative to the total, but also the shift to higher-quality goods that has been forced on exporters such as Hong Kong by the MFA may enhance the role of tariffs in the years ahead. Nonetheless, quantitative restrictions on trade have been and will continue to be the main instrument of protection employed by the developed countries against cheap imports from the Third World. The two successive renegotiations of the MFA now mean that in July 1986 (the expiry date of the current agreement) the world will celebrate the twenty fifth anniversary of a series of accords to restrict trade that were meant to be temporary and intended to facilitate an orderly transition to unrestricted trade. What is left of this intention was revealed in a statement in 1981 by the Community authorities: 'It seems that a return to free trade and competition [in textiles and clothing products] remains a very unlikely eventuality.'[11]

National Adjustment Policies

The experience of the eight countries in the study is derived from a broad variety of public approaches to the problem of facilitating adjustment in the industry. Apart from the general protective mantle provided by the MFA, governments have employed a broad spectrum of policies either to prod their domestic industries to regain competitiveness or to shield them from the most devastating effects of external competition. Acting in response to a deteriorating social and political climate, or buoyed by the hopes of economic recovery, government policies have oscillated between these extremes. By the end of the decade, however, it had become generally accepted that adjustment should be encouraged and that, other than in the trade field, domestic policies ought to be geared to this goal.

Industrial Policy in the European Community

As it has done in the trade area (but to a considerably lesser extent), the European Community has defined the limits within which national industrial policies should operate. The founders of the Community, not satisfied with a design that would simply eliminate mutual trade barriers, sought assurances that member countries would not provide special aid to their domestic firms if this were 'to distort competition ... in so far as it affects trade between member states'. Yet the same articles in the Treaty of Rome that contain these safeguards (Articles

92 and 93) also recognise that specific circumstances may give rise to state aids that 'may be considered to be compatible with the common market'. Choosing a dividing line in the face of this ambiguity has taken up a considerable amount of time and energy in recent years.

The early efforts by the Commission of the European Community to make legitimate needs for state intervention in industry compatible with the maintenance of competition among the industries of member countries led to the emergence in 1972 of a set of guidelines which included the following criteria for government assistance:

(a) It must be selectively focussed on firms and sectors with a significant potential for positive adjustment.

(b) It must be temporary and diminishing over time, so as not to encourage dependency and should continue to provide a stimulus for change.

(c) It must be as transparent as possible, so that its impact on competition can be assessed correctly.

(d) It must be consistent with the stated objectives while no stronger than absolutely necessary.[12]

These general views echoed the guidelines issued on 22 July 1971 on aid to the textile sector.[13] After reviewing the importance of the sector to the Community and its highly competitive nature, the Commission concluded that any aid to the industry must fall within a given framework:

(a) Rising productivity should be the basis upon which the industry would remain sufficiently competitive, even in a market that would be increasingly open to imports from developing countries.

(b) Governments should assure the necessary conditions for this transformation while mitigating the social or regional difficulties that might result from it.

(c) The Community's trade policy should encourage a gradual opening of the internal market consistent with the need for restructuring the sector in the medium term. To further this aim, the document set out a timetable whereby the establishment of preferential tariffs for developing countries was to be accomplished within a five-year period, and laid down criteria for the progressive elimination of all quantitative restrictions.

(d) The Commission would undertake certain common projects in such areas as research and development, the use of social-security funds, regional assistance and the creation of an 'observatory' capable of providing the industry with timely and relevant data for adjustment purposes.

(e) Finally, the Commission would continue to monitor national aid to the industry with the purpose of: (i) opposing all aid having a direct impact on costs or prices or resulting in capacity increases; (ii) favouring, instead, subsidies for collective projects, reductions in installed capacity, shifts in product orientation away from non-competitive lines and vertical integration or horizontal concentration; and (iii) discouraging investment subsidies, even when their objectives were to be modernisation, except where severe social conditions prevailed and only then if their application were temporary, limited to seriously affected areas and targeted to firms with difficult restructuring problems. When these criteria were satisfied, an assessment of the Community's interest was still necessary before any aid could be granted.

These guidelines read like a litany of the principles embodied in positive adjustment. While the expressed desire for an early return to unimpeded trade became a casualty of the economic crisis of the post-1974 era, the Commission fought hard against distortions to competition brought about by the tax and subsidy policies of a number of governments.[14]

In June 1970, the Commission of the European Community expressed certain reservations about the Italian Draft Law No. 1011, which granted reductions in the social-security contributions paid by textile firms.[15] This marked the beginning of a tug-of-war between the Commission and the Italian Government which highlighted the practical limits of the 1971 guidelines. The major issue surrounding Law No. 1011, adopted on 1 December 1971, concerned point 'e' above: relief from social-security contributions would have a direct effect on operating costs and, therefore, on prices and competition.[16] On 31 July 1972, the Commission simultaneously allowed the Italian Government to extend an extraordinary aid programme to industry in certain depressed areas and began procedures against Law No. 1011 under Article 93(2) of the Treaty of Rome.[17] A year later, the Commission issued an interim decision abolishing the specified reductions in social-security charges benefiting the industry, arguing that:

> 'The aid in question is operating aid to which the Commission is generally opposed on the grounds that it is not an effective incentive to recipient firms to carry out the necessary reconversion operations. In the particular case of the Italian textile industry, the operating aid is not consistent with what should be the aim of resolving the structural difficulties apparent in certain branches or firms, since it is granted indiscriminately to all textile firms. Furthermore, this type of aid is liable to have a direct effect upon competition and intra-Community trade, since it is reflected immediately in the cost price and, consequently, in the competitiveness of firms...'[18]

The Italian Government appealed against the decision to the European Court of Justice and was turned down on 2 July 1974. Law No. 1011 was subsequently amended and on 7 March 1975 the Commission closed its case on the basis that the modifications adopted by the Italian Government rendered the programme compatible with the Treaty of Rome.[19] Thus a major foundation stone of the Community's policy on restructuring was set firmly in place.

A second area of conflict concerned the competitive effects of large-scale government intervention through state holding companies. The issue was first raised in early 1972 upon the creation of Gestioni e Partecipazioni Industriali (GEPI) in Italy, a holding company designed to enter into 'salvage' operations particularly in the textile industry in the Mezzogiorno (the southern part of Italy). It was highlighted in a statement by Mr A. Borschette, then responsible for competition policy at the Commission of the European Community, when he claimed that 'the Commission is paying close attention to the effects on competition of temporary holdings taken by state-controlled bodies'.[20] The first skirmish on this front took place in parallel with the action on Law No. 1011, as the Commission also began to act under procedure 93(2) against Draft Law No. 946, which increased by 15 billion lire the budget appropriations for the Istituto Mobiliare Italiano (IMI) in order to provide aid to 'industrial firms which are experiencing difficulties'. Eventually abiding by the 1972 framework, the Italian Government agreed to limit the IMI loans to restructuring projects being undertaken during existing programmes or with prior notification to the Commission.[21] The Commission then suspended its procedure 93(2) action on 24 June 1974, but left the broader question of take-overs by state-owned holding companies open for future resolution.

Six years later, on 26 June 1980, the Commission of the European Community took a major step in the direction of controlling public corporations when it issued a directive calling for greater transparency in financial dealings between the state and its public undertakings.[22] Exemptions from such requirements, disclosing the sources and disposition of state funds by public companies, were made for non-traded services, small corporations as well as those engaged in water supply, energy and transportation, and for public credit institutions. France, Italy and the United Kingdom rejected the Commission's arguments on several grounds and denied its applicability to their respective undertakings. The European Court of Justice, however, upheld the Commission's rights and competence in this domain and rejected the appeal from the three countries in its entirety.[23] The Commission subsequently announced in December 1982 that it would begin a detailed investigation of the possible anti-competitive effects of state ownership in five sensitive sectors of industry: automobiles, synthetic fibres, textile machinery, cigarettes and tobacco products and shipbuilding.[24]

The third area of contention involved the granting of export aids. Here the Commission was on very solid legal ground when it initiated proceedings against the Italian Government early in 1976 for providing export assistance to companies in the toy, textile and footwear industries. Arguing that these measures were incompatible with the basic principles of the 'common market', the Commission decided on 8 September 1976 to require that the Italian Government adopt the measures necessary to ensure that the Istituto de Commercio Estero (the government export department) discontinued any export assistance to sales made to other member states.[25] Again, a strong precedent was established on this issue.

Not all decisions made by the Commission of the European Community were negative or reactive. In December 1975, the Commission concluded it had no objections to a British scheme for aiding its clothing industry after the British Government assured the Commission that there was 'no question of increasing production capacity'. A month later, the Commission also found the Dutch Government's measures for the reorganisation of the textile industry compatible with the requirement for no increases in capacity.[26] Prior to these decisions, the Commission had moved to consolidate the 1971 guidelines (which it did in January 1974) and launch its first common programme on research and development for the industry. Approved in September 1974 by the Commission and confirmed by a decision of the Council of Ministers in April 1975, the programme proposed to tackle three main projects: thermal treatment of chemical fibres, processing of textiles by organic solvents and fireproofing. The Community would contribute 250,000 European units of account (EUA) which corresponded to a third of the total expected expenditure.[27] With this programme and the British and Dutch decisions, the Commission appeared to signal an alternative to disruptive subsidy schemes in a movement towards positive adjustment policies.

The first and only attempt to date by the Commission of the European Community to influence the adjustment process directly was its recommendation in September 1976 of a concerted approach to the ladies' stockings and tights sub-sector. Excess capacity at the time was estimated at 45 per cent of installed capacity and the Commission began a series of consultations with member governments on how to limit or reduce capacity in the sub-sector so as to avoid the threat of destructive price competition. By 1977, however, the Commission's attention had shifted to the problems of the synthetic-fibre sector where a number of crisis plans were elaborated (none of which fully satisfied the Directorate-General of Competition) and to the renegotiation of the MFA. The urgency of the latter was highlighted in December 1977 when, as negotiations dragged on, the

European Parliament warned that 'the Community textile industry can remain strong and an efficient employer only if urgent steps are taken to restrict the detrimental effects of imports from low-cost countries' and that failing a successful conclusion of the MFA unilateral action should be taken.

In May 1978, the Commission of the European Community sent a communication to the Council of Ministers outlining its policy on aid schemes for industry.[28] It underlined the basic principles that (i) aid should be only of an emergency nature; (ii) it should not safeguard the private capitalist from risk; and (iii) it should not attempt to preserve the *status quo*. Two months later, the Commission re-interpreted its 1971 and 1974 guidelines reaffirming its commitments to three objectives:

> '1. Companies' own industrial drive [is] the prime mover of progress and adaptation in the industry... This implies close coordination between the policies of the member states and adherence to a framework of aids [that] do not distort the conditions of competition but do facilitate the necessary adaptations.
>
> '2. Greater competitiveness ... might in some instances require cuts in the present number of jobs. It will, therefore, be necessary to provide aid for converting undertakings, job creation, retraining and other social measures...
>
> '3. The industry must be fully integrated into the international trade system.'[29]

On this last point, the document insisted that 'the very stringent agreements [negotiated in the MFA] give the Community's industry breathing space until 1982, which it must use to launch or speed up its efforts to adapt to the conditions of both Community and international competition' and that 'there is no doubt that workable competition is the fastest and most reliable instrument for adapting an industry made up of so many undertakings'.

With this in mind, the Commission of the European Community intervened directly whenever it thought it saw instances of market failure obstructing adjustment. One such area is research and development. In April 1979, it launched its second common research-and-development programme to cover five areas (garment construction, knitted fabrics, wool spinning, improvement of linen usage and pollution control) over three years. The Commission allocated a budget of 8 million EUA to which contributions from the industry would be added.[30] Shortly thereafter, the Commission contracted with a major firm of textile consultants to examine the opportunities for the utilisation of new technologies and the implications for investment and the structure of the industry.[31] On the expiry of the 1979 programme, the Commission launched a new request for proposals in April 1982. Eventually, 36 projects in four of the above five areas were accepted as eligible for a total Community contribution of 3.5 million EUA.[32]

Another area of action by the European Community was 'improving the flow of economic and commercial information' that would enable firms to assess their own strategies for adjustment. In 1978, the Commission proposed a quarterly report with up-to-date and detailed production and consumption data. After extensive consultations, a proposal was made for a comprehensive industry data bank organised by the Union Textile de France with the collaboration of the Commission and the two major industry associations in Western Europe, Comitextil and the European Clothing Manufacturers Association (AEIH). Progress on this matter, however, has been slow.

To examine progress in both areas (research and development and information flows) as well as in preparation for the 1981 MFA negotiations, the European Community, under the leadership of Viscount Etienne Davignon, as Commissioner for Industry, initiated a major series of meetings and consultations between Community officials, academics and management and labour representatives from all branches of the industry. Between November 1978 and December 1981, nearly two dozen official meetings were held to deal with such matters as the selection of topics for research, the development of the information data bank, the MFA and its renegotiations, the level of Community funding and a number of specific problems such as the issue of country-of-origin markings and the difficulties that might be posed by the Community's future enlargement.

On 30 July 1981, the Commission of the European Community once more confirmed its general orientation towards the industry in a detailed communication sent to the Council of Ministers. Following the Commission's proposal in April on the need to reduce the flexibility of the MFA provisions and bring the current trade flows with preferential-access countries under regulated administrative control,[33] the communication of 30 July emphasised the need to reinforce measures that would stimulate industrial adjustment in the sector.[34] Once again, the Commission underlined the importance of a large open market in which 'all barriers between member states are removed' and where all companies can operate under 'equitable competitive conditions'; that is, in a competitive arena where no artificial distortions are introduced by member governments which may delay effective adjustment or lead to an escalation of competitive subsidies. Among the proposals made, the Commission emphasised the need for the following:

(a) more cooperation between firms in such a fragmented industry;

(b) easier access to capital at reasonable cost;

(c) intensification of research-and-development efforts and innovation in both products and processes;

(d) a major effort to develop a comprehensive data bank that would help industry and government in their decision making;

(e) renewal of the MFA and the corresponding bilateral agreements, as well as accommodating preferential trade relationships with a policy of gradual change;

(f) opening third-country markets to Community exports;

(g) greater utilisation of 'outward processing' as a mechanism for adjustment and for North-South cooperation;[35] and

(h) intensification of all possible acts that would ease the human adjustment problem; in other words, providing assistance for training and relocation and stimulating opportunities for alternative employment in the most seriously affected regions of the Community.

Belgium: the Claes Plan

Badly affected by the crisis, Belgian clothing manufacturers began to press the Government in 1974 to offer some kind of relief. To present their case, the manufacturers used the long-standing Conseil Professionel du Textile et du Vêtement, a tripartite body especially concerned with facilitating communications between government, industry and labour unions. The Government's initial response in 1975 was to provide direct relief in the form of an interest-free loan of 15,000 Belgian francs per worker, to be made available to companies in the clothing sector upon several conditions. First, the companies benefiting from the loan programme had to agree to maintain employment during the year following 30 June 1975 at a level of at least 90 per cent of their labour force as of that date. Second, they had to submit to the Ministry of Economic Affairs a copy of their annual accounts and also refund the loan before distributing any profits to their shareholders. (The loans were repayable in any case by June 1983.) Subscriptions, however, were rather modest and the Commission of the European Community refrained from taking any action, apparently due to the gravity of the social situation.[36]

The continuing deterioration in employment and trading conditions led the Belgian Government to formulate the outline of a 'safeguard plan' in October 1977 aimed at restructuring the clothing industry. While the plan did not create any specific instruments for assistance, it elaborated guidelines and recommended certain specific actions to improve the competitiveness of the clothing and textile industries. The emphasis was placed on high technology and non-standardised production, for the plan explicitly acknowledged that Belgian manufacturers were unable to produce undifferentiated goods economically. The safeguard plan had four main features:

(a) It called for a new and more restrictive MFA, for better control of certificates of origin and of existing trade agreements and for the reservation of 80 per cent of any 'outward-processing' quotas to national producers.

(b) A second interest-free loan of BF15,000 per worker would be made available in 1978 (BF20,000 per worker to firms not having benefited from the earlier loan). This new loan was to be used to pay part of the social-security charges incurred by the companies. The face amount of these loans, however, represented less than 10 per cent of the annual labour cost per worker and were repayable, being effectively a subsidy of 1-2 per cent of employment costs.

(c) Investment assistance would be provided only to firms rationalising their production processes within the framework of a comprehensive restructuring plan; assistance would not be given to firms which sought simply to expand production capacity.

(d) Measures would be reinforced to promote exports (such as improved export credit facilities), as would subsidies given to the industry association by the Belgian foreign trade office to help Belgian producers participate in foreign trade fairs and promote Belgian products abroad.

What followed was probably one of the most intensive conflicts to date between the European Community and a member country on a specific programme of industrial restructuring. The Commission first reacted to the 'safeguard plan' on 29 March 1978 by initiating proceedings under Article 93(2), particularly against the interest-free loans. The Commission argued that its adoption infringed the notification provisions of Article 93(2) and that there was insufficient information on the selective criteria (if any) to be applied for the granting of financial assistance. Soon thereafter, the Commission spelled out its requirements on selectivity, adding that any firm benefiting from the loans would have to accept a timetable for reconversion; that the Government must announce a general programme of restructuring for the sector within six months; and that there should be no compounding with other assistance schemes such as existing regional programmes. On 2 March 1979, after noting the Belgian Government's acceptance of these conditions, procedure 93(2) was closed.[37]

In order to comply with the Commission's requirements, the Belgian Government contracted with a major international consultancy firm to conduct a thorough study of the textile and clothing sectors and make recommendations for public policy.[38] Completed in June 1980, the report forecast the likely condition of each of the three industries by 1984 (textile fibres had been added) in the absence of any major change in public or private policy. It then set a series of objectives for increasing the Belgian industry's share of European production relative to the 1984 levels previously estimated (for example, the goal was for clothing production to rise from a projected 2.9 per cent of European output under the 'do-nothing' alternative to 3.7 per cent). If achieved, these goals would result in a net saving of 21,200 jobs (out of a total of 98,400) in all three industries and require a significant increase in commercial efforts (BF10.7 billion in textiles and BF6.8 billion in clothing by 1984) to be met by comparable reductions in fixed and variable costs. The financial support necessary to bring about these results and keep the industry financially viable (that is, a debt-to-equity ratio no higher than 1.0) called for a public commitment of annual financial support over five years (in current 1980 francs) of BF6 to 9 billion. Finally, the report emphasised the need to back adjustment efforts selectively, based more on the strength of the individual company's restructuring plan than on the viability of the sub-sector itself. It argued that a well-conceived strategy in a weak sub-sector was more likely to succeed than a mediocre strategy in a strong sub-sector. For this reason, a significant proportion of the assistance budget should be allocated to defining the adjustment strategy (with costs shared by the company) and only projects of significant size undertaken.

As the study was under way, the Commission of the European Community re-opened procedure 93(2) against the 1977 Royal Order in April 1980, and asked for the detailed restructuring plan to be submitted within three months. In August, the Claes Plan, named after the Belgian Minister for Economic Affairs who had sponsored it, was tentatively accepted by the Commission until such time as the specifics became available, subject to prior notification in each instance.[39] The details of the restructuring plan were submitted to the Commission the following year. They followed the lines established in the consultancy study and projected a net saving of 30,000 jobs over the next five years. The Commission responded by establishing the following conditions:

(a) Assistance could be provided only to viable companies.

(b) No increase in capacity must result.

(c) No mingling with other aids (sectoral, regional or general) was to be permitted.

(d) A maximum expenditure of BF6.8 billion was established for the first year.

(e) A company's share of any investment must be higher than 30 per cent (25 per cent in special circumstances with prior notification), while the government's share could not exceed 45 per cent.

(f) The synthetic fibre industry was excluded.

(g) Projects in three sub-sectors — men's ready-to-wear, women's stockings and wool yarn and filament — with significant surplus capacity in the Community as a whole would require prior notification if any firm with more than 50 employees were to benefit.

(h) Prior notification was also necessary for all companies with over 50 employees where Belgium was considered to be competitive (for example, carpets, velours and home furnishings).

(i) A thorough review of the programme would take place after its first year.

In December 1981, the Belgian Government agreed to all the stipulated conditions and the project was launched on a one-year trial basis.[40]

Three months later, the Belgian Government proposed a series of modifications to the programme whose aim was to soften the impact of the conditions imposed in

December. Once more, the Commission established its opposition by opening a 93(2) procedure and asked other governments to comment. In the meantime, a number of aid proposals for firms in sensitive or competitive sub-sectors subject to prior-notification requirements was presented to the Commission. These elicited significant opposition from other member countries, national federations and individual competing firms, which forced the Commission to conclude that no derogation of Article 93(2) was possible since the proposed aids were incompatible with the conditions established for the programme.[41] Finally, in February 1983, the Commission imposed a new series of restrictive conditions on the modifications proposed by the Belgian Government for its 1983 programme. The new additional conditions excluded altogether a number of sensitive or competitive sub-sectors from access to the aid programme, extended prior-notification requirements to eleven other sub-sectors, limited the total budget to BF4 billion and raised the minimum corporate share to 50 per cent of investment.[42]

While it is too early to judge the impact of the programme, it is evident that the Commission of the European Community has played a vital role in limiting its scope. Not only were sub-sectors which had either extensive over-capacity or contained many healthy competitive firms excluded from indiscriminate access to aid, but the Commission also insisted that only viable firms with sensible adjustment plans be supported and that they be made to share a significant portion of the risks. Public resources were thus aimed at the middle range of the industry's structure where they could be expected to have the greatest impact.

France: Modernisation Efforts

In 1973, France's net exports of clothing represented over 11 per cent of domestic consumption, up from 7 per cent in 1963. Throughout this period, French goods enjoyed an unsurpassed reputation for quality and design. It was felt that this distinctive characteristic would more than compensate for high costs and the industry's performance through the mid-1970s verified this. Subsequently, however, both employment and net trade in the French clothing industry deteriorated rapidly. Government reaction consisted primarily of providing strong support to the industry's demand for protection in the 1977 MFA negotiations. Other than this, clothing firms could make use of general programmes aimed at productivity improvements and benefit from a large assortment of general and regional industrial development projects.

Among the various schemes offered by government agencies, reduced-interest loans for investment for small firms were the most significant for the clothing industry. In 1976, for example, nearly 10 per cent of all loans granted under this programme benefited clothing and textile firms (FF40 million out of FF460 million). Although assistance was granted only in the context of a restructuring programme presented by the firms, the grants represented a significant proportion of total investment by the clothing industry of nearly FF600 million during the same year. In addition, a total of FF508 million in premiums was granted for regional investment programmes in 1976, fostering the creation of 35,700 new jobs, and private investments of FF4.5 billion benefited from tax relief, creating another 31,365 new jobs. Clothing firms received about 9 per cent of these benefits, which was not out of proportion with their economic significance.

Increases in value added per worker during the 1970s had not been particularly impressive among French clothing manufacturers. Government response centred on two quasi-governmental institutions. The Centre d'Etudes Techniques des Industries de l'Habillement (CETIH) is a research institute established in 1948 financed by a special 'para-fiscal' levy on the domestic industry, which covers 60 per cent of its budget, government subsidies and corporate research contracts and services. (The levy is mandatory, the proceeds of which are directly assigned to a trade association or related institution.) The Centre's programmes focussed on raising productivity by improving quality, the organisation of production and manufacturing technology. To disseminate its findings and assist firms in their implementation, the Centre ran a number of training programmes for all levels of management and offered direct help to any firm requesting it. The Centre Interprofessionel de Recherche des Industries Textiles (CIRIT), similarly funded through para-fiscal levies, can provide assistance on mergers, on production rationalisation and on any collective project (that is, involving several firms on a cooperative basis) aimed at modernisation and improved productivity.

In September 1978, the French Government launched an ambitious programme of industrial restructuring aimed at depressed regions characterised by declining industries (steel, shipbuilding and textiles). The Fond Spécial pour l'Ajustement Industriel (FSAI) was given funds of FF3 billion and was to link assistance to productive investment, *not* to the number of jobs created. The fact that the Government failed to come to the aid of the textile giant, Boussac, while providing for regional assistance through FSAI and the Vosges Plan of 1978, was a sign of the shift away from sectoral support to infrastructure development and the generation of alternative employment opportunities.[43] Nonetheless, between 1975 and 1977, textile and clothing firms benefited from various loan schemes available for industrial restructuring to the tune of over FF500 million.[44]

Soon after the creation of FSAI, the Commission of the European Community opened 93(2) proceedings against the programme of subsidies and parallel loans. An appropriate method of estimation of their joint effect was established by the Commission and, once the French Government agreed to respect the limits established for regional aids on the basis of this formula, the proceedings were lifted.[45] In December 1979, however, the Commission started 93(2) proceedings against an amendment to the French regional development aid scheme and, most importantly, against a draft decree proposing an aid scheme for the textile and clothing industries. The scheme was to be funded by a single tax levied through the value-added tax (VAT) machinery: it would finance joint research projects and 'facilitate the modernisation of textile and clothing firms with a view to improving competitiveness'.[46] Yet the Commission had been surprisingly quiet on an 'arrangement' sponsored by the French Government in February 1978. Noting the existing imbalance between manufacturers' and retailers' profit margins (a retail margin of 60-80 per cent was common practice for standard goods and higher margins prevailed for goods with higher fashion content), the Government felt that this situation encouraged a proliferation of small clothing shops selling at relatively high prices, while large volume-oriented retailers turned to imported goods. With this in mind, the Ministry of Industry sponsored an agreement between the industry associations representing retailers and clothing manufacturers whereby each association would recommend to their members policies that would reduce the internationalisation of competition (presumably beyond the Community). Given the voluntary nature of the proposal, it was probably felt that such an agreement would be of little consequence.

From this time, the level and intensity of French intervention on behalf of the clothing and textile industry rose dramatically. Faced with a rapidly growing crisis evidenced by the deteriorating trade balance in clothing, and with the public pressures generated by a series of national elections, the conservative Government of Giscard d'Estaing took the first steps. First came the 'Cotton Plan' in 1977, then a 'Yarn and Texturising Plan' the following year, a plan for the wool filament sector in 1979 and, most important of all, the 'Codis' Plan of 1980. Under the last, the textile and clothing industries joined six high-technology sectors identified by the French Government as the 'industries of the future'. The inclusion of textiles and clothing, in addition to the obvious political implications, was justified on the basis that they constituted 'infant' industries in the sense that they had never gone through the technological transformation that had modernised other industrial sectors. The Codis Plan was thus oriented towards capital investment in support of this 'strategic' sector.

The change of government in May 1981, following the election of François Mitterrand as President, brought about a continuation of this shift in policy. In December, the new Government launched a textile plan the major characteristics of which were:

(a) A sum of FF1.3 billion was set aside for investment loans at preferential rates (following the logic of the previous Codis Plan).

(b) A reduction of FF3-4 billion was granted in social-security charges paid by the employers (in exchange for no redundancies).

(c) A substantial increase in research-and-development budgets was to be regionally administered and financed by the Ministry of Industry and the CIRIT.

(d) A tough position was taken on the forthcoming bilateral negotiations under the MFA, which was in marked contrast to the Government's exaltation of the Third World in foreign policy pronouncements.

(e) Certificate-of-origin legislation was promoted (aimed at West German imports finished by 'outward processing') and there was severe prosecution of cases of false labelling.

(f) A Maison de la Mode was established in Paris to serve both as a training centre and to support the Paris image as the world's fashion centre.

(g) A group of 'clubs' was created in various sub-sectors (for example, men's wear, shirts *et cetera*) to provide advice to the industry and exert considerable influence on policy at the company level since all CIRIT credits were to require the approval of the corresponding 'club'.

The plan, therefore, had elements both of operational support and of the restructuring and adaptation of the sector.

In May 1982, the Commission of the European Community pronounced itself against some aspects of the measure and opened an investigation under the 93(2) procedure. The argument put forth by the Commission was that the reductions in social-security charges granted to firms in the industry were in no way related to the viability of the firms or to their having agreed to some sort of restructuring plan. Furthermore, given the existing level of regional and general aid benefiting the industry, the cumulative effect of the measures might cause serious distortion of intra-Community trade and competition. After receiving expressions of significant opposition from other quarters, the Commission concluded in January 1983 that the reduction in social-security charges constituted an operational aid not tied to a plan of restructuring and was, therefore, incompatible with the Community guidelines and should not be granted.[47] The other aspects of the 1982 plan were not affected, however, and it was estimated that 80 per cent of the firms in the industry had signed 'solidarity' contracts with the government whereby they agreed to invest in modernisation while maintaining constant employment levels. A surge in clothing demand in 1982 (3 per cent versus the 1-2 per cent predicted) had helped to keep the accords in effect, but continuing import penetration (up 24 per cent in women's ready-to-wear) threatened the long-term prospects of the employment guarantees.[48]

Federal Republic of Germany: an Anomaly

There have been no direct subsidy schemes to aid the textile and clothing industries in the Federal Republic of Germany. To conclude from this observation that these sectors have succeeded in adjusting to international competition without government assistance is to ignore the large impact that protection and other general assistance programmes have had on the industry.

The West German clothing industry is somewhat of an anomaly in an economy oriented towards liberal trade. Since the early 1960s, the industry has enjoyed one of the highest rates of effective protection of any sector in West Germany (averaging about 21 per cent during the early 1970s), a distinction it shares with textiles, iron and steel, non-ferrous metals and pulp and paper.[49] In addition, it has been estimated that the quantitative import restrictions imposed on a large number of clothing products represent a tariff-equivalent level of protection of 45 per cent.[50] The Government, however, has never felt comfortable with this level of protection,[51] particularly in view of the nation's dependence on developing countries for a significant share of her export earnings and her capacity (as discussed earlier) to absorb displaced workers in other industries. Thus there is reason to suspect, as industry representatives claimed privately, that West Germany was less meticulous in implementing the bilateral agreements under the 1977 MFA than her European partners.

West Germany's policy towards industry was relatively non-interventionist throughout the 1950s and 1960s.

Except for a number of specific areas of political or economic concern (for example, agriculture, coal mining, minerals, transport and housing), the Government's role was limited to promoting competition and providing a sound infrastructure and macro-economic environment. Regional policy was only important in West Berlin and the Saar, and research-and-development support was limited to those sectors (aerospace, nuclear energy and, later, data processing) where an overwhelming national interest was thought to exist.[52] In the early 1970s, particularly after the creation in 1972 of the Ministry for Research and Technology, a more active industrial policy followed. Its instruments included major efforts to improve the quantity and quality of available economic information, to encourage labour mobility and entrepreneurship, as well as an active competition policy. Sectoral and regional aid also rose sharply to 5.6 per cent of gross national product (GNP) in 1974, or 9.2 per cent of value added in all affected sectors net of the assistance (a sort of 'internal rate of protection' measure). But the vast majority of this assistance went to non-manufacturing sectors. In fact, the internal rate of protection for manufacturing industries was only 2.5 per cent in the same year.

Table 4.3 presents a summary of some of the data from a study carried out by the Institut für Weltwirtschaft at the University of Kiel.[53] The data show the relatively low level of financial support given the clothing industry amounting to about 40 per cent of the average for all manufacturing. By contrast, tariff protection was among the highest, in keeping with the view that protection 'has always favoured the production of [unskilled] labour-intensive and raw-material-intensive lines of production'.[54] The data also appear to contradict the commonly held belief that regional aid was the clothing industry's mainstay in West Germany. At 173 German marks per employee in 1974, this sort of aid was below the national average for all industries. The labour-intensive clothing sector did, however, benefit more than was proportionate to its economic weight in terms of value added. Also, there have been significant changes in the overall levels of support available both regionally and nationally since 1974.

The authorities in the Federal Republic were able to utilise the infrastructure set up to channel assistance from the Marshall Plan for their own assistance programmes. This was made possible by a Law passed in 1953 (the Economic Recovery Programme [ERP] Development Law), which grouped under its umbrella all government intervention towards industry. In 1978, total assistance under the ERP amounted to DM3,365 million, 95 per cent of which was distributed through five main programmes: assistance to small businesses (DM975 million), assistance to structural adaptation (DM412 million), an environmental-control programme (DM365 million), special aids for Berlin (DM703 million) and export promotion and development assistance (DM725 million). The proportion of these funds allocated to the textile and clothing industries varied from year to year, but one estimate contrary to the findings of the Institut für Weltwirtschaft is that, between 1969 and 1972, as much as 45 per cent of the available funds were granted to the two sectors, a figure disproportionate to their economic weight by *any* measure.[55]

Each province or *Land* enjoyed substantial latitude to manage its own industrial-assistance programmes. Subsidies to industrial investment and loan guarantees to firms not able to borrow directly from commercial sources were standard features of these programmes. There were more than 108 different programmes run by the eleven German provinces in 1978. Table 4.4 summarises the main areas of activity covered by them for each province. It is difficult to assess the impact of these programmes on the evolution of the industry

Table 4.3
Industrial Subsidies and Effective Protection in West German Industry,[a] 1974

	(million marks)			(marks per employee)		
Subsidies by:	*Clothing*	*Textiles*	*All industry*	*Clothing*	*Textiles*	*All industry*
Type of grant						
Interest grant	17.8	35.1	374.5	44.5	80.1	38.0
Current transfers	0.1	0.3	1,418.9	0.2	0.7	144.1
Investment grants	16.8	52.8	2,355.4	42.0	120.5	239.3
Special tax allowances	69.3	38.8	2,151.2	173.2	88.6	218.5
Policy area						
Research and development	...	0.5	859.8	...	1.1	87.3
Regional development	69.1	70.4	2,068.4	172.8	160.7	210.1
Other	34.9	56.1	3,371.8	87.2	128.1	342.5
Source of funds						
Federal government	66.8	80.0	4,205.8	167.0	182.6	427.2
Provincial government	34.9	44.5	2,015.7	87.2	101.6	204.8
Local government	2.3	2.5	78.5	5.8	5.7	8.0

Totals[b]	104.0	127.0	6,300.0	260.0	290.0	640.0
Total subsidies as % of value added	1.5	1.2	2.1	...	...	...
Tariff protection: equivalent subsidy value[c]	1,879	1,942	25,201	4,000	3,760	2,860
Effective rate of protection (%)	20.7	20.8	10.0	...	...	...

SOURCE: Ernst-Jürgen Horn, *Management of Industrial Change in Germany*, Sussex European Papers No. 13 (Brighton: European Research Centre, University of Sussex, 1982) Tables A9-A12.

NOTE: In the table '...' signifies 'not significant'.

[a]Includes all manufacturing and mining sectors.

[b]The five sectors with the highest level of subsidy support were aircraft, extractive industries (oil and minerals), data-processing equipment, shipbuilding and printing. All of these exceeded 1,000 marks per employee in 1974.

[c]Only eight sectors exceeded an equivalent subsidy value of 3,500 marks per employee. Other than textiles and clothing, the two highest levels of effective protection were in pulp and paper products (29.6 per cent) and non-ferrous metals (22 per cent).

Table 4.4
Major Assistance Programmes of West German Provincial Authorities, 1978

Types of assistance	*Baden-Wurttemberg*	*Bayern*	*Bremen*	*Hamburg*	*Hessen*	*Niedersachsen*	*Nordrhein-Westfalen*	*Rheinland-Pfalz*	*Saarland*	*Schleswig-Holstein*
For new industrial investments:										
Direct grants	x	x	x	x	x	x	x	x	x	x
Direct loans		x		x			x			x
Loan guarantees	x	x	x	x	x	x	x	x	x	x
Interest subsidies										x
R&D subsidies	x						x			
Employment-creation premium							x			
Export guarantees	x					x		x		
Special aids to small firms:										
Direct grants		x								
Direct loans	x	x			x	x	x		x	x
Liquidity assistance	x									
Interest subsidies			x	x		x		x		
Export assistance		x							x	

Source: José de la Torre and Michel Bacchetta, 'The Uncommon Market: European Policies Towards the Clothing Industry in the 1970s', *Journal of Common Market Studies*, Oxford, December 1980.

without further detailed studies. One can note, however, the particular orientation of the Bavarian programmes towards assistance to small firms to promote both investment and exports, which may partly explain the propensity of the clothing industry to locate in this province.[56] Since all regional programmes were managed locally, they favoured small firms that might otherwise be frightened away by the cumbersome administrative framework surrounding national programmes.

In sum, public policy in the Federal Republic of Germany towards the industry seemed to be dominated by a bias towards market forces, albeit somewhat constrained by the European Community's trade policies, on the one hand, and the more interventionist policies of provincial governments, on the other. Nonetheless, the evidence confirms the widely-held belief that these general aid programmes (other than trade protection) have been used sparingly and that official policy has been to let the industry adjust as it can to the rigours of international competition. The extensive use of 'outward processing' by the West German industry, the rapid decline in the sector's overall employment and output and the rise of productivity and market differentiation in the surviving firms have been the result of this policy. What survives, then, is a much reduced but stronger industry capable of holding its own, at least under current competitive conditions.

Italy: Direct State Participation

The Italian economic miracle of the 1960s had begun to show signs of losing its impetus by the decade's end and the severe problems of central and southern Italy were already fostering turbulent conditions for industry before the 1973-74 crisis. In 1961, 22.9 per cent of clothing employment was located in the south. After a decade of special programmes to promote industrial development in the Mezzogiorno, only 18.5 per cent of clothing employment could be found there. As growth began to slow down in the early 1970s, the industry, with its high employment and regional significance, became the object of many of the government's direct-intervention schemes, as well as the beneficiary of several laws designed to encourage industrial activity in general and in the south in particular. The continuous decline of the lira throughout the late 1970s also served to sustain the competitiveness of the Italian clothing industry, especially because the European Community's trade policies served to provide a sheltered European market for the lowest-cost internal producers. The most significant mode of intervention by the Italian Government, however, and one that was unique in the Community was the high level of direct state participation in the industry through the acquisition of bankrupt and failing companies.

Direct intervention by the state in the textile sector began with the acquisition in 1957 by the Istituto per la Ricostruzione Industriale (IRI) — one of the two largest state-owned holding companies with diversified investments throughout Italy — of a cotton manufacturing firm near Naples which had lost over 10 billion lire between 1950 and 1955.[57] In 1962, the giant Italian petrochemical holding company Ente Nazionale d'Idrocarburi (ENI) acquired Lanerossi, based in Venice, one of the most important textile groups in the country. ENI's diversification strategy was exposed to the difficulties experienced by the textile sector after 1969 and became the object of increasing pressure for state intervention. Numerous 'salvage operations' took place between 1969 and 1973 during which time the Lanerossi-group operations more than doubled in size to over L200 billion in sales and 23,000 employees. By 1977, this group controlled about 8.5 per cent of Italian wool-textile production, 4.5 per cent of clothing production and 2.3 per cent of production in cotton goods. The clothing sector alone accounted for about 32 per cent of sales and 45 per cent of employment of the Lanerossi group.

During the late 1960s, there was considerable debate in Italy about the appropriateness of the 'salvage' approach undertaken by the Government in other industrial sectors. The result was the creation of GEPI, a public financial holding company, owned by IRI, ENI and two other state holding companies, whose task was to devote itself exclusively to salvage operations. GEPI was to acquire companies which were bankrupt or nearly so, put into practice a restructuring or reconversion plan and re-sell the companies to private owners as quickly as possible. Soon after its creation, a considerable proportion of GEPI's resources was directed towards the textile and clothing sector in both central and southern Italy. Political pressures became paramount as the recession deepened in 1975 and elections were called. The original limit placed on GEPI that it should not acquire more than 30 companies was soon forgotten. By late 1975, it owned 110 bankrupt enterprises, employing over 40,000 people, of which about 50 per cent were in the textile and clothing industries.

As Table 4.5 indicates, the losses of both the Lanerossi and GEPI clothing groups were staggering throughout the period covered (1974-77). Their combined losses in 1977, on a per-capita basis, represented approximately 52 per cent of their average labour costs. It was not surprising, therefore, that the loudest criticism of the state's public holdings (which accounted for 11 per cent of total clothing-industry employment by 1978) came from the private sector, which claimed it was unable to compete on a fair basis with these heavily subsidised firms.[58] The Commission of the European Community, on the other hand, heavily preoccupied with rescue efforts for the synthetic fibre sector, had not pursued its earlier concern about the growth of state holdings and the potential impact such growth would have on competition.

TABLE 4.5

Public Ownership in the Italian Clothing Industry, 1974-77

	ENI-Lanerossi-TESCON				*GEPI*			
	1974	*1975*	*1976*	*1977*	*1974*	*1975*	*1976*	*1977*
No. of companies owned	4	5	5	na	21	24	na	na
No. of employees	8,678	10,686	10,468	10,371	9,093	8,566	8,400	8,021
Sales (billion lire)	46.4	56.8	104.2	129.8	45.5	52.4	69.0	98.0
Net losses (billion lire)	2.0	10.7	11.0	44.0	10.4	19.5	14.1	12.8
Losses on sales (%)	4.3	18.8	10.6	33.9	22.9	37.2	20.4	13.0
Losses per employee:								
in million lire	0.23	1.0	1.05	4.24	1.14	2.28	1.68	1.60
in US dollars	355	1,536	1,263	4,810	1,760	3,491	2,018	1,809

SOURCE: *Risultati delle aziende pubbliche italiane del settore abbigliamento* (Milan: Associazione Italiana Industriali Abbigliamento, 1979).
NOTE: In the table 'na' signifies 'not available'.

By mid-1978, GEPI had sold a total of 33 of the 110 companies it had acquired since 1971, including three small clothing manufacturers employing less than 100 workers each. During this period, GEPI invested a total of L800 billion in its various rescue operations, 80 billion of which went to the clothing sector. The initial goal of careful selection in the salvage process had quickly been abandoned in favour of criteria based purely on political and social imperatives. GEPI's staff soon realised that they had little influence over final decisions, which were often reached by direct agreement between the government and the national unions and imposed on GEPI through the national planning agency (CIPE). Whether a company could be restructured profitably was not an important criterion. In fact, GEPI found itself acquiring parts of companies as they streamlined their operations and sold off unprofitable or troubled activities. The end result was a collection of unrelated parts with no coherence in terms of product lines or capabilities and with little scope for economies of scale.[59]

After 1976, GEPI obtained from the government an 'understanding' (although not an explicit policy) that no more rescue operations would be undertaken in the north of Italy. GEPI's management felt committed to the goals of regional development (direct labour costs in the south were about 60 per cent of those in the north) and they argued that the problem consisted of attracting qualified managers willing to relocate. Given GEPI's operational 'disadvantage' of having to employ labour which was largely unionised (and its inability to utilise black-market labour), the south offered, in management's view, the only solution to its difficult situation.

In August 1977, a new law (No. 675) was adopted to replace most existing legislation dealing with industrial expansion and adjustment, particularly Law No. 1011.[60] It created a new inter-ministerial body, the Comité

Interministeriale de Politica Industriale (CIPI), in charge of coordinating and responsible for administering industrial policy. The new legislation established a fund for industrial restructuring (L2,630 billion or about US$3 billion over three years) and a fund for improvements in labour mobility. The law also reorganised the structure of direct public intervention in industry, for example limiting GEPI's operations in the south of the country. In December 1976, the Commission of the European Community had opened proceedings under Article 93(2) against the proposed 'industrial reconversion fund'. By December 1977, however, the Italian Government agreed to keep the Commission informed on CIPI's criteria for allocating the fund's resources, on actual annual disbursements, and on the sectoral and regional distribution of all such grants.[61]

One of CIPI's first tasks was to sponsor a study of the clothing and textile industry, which was published in June 1978 under the title 'Sistema Moda'. The future strategy for the industry, according to the report, should be based on the quality and creativity of fashion labelled 'Made in Italy' and on a programme of diversification into new product and market niches. The industry's structure was to evolve towards greater integration of financial and commercial functions together with greater scale and specialisation at the plant level. To achieve these goals and to maintain the level of employment and a surplus in the balance of trade, the following measures were proposed:

(a) the absorption of social-welfare charges into the general tax system and a stronger enforcement of fiscal and labour legislation; and

(b) the creation of credit facilities in order to encourage diversification of clothing and textile firms within and without the sector.

These facilities would be granted only on meeting the following conditions: closure of inefficient plants and certification by requesting firms that they were not investing abroad in 'outward-processing' plants and would observe all relevant tax and labour laws.[62]

A third element of Italy's policy of structural assistance consisted of a special fund designed to keep workers at their posts through periods of temporary slack. The 'wages integration fund' (Cassa de Integrazione Guadagni) provided up to 50 per cent of any reductions in the workers' wages for a maximum of one year over any two-year period in case of either redundancy or short hours, provided they were retained as employees by their companies. The number of man-hours thus subsidised increased drastically during 1978 to about 3.5 million per month, particularly in the clothing and footwear industries. Later that year, the Italian Government introduced a scheme to reduce the burden of employers' contributions to health insurance which followed the general lines of the CIPI's strategy. The scheme, however, favoured female employees by granting their employers a much larger exemption (L64,000 per month versus L24,500 for male employees). The Commission of the European Community considered the differential treatment to be a 'state aid, within the meaning of Article 92(1) of the Treaty' since it would reflect positively on firms in the textile, clothing and footwear industries which were predominantly employers of female labour. In December 1979, therefore, the Commission opened procedures under Article 93(2) against the tax-relief programme. In September 1980, a final ruling was issued requiring no differentiation between tax-relief allowances for male and female workers.[63]

Italy's approach to adjustment in her clothing industry can be summarised as consisting of a series of fire-fighting operations. Not until the publication of the 1978 report by CIPI was there any overall sense of what objectives were being pursued and at what cost. Fortunate to have one of Western Europe's most cost-efficient and design-intensive industries, the Government nonetheless devoted considerable resources in a pointless attempt to preserve every possible job in the sector. Through direct state take-overs or instruments, such as the 'wages integration fund' and tax-relief allowances, the Government spared no effort to guarantee employment in the sector. The costs were extremely high and, had it not been for continuous monitoring by the Commission of the European Community, would have been higher still. It is therefore remarkable that, parallel to this policy of state intervention and paternalism, Western Europe's most competitive clothing industry prospered. In spite of benefiting from some of these programmes, the private sector was penalised by the additional competition of subsidised firms. Yet they successfully searched abroad (in Western Europe and elsewhere) for the opportunities for growth and profit denied by their Government at home.

Netherlands: Collapse of Consensus

Until the late 1960s, any assistance given to industry by the Dutch Government was intended primarily to support certain broad economic objectives, among which the continued expansion of the country's industries ranked high. This was a period of rapid industrial growth. Job opportunities multiplied in the chemical, electronics and other manufacturing sectors, attracting workers away from more traditional and lower-wage activities. The textile and clothing industries were among those hardest hit by the competition for workers which this economic boom engendered. The wage explosion, which began in 1964 fuelled by the large increases in productivity possible in the new industries, forced many Dutch clothing manufacturers to look across the border to northern Belgium for alternative manufacturing locations. As this avenue offered limited opportunities, sub-contracting operations were next begun in Eastern Europe and, in the early 1970s, expanded to the developing countries of the Mediterranean basin.[64]

Beginning in 1970, as a number of industrial sectors showed signs of declining competitiveness, the Dutch Government was moved to reconsider the scope of providing direct assistance to these ailing industries. As a first step, a series of sectoral analyses was launched in order to discover appropriate intervention programmes. A 1972 report on the prospects for the clothing industry by a Rotterdam firm of management consultants predicted that trade with developing countries would expand on a broad scale to the detriment of the Dutch industry. Since 'the Netherlands play a leading part in promoting trade with LDCs [less developed countries] because of its traditional free-trade policy, its many ties with overseas countries and ... because the Netherlands are a gateway for the entire North European foreign trade', any attempt to interfere with this process by resorting to protection was judged unwise and improbable. Instead, the report continued: '"Outward-processing" activities that would compete with imports and not with home production should be given preferential treatment and the state should encourage any general measures that would improve productivity, export sales and employment.'[65]

The recommendations of the 1972 report were not designed to cope with the near collapse of the industry that occurred after 1973. Both employers and labour unions asked the Government for immediate assistance and, together, all three established the tripartite group of advisers that became known as the 'steering group'. The group published its recommendations in a 1974 report in which they advocated drastic limitations on imports, quantitative restrictions on 'outward processing', financial assistance from the government, wage subsidies (especially for older and less productive workers) and subsidies for phasing out non-viable firms. The proposed programme, if implemented, would have represented a financial burden to the Government of 60 million guilders (Dfl.) over the next three years. After much debate the following set of measures emerged:

(a) A subsidy of Dfl.1,000 per worker (about 6 per cent of average yearly labour costs) was granted to clothing firms on condition that they did not reduce the number of their employees during 1975 by more than 10 per cent. (A total of Dfl.20.2 million was granted under this scheme.) The following year, a 600-guilder subsidy was added under the same conditions, leading to additional disbursements by the government of Dfl.11.4 million.

(b) A licensing system was set up to control imports of clothing from outside the original six member countries of the European Community.

(c) A tripartite organisation, Wercon, was created to facilitate re-employing dismissed clothing workers either inside or outside the industry and a second tripartite body, Strucon, was charged with the responsibility for transforming the clothing industry into a more competitive sector.

The members of Strucon were the employers, the unions, the concerned ministries (Economic and Social Affairs) and the Nederlandse Herstructureringsmaatschappij (NEHEM). This last was also a tripartite body (founded in 1972 as an independent organisation) which was financed and empowered by the Government to promote and restructure industry in the Netherlands along more competitive lines. NEHEM's role was to consult various elements in the sector concerned, gather all relevant data, define the lines along which the restructuring of the industry should take place, and act as the operational and administrative agent behind any eventual effort at restructuring. In the case of the clothing industry, responsibility for any final decision was to remain with Strucon, which would take into account NEHEM's recommendations. In order to fulfil its advisory role, NEHEM divided the industry into seven main branches and prepared a detailed report on each.[66] These reports explored possible development strategies for each sub-sector, based on a detailed review of the strengths and weaknesses of the principal firms involved, and on likely scenarios of both intra-Community and extra-Community competition for the 1980s. The main purpose of the studies was to judge and guide the adjustment plans presented by individual firms which sought to benefit from the financial assistance that would be made available. Once a company's plan was approved by Strucon, assistance would be channelled through two schemes:

(a) The Kaderregeling Confectie-Industrie had been adopted in 1976 to improve productivity and product quality, decrease production costs and promote cooperation between firms. The instruments employed were credit facilities and subsidies for projects costing more than Dfl. 50,000 for machinery, equipment and consultant expenses (the subsidies were limited to a maximum of 20 per cent of the expenses incurred and could not exceed Dfl.250,000 per firm).

(b) The Aktieplan Confectie-Industrie established an agreement procedure between NEHEM and the companies and provided flexible assistance which included subsidies of 40-50 per cent of expenses related to an approved restructuring effort, the capacity to facilitate and expedite any subsidies granted through the Kaderregeling scheme and subsidies of up to two thirds of the costs of general interest projects undertaken directly by Strucon in areas such as research and development and technological improvements, automation, improvement of work methods and working conditions, new-product and market research, export assistance and so forth.

The budget earmarked for these schemes amounted to Dfl.15 million for the Kaderregeling for the 1976-78 period (an additional Dfl.10-15 million was allocated for 1979-80) and Dfl.11.5 million for the Aktieplan for the 1979-80 period.

On 26 October 1977, the Commission of the European Community opened proceedings under Article 93(2) against the Dutch programmes for the clothing industry. The Commission argued that it was the third such measure since 1975 and that, although its aims appeared to be in line with the Commission's objectives, insufficient details were available for a judgment to be made on what the competitive effects within the Community would be. The Dutch Government responded with assurances that the scheme was not designed to create new capacity or support inefficient firms and agreed to keep the Commission informed on the application of the scheme during the 1978-80 period, particularly in terms of the number of firms aided and the size and number of investments undertaken. On 27 October 1978, the Commission lifted the proceedings and permitted the schemes to go into operation.[67]

The depth of the recession moved the Government to intervene in other ways in order to sustain employment. To this end, the Employment Fund was created in 1974 to provide loans without guarantee and capital assistance to ailing firms, especially in depressed regions. The fund was not linked to any restructuring programme. In addition, all existing programmes aimed at promoting investment in the Netherlands had been consolidated in April 1978 by the Investment Account Bill (Wet Investeringsrekening or WIR) which encompassed many different measures dealing with employment, small-scale enterprises, regional development, town and country planning and other major projects.[68]

The Dutch Government's approach to the clothing industry appears to have been based on practical rationalisation and a minimum of artificial support, coupled with a measure of import protection and heavy direct subsidies to employment. All clothing firms in the Netherlands had been classified according to the criteria developed by NEHEM into three categories: 'healthy' firms employing around 7,000 people which did not require any assistance; 'middle' firms, employing 10,000-12,000 people, which needed assistance to become more competitive (the Aktieplan had been especially designed for them); and 'helpless' firms, employing 4,000-5,000 people. These helpless firms were not eligible to receive any assistance through the Aktieplan and were destined to be phased out. Their workers could still benefit from the Employment Fund, but the Fund's budget had melted away: down from Dfl.600 million in 1975 to Dfl.50 million in 1978.

NEHEM had estimated that a total internationalisation of production (that is to say, a continuation of present trends) would result in only 4,000-5,000 jobs remaining in the Netherlands. As part of the strategy of adjustment for the industry, certain market segments had been identified as high priority to guide in the implementation of individual adjustment plans. Producers were expected to concentrate on 'in-season sales' with short delivery times, which could add 8,000-9,000 jobs, and on high-fashion products, thought to be less sensitive to low-cost competition, which could add another 7,000 jobs. It was expected that this might yield a stable employment level of about 20,000 people for the industry, or a net gain of about 15,000. The clothing industry in the Netherlands was approaching these levels of employment in 1978.[69]

By that time, however, the principal consensus-building structure behind the aid and restructuring schemes had suffered several major blows. The retraining programme organised by Wercon had made a good start: during its first year of operations it trained 2,400 redundant employees in the textile and clothing industries and 75 per cent of these were successful in obtaining new jobs.[70] In 1978, however, the programme was unexpectedly cancelled. A possible explanation was to be found in the gradual disintegration of the tripartite consensus which had been evident since 1977. Following the dismissal that year of 170 workers by a men's suit manufacturer (which had closed its doors while the sector was under study by Strucon), the main labour-union representatives resigned from Strucon in December 1977. This action, together with widely-spread dissatisfaction in union circles with the painful sacrifices required by most of NEHEM's plans, undermined the broad support necessary for any rationalisation programme. While the Ministry of Social Affairs continued to allocate funds unilaterally for worker retraining in the clothing industry (Dfl.26 million for 1976-78), the Ministry of Economic Affairs withdrew its support from other related programmes. Thus a cooperative organisation set up in 1977, which had united about 10 per cent of the clothing industry in a joint marketing programme, was cut off from any further funding after 1979.

During the 1975-80 period, the clothing industry of the Netherlands had been the beneficiary of over Dfl.200 million in public assistance: an unprecedented rate in the history of the country. Spread over many programmes, often of short duration and involving several, frequently conflicting, policy instruments, the government's policy had veered between one objective and another. By the end of the decade, it was clear that a new approach was necessary.[71]

From December 1979, the Dutch Government changed its strategy on industrial adjustment. It would no longer emphasise the restructuring of declining sectors, but would focus instead on stimulating the skill-intensive and technology-intensive industries that were at the core of the country's exports and future competitiveness. Table 4.6 illustrates the financial consequences of this shift in emphasis. Individual firms were to be supported only in districts where unemployment was significantly above the national level (the barrier was then set at 7 per cent), or whenever the impact on the labour market was judged to have major consequences (that is, from over 500 to over 1,000 job losses, depending on the region). Support for an individual firm would not be granted, however, outside the framework of a sectoral restructuring plan for those industries (including clothing) where such a plan was in effect. Furthermore, NEHEM, from which most major trade unions had withdrawn in late 1977, was to be replaced by a new organisation sponsored by the Ministry of Economic Affairs and constituted of civil servants and independent experts.[72]

United Kingdom: from Jobs to Investment

The United Kingdom has probably the longest history of intervention in the textile sector dating from the adoption of the Cotton Spinning Act of 1936. This first attempt at rationalisation was followed by various other measures in the early post-war years, none of which managed to deal effectively with the problem of surplus capacity. The 1959 Cotton Industry Act was the first comprehensive programme of adjustment assistance which clearly 'intended to help the industry to adapt to new circumstances in which large-scale imports were a fact of life'.[73] It succeeded in reducing the industry's capacity considerably, but it did not halt the continuing decline of employment and exports which had been in evidence since 1924.

In the mid-1970s, the United Kingdom was experiencing one of its darkest economic moments: its external sector was dangerously out of balance, industry

TABLE 4.6

Industrial Subsidies in the Netherlands by Type of Aid, Actual Commitments for 1975-78 and Projections for 1980-84
(million guilders and per cent)

	Sectoral support	*Development credits*	*Promotion of innovation and advanced activities*	*Support of individual enterprises*	*Total*
Actual commitments, 1975-78					
Textile, clothing, leather and footwear	365.6	0.8	...	303.0	669.4
% of category total	22.3	0.3	...	13.3	14.0
Metal and electronics	47.7	212.0	217.5	614.5	1,091.7
Transport equipment	937.2	22.0	321.2	738.0	2,018.4
All others	288.3	80.3	8.5	630.9	1,008.0
Total	1,638.8	315.1	547.2	2,286.4	4,787.5
% distribution	34.2	6.6	11.4	47.8	100.0
Projections for 1980-84					
Total	4,503.0	...	2,129.0	260.0	6,892.0
% distribution	65.3	...	30.9	3.8	100.0

SOURCE: Ben Evers and Gerard de Groot, 'The Netherlands', in Geoffrey Renshaw (ed.), *Employment, Trade and North-South Cooperation* (Geneva: International Labour Office, 1981) Tables 16 and 17.
NOTE: In the table '...' signifies 'not significant'.

was in disarray, inflation was running at more than 25 per cent annually and unemployment rose daily. After the 1974 election confirmed the Labour Party's hold on the Government, Harold Wilson's priorities as Prime Minister turned to a resolution of the economic crisis through budgetary restraints and the introduction in 1975 of an incomes policy designed to break the inflationary spiral. Simultaneously, the Government had to face urgent industrial policy issues in the automotive, steel, shipbuilding, aerospace and mechanical and engineering industries. As the Government's new industrial policy was announced in 1975 (and, some would argue, immediately repudiated by the Chrysler salvage operation), the clothing industry represented a rather small issue in the broader political and economic context.

Nonetheless, one of the results of this emerging industrial policy was to give new life to the National Economic Development Council (NEDC), a tripartite (government, business and labour) forum created by the Conservative Government in the early 1960s but dormant since 1971. The NEDC had its administrative organ in the National Economic Development Office (NEDO) which provided planning and industrial staff to a series of sectoral economic development committees (EDCs or 'Little Neddies'), of which 21 existed in 1967, representing more than 80 per cent of the private-sector labour force. After two changes of government and a number of administrative reorganisations, only nine EDCs were still fully functioning in 1971.

Within this context, the British clothing industry was able to benefit from a series of government measures of an emergency nature as well as from a general sense that a coherent long-term strategy was essential to overcome Britain's economic malaise. Four major aspects of the evolving relationship between the industry and the Government deserve note: job preservation, a sector-specific programme for improving the industry's competitiveness, protection from low-cost producers and continued access to regional development and other generalised industrial grants.

The first measure corresponded closely to similar programmes adopted in Belgium, Italy and the Netherlands. The temporary employment subsidy (TES) was an emergency measure adopted by the Government in August 1975 to encourage companies to defer threatened redundancies affecting ten or more workers in any given establishment. The programme made a direct grant of 20 pounds sterling per week for each worker kept in full-time employment who would, in the absence of a subsidy, otherwise be made redundant. The subsidy was payable for a full year at its normal rate and extendable for six months at £10 per week. In December 1975, the Commission of the European Community declared it had no objections to the TES as long as the structure of beneficiary firms was sound and the programme was temporary in nature.[74]

It soon became clear that the textile and clothing industries were the major beneficiaries of the TES. Nearly half of all TES applications received until July 1978 came from these sectors, and payments to them under the job-support scheme totalled more than £100 million during its first three years of operation. It was estimated that more than 80,000 workers in the textile and clothing industries (or just under 10 per cent of the total employment in both sectors) were being kept in their jobs by the programme. Considering that annual TES payments represented 59 per cent of the average annual earnings per employee in the clothing industry (and 37 per cent of the value added per employee), it was not surprising that the Commission of the European Community reconsidered its earlier position.

By the end of 1977, the Commission had raised several objections to the scheme: it had been renewed six times, TES assistance had been made available indiscriminately throughout the country and the budgetary allocations had risen from £7 million in 1975 to a projected £431 million for 1978-79. In the Commission's view, the TES was keeping firms artificially alive in declining sectors and this, given the concentration of aid in textiles, clothing and footwear, had clearly anti-competitive effects. After three months of intensive negotiations, the Commission approved a one-year extension of the TES, subject to several conditions:[75]

(a) funding for 1978-79 was to be reduced to £135 million compared with £222 million for 1977-78;

(b) the textile, clothing and footwear sectors were to be limited to £55 million (as against £106 million in the previous year) of assistance;

(c) for these three sectors, assistance was to be limited to 70 per cent of eligible workers for the first six months and 50 per cent for the subsequent six months;

(d) any extension of the TES beyond six months would have to be accompanied by a restructuring plan;

(e) new recipients were to be limited to a maximum of twelve months assistance; and

(f) no firm or division of a firm could receive assistance more than once.

These restrictions were intended to alleviate the negative effects the programme might have on labour mobility and the adjustment process and render it consistent with other similar decisions.[76] In addition, the Commission imposed a strict monitoring system of quarterly reports and prior notification for significant cases and made it clear that no extension would be granted beyond March 1978. Eventually the programme was replaced by the Temporary Short-time Working Compensation Scheme, whose aim was to encourage firms not to make excess labour redundant but to allocate the available work among the firms' total workforce through a shorter working week. While technically less objectionable than the TES, both these programmes had the effect of reducing the worker displacement normally associated with the sector's contraction and, therefore, slowing down the adjustment process.

After the 1975 launching of the 'new industrial strategy' in the United Kingdom, a series of deliberations were held within the Clothing Industry Economic Development Committee, one of the 37 sectoral EDCs which had re-emerged under the aegis of the NEDC-NEDO complex. The tripartite clothing EDC developed a sectoral strategy whose aims were:

'— continuing to accelerate improvements in productivity;

'— ensuring an effective control over the rate of import penetration of the home market (as a basis for renewed confidence for investment in the British industry); and

'— a concerted approach to expand exports substantially'.[77]

There were a number of aspects to the EDC's strategy, the most central being the Clothing Industry Development Scheme (CIDS), introduced late in 1975 under Section 8 of the 1972 Industry Act.[78] The CIDS sought to encourage the rationalisation of production and a greater concentration of activity in more efficient units without an increase in available capacity. Financial assistance was offered at varying rates for 'the employment of consultants that would investigate and/or implement measures to increase productivity and efficiency; the introduction of new machinery designed to increase productivity; and projects involving reorganisation or restructuring, including company mergers'.

The CIDS was to operate selectively using as its criterion the judgment of the Department of Industry as to whether or not the project under consideration was consistent with the objectives of the industrial strategy, 'was commercially and technically viable, was appropriate to the managerial and financial resources of the applicant firm and will significantly improve productivity and efficiency'. The Government allocated £20 million to CIDS to subsidise 50 per cent of corporate expenditures in the first category above (consultants) and 20 per cent (later increased to 25 per cent after December 1976) in the last two (investments in productivity and restructuring). By the closing date of 31 December 1977, enough applications had been received to guarantee that the full amount allocated would be spent. Table 4.7 summarises expenditures under the CIDS programme.

A 1981 review conducted by the Department of Industry was guardedly optimistic in evaluating the results of the programme.[79] In general, the participating companies had performed better than the industry as a whole, but this could be attributed to a number of factors. For example, while nearly one fifth of the establishments in the British clothing industry had received assistance, they represented over one fourth of total industry employment; that is, larger firms tended to benefit disproportionately. In addition, the participating companies, as their larger size alone would predict, tended to have a better prior record of performance than the industry. The report also recognised the modest impact of the scheme. The £13 million granted for investment assistance represented approximately 7 per cent of aggregate investment in plant and equipment for the years 1976-79. In fact, regression estimates carried out by the Department of Industry indicated that the 'additionality effect' of the scheme was to induce an incremental investment of £20 million, or 15-20 per cent of fixed capital formation for the industry in three years. While induced projects performed slightly less well than those which, although provided assistance, would have been carried out in its absence, the difference

TABLE 4.7

Expenditure under the United Kingdom's Clothing Industry Development Scheme (£ thousands)

	Applications received		*Applications rejected or withdrawn*		*Applications accepted*			
	No. of projects	*Value of projects*	*No. of projects*	*Value of projects*	*No. of projects*	*Value of projects*	*Assistance offered*	*Grants*[a] *paid*
Category I: Consultancy	296	2,791	53	505	243	2,285	1,138	849
Categories II and III Investment and rationalisation	818	119,776	144	28,611	674	91,165	19,734[b]	12,534

SOURCES: *Annual Report by the Secretary of State for Trade and Industry under the Industry Act of 1972,* House of Commons Paper No. 460, Session 1980-81 (London: Her Majesty's Stationery Office, 1981); and *Annual Report by the Secretary of State for Trade and Industry under the Industry Act of 1972*, House of Commons Paper No. 503, Session 1981-82 (London: Her Majesty's Stationery Office, 1982).

[a]As of 31 March 1981. Subsequent payments have brought up the total figure to just over £14 million, which represents a take-up rate of approximately 66 per cent of the assistance offered.

[b]These are mainly investment projects. A total of £776,000 was offered for projects involving only rationalisation and restructuring.

was not significant. Perhaps the most lasting contribution of the scheme is the most elusive to measure. Many companies reported that the process of participating in the programme had forced them to clarify their plans and subject them to critical review and that this experience was likely to be continued as they embraced a more rigorous planning methodology for the future.

While the CIDS had a definite production and technological orientation, other aspects of the sectoral strategy dealt with improved promotional efforts, particularly in terms of export expansion. The Clothing Export Council (a privately-sponsored body) brought together a number of separate efforts by the trade association and set a target of £1 billion of clothing exports by 1980. Its services included advice on markets and foreign agents, dissemination of information on export opportunities and distributors, market research for specific product categories, participation in exhibitions, fairs and fashion shows and other specialised activities. The Council also served to facilitate the industry's liaison with certain government bodies engaged in export promotion, such as the Export Credits Guarantee Department and the British Overseas Trade Board, which also assisted in the conduct of overseas market research, participation in fairs and travel support.

At the instigation of the Central Policy Review Staff, an independent 'think tank' set up by Edward Heath's Government to develop economic policy alternatives for the Government's consideration (and disbanded by Margaret Thatcher's Government in 1983), a number of sectoral Requirement Boards were set up during the early 1970s. Covering many branches of industry, these Boards were part of the Government's research and development policy and were specifically charged with the objective of orienting research to user requirements and providing financial support to such activities. The Garment and Allied Industries Requirements Board

(GARB) was set up in 1975 and had a budget for 1978-79 of £1.75 million, with responsibility for the clothing, footwear, leather and textile industries, together with their associated machinery industries. Among its various projects, GARB had granted £38,000 in 1977 to the Clothing Institute's Technology Centre for the latter's programme of promoting technology transfer and diffusion to the industry.

The Clothing and Allied Products Industry Training Board was an industry-sponsored body which provided training programmes for management and operatives at all levels of specialisation. Partly financed through a levy on the industry, it balanced its budget through programme fees. Since 1975, though, the industry had been arguing for a more intensive research and technological effort to meet its needs for increased productivity. The existence of the Clothing Industry Economic Development Committee provided the platform for the creation in 1978 of the Clothing Industry Productivity Resources Agency (CIPRA) which was to harness and develop the technical research available to the industry from many different fields. With a five-year initial funding of £450,000 from the CIDS, CIPRA was to act as broker for services and as a communications centre for promoting marketing, product and technical research and innovation. CIPRA was expected to become partially self-financing after an initial period of three years, at which point its modest fees were expected to cover 50 per cent of its costs.

Import protection was the third element in the Government's approach to the industry.[80] The basket provisions and 'trigger' import levels included in the 1977 MFA had been major victories for the clothing industry, which did not view the arrangement as protectionist, but, rather, as permitting 'an orderly expansion of imports' at rates 'greater than the growth in the domestic market'. Evidence of the Government's determination to ensure that the agreement was enforced was the sympathetic reaction of the Department of Industry to the requests for action put to them by the British Clothing Industry's Council for Europe when 'trigger' levels or other limits stipulated by the MFA had been exceeded. Based on analyses of imports in January-March 1978 (the first three months under the new agreement) the industry found 93 instances (product categories) involving 27 countries which were judged as 'cause for concern'. The Department of Industry agreed either to exert pressure on the European Community to operate the 'basket extractor' mechanism and introduce quotas (on, for example, imports of trousers from Singapore, India and the Philippines), open bilateral negotiations with certain countries (such as Malta and Portugal) or continue to survey the situation closely. This close support contrasted sharply with the situation in West Germany.

Finally, there were a number of general and regional development programmes available to clothing firms. The 1972 Industry Act, Section 7, on Selective Financial Assistance, was a general industrial development law designed to promote employment. The Department of Industry estimated that this programme alone had created about 13,000 new jobs in industry since its inception. The 'selective' nature of the programme had to do with the criteria employed for awarding grants, which favoured investment in labour-intensive industries. The clothing industry, however, had received only £4.1 million in assistance from this programme out of a total expenditure of £421 million. There were also a number of regional schemes open to the clothing industry in terms of employment-training grants, investment subsidies under Section 8 of the 1972 Industry Act (from 1972 to 1978, £15.4 million had been granted to the clothing industry out of a total expenditure of £1,548 million) and certain government purchasing-preference schemes.

The impact of these programmes on the clothing industry had been insignificant because of the small size of the units (the Selective Investment Scheme, for instance, designed as a counter-cyclical measure, required investments of more than £500,000 to qualify for assistance), their inability or unwillingness to deal with the required paperwork and the regional distribution in the industry, which was not heavily biased towards the special development or intermediate areas enjoying enhanced benefits. Finally, the Finance Act of 1972 provided several special incentives for investment and stock building which have on occasion benefited the industry.

The British adjustment strategy for its clothing industry seemed to be predicated on two important elements. First, protection would provide the time necessary to implement some basic changes in the industry's competitiveness. Second, a programme such as the CIDS was meant to show the way to the industry, to restore its confidence so that the necessary investments would be made, productivity improved and competitiveness enhanced.

The British industry possessed some powerful competitive advantages. It was the only country in the sample with a number of large and financially strong groups (Courtaulds, Coats Paton, Tootal and Carrington Viyella) which were integrated from fibre through to clothing and even retailing. Second, extremely close relations existed between domestic manufacturers and several large retailing organisations. The efforts of companies such as Marks and Spencer to work with domestic producers were, perhaps, responsible for the fact that a significant proportion of domestic demand did not fall into the hands of foreign suppliers.[81] Finally, labour costs in the United Kingdom were lower than in any other country in the European Community. While the rise in the value of the pound in 1978-80 hurt the industry considerably, British labour costs were at least 10-20 per cent below those in France, 40 per cent below those in Italy and 50 per cent of those in Belgium, West Germany and the Netherlands.

In general, the Clothing Industry Development Scheme was too modest an effort to result in dramatic change. Its consultancy assistance, for example, was limited to smaller firms (establishments of fewer than 300 full-time employees belonging to firms not employing more than 1,000 people) and to assignments covering 'advice on production, management, finance, administration, control systems and the scope for possible mergers or common service projects'. Furthermore, 'the Department of Industry must be satisfied that there is a reasonable prospect of a Category 2 or 3 project [investment in productivity] emerging from the consultants' work or that, where such an outcome is inappropriate, alternative means of improving productivity and efficiency can be achieved'.

This relative lack of concern for product positioning or for the impact of changes in a firm's marketing strategy was somewhat puzzling. While aware of the importance of factors other than production (as evidenced in several documents emanating from the Clothing Industry Economic Development Committee), the focus of the assistance programme was on technology and on increasing productivity. This is clearly not enough. The ability to apply coherent market differentiation strategies *and* attain increases in productivity would together determine which parts of the clothing industry in the United Kingdom, as in other industrial countries, would survive and under what conditions.

United States: Protecting a Large Domestic Market

The fundamental factor which has conditioned public response to the need for adjustment in the American clothing industry is the existence of a large domestic market capable of sustaining a broadly diversified industry without any losses arising from small scale or inefficiency. This and the overwhelming worldwide dominance of the American industry immediately after World War II led to a mentality among American firms that the best solution to their competitive problems, as these emerged in the late 1950s, was to be found in the domestic market. The rise of West European and South-east Asian competitors at the time coincided with rapid gains in American productivity (and, therefore, downward pressures on employment), an overvalued dollar and a steady decline in the proportion of the average American household budget spent on clothing. In addition, various United States administrations played a major role in accentuating the industry's demand for protection.

Government policy had not been particularly favourable towards the industry, beginning with the establishment, in 1933, of a system for supporting the price of domestic cotton above the prevailing world price (the result of depressed prices at home and the need to maintain agricultural incomes during the Great Depression). American textile producers, who were prohibited from importing low-priced foreign cotton, operated at a significant disadvantage *vis-à-vis* manufacturers elsewhere. Matters deteriorated in 1956 with the establishment of a two-tier cotton price system. Then, foreign textile producers could buy subsidised American cotton at prices which averaged 25 per cent below those prevailing in the domestic market.[82] It was no coincidence that pressures mounted for Japan to restrain her exports of cotton fabrics and clothing to the United States, most of which were made of American cotton, culminating in the 1957 VER. Other government policies of the early post-war period had equally negative effects on the industry.[83] The Administration unwittingly pursued a broad set of policies including prohibitions on mergers which preserved the fragmented nature of the industry, minimum-wage legislation affecting, primarily, the low-skilled workers who constituted the bulk of the industry's workforce and foreign-aid policies which encouraged industrialisation, particularly a textile-led one in countries as diverse as Japan and Colombia.

As the competitiveness of the industry deteriorated in the late 1950s, the focus turned to protection that would preserve the large domestic market for local industry. The bilateral agreement with Japan on cotton textiles had helped spread textile production to other countries not covered by the export limitation and had forged a closer link between the textile and the clothing industries. Once the former was protected, the latter had no choice but to join in or face lower-cost competition.

American leadership in negotiating the textile arrangements has been described above, but less well known are some of the early attempts to involve the Administration in a concerted effort to facilitate adjustment in the industry. In 1959, a Congressional committee reviewing textile trade set aside two recommendations put forth by the Textile Workers Union of America:[84]

(a) the establishment of a permanent textile development agency to engage in research and development, to administer a short working week and to finance the movement of workers and retraining and retirement benefits; and

(b) the creation of a special board to administer labour disputes and mediation in the industry.

Industry was adamantly opposed to both these recommendations, seeing that their independence would be reduced at the hands of both the state and the labour unions. Besides, the industry stood to gain on the issue of protection in any event, since labour-union interests were allied to their own. Without the support of the industry the adjustment initiative failed to gain momentum.

A second attempt at introducing adjustment assistance to the industry was the Kennedy Plan of 1962. It consisted of seven measures:

(a) an expanded programme of research, covering new products, processes and markets, to be carried out by the Department of Commerce in cooperation with labour-union and management groups;

(b) a proposal to change the depreciation allowances on textile machinery;

(c) aid from the Small Business Administration to 'assist the cotton textile industry to obtain … financing for modernisation of its equipment';

(d) a directive to the Department of Agriculture to recommend ways to offset the differential arising from the two-price cotton system;

(e) an assistance programme for industries experiencing or being threatened by injury because of growing imports;

(f) a conference between exporters and importers of textile products to seek an understanding to provide a basis for trade without undue disruption of established industries; and

(g) a statement that any application by the textile industry under the escape clause or national-security provisions of the Trade Agreements Extension would be carefully considered on its merits.[85]

Other than in the trade area, where the LTA was put into effect in that year, little progress was made on the overall adjustment plan. The research programme was limited to fact-finding and statistical analyses of little consequence. The accelerated-depreciation provisions which were enacted were later extended to all industry.

These had some positive short-term effects in that the textile and clothing industries' average rate of profitability (as a percentage of the average for all manufacturing industry) rose from 60 per cent and 83 per cent, respectively, for the years 1961-63 to 76 per cent and 94 per cent, respectively, for 1964-66, the years immediately after the new provisions went into effect. But the longer-term effect was to increase domestic capacity and aggravate the problem of diminished competitiveness during the next recession. The two-price system for cotton was eventually abolished in 1964 which, although too late to mend the damage caused, did contribute to the subsequent profit improvement. Finally, the Trade Expansion Act (TEA) of 1962, which prepared the ground for the forthcoming Kennedy Round of multilateral trade negotiations, introduced the concept of trade-related adjustment assistance for both firms and workers. The conditions for eligibility were so worded, though, that the United States Tariff Commission (the body charged with certification) denied all fourteen industry petitions and all seven individual company petitions for determination of trade-related injury that were presented to it up to and including December 1969.

Even after conditions were relaxed in 1970, the Tariff Commission reviewed thirteen additional industry-wide petitions for certification and 60 individual firm petitions until the expiration of its authority in March 1975. Of these, only five industries were declared eligible for assistance (which meant that member firms could apply for benefits on an accelerated basis) — barber's chairs, marble products, earthenware, sheet glass and pianos — and 25 individual applications (including five in textile and clothing) were approved. The total funds disbursed to the 36 eligible firms, during the eleven years the programme was in effect, took an average 26 months to process and amounted to about US$45 million.[86] Equally, no worker-assistance petitions were granted under the first eight years of the TEA, which, together with the extraordinary delays in obtaining any response, prompted union officials to rename the programme 'burial assistance'.

The failure to introduce any meaningful assistance programme and the shift by most exporting countries to man-made fibres during the 1960s brought out a broader coalition of labour and capital in favour of greater and more comprehensive protection. In evaluating the American position up to the signing of the 1973 MFA, one analyst observed:

> 'Throughout the international negotiations, the US textile and apparel industries demonstrated that they could block any concessions that they viewed as unfavourable. Because the US government had failed to develop an industrial policy — and equally important, a political coalition to support it — it was forced to follow industry's lead. Ironically, the only constraint on the demands of the domestic industry [for more protection] was international.'[87]

Eventually, the international opposition collapsed as the signing of bilateral VERs on man-made fibres by the United States with the major South-east Asian producers left Western Europe wide open for their assault.

The passage of the 1974 Trade Act was an attempt to remedy the miserable experience with trade adjustment assistance (TAA) since the 1962 TEA. The conditions of eligibility were simplified (some might say perverted), benefit levels were increased and, for the first time, communities became eligible for assistance if a significant proportion of workers in the area lost their jobs through increased imports. After a slow start, response by companies and workers accelerated. Technical assistance for consulting services, for example, in amounts of $10,000-25,000 per firm could be allocated immediately after certification in order to aid in preparation for an adjustment plan. Once the plan was approved, direct loans of up to $1 million could be made at favourable rates (based on the average cost of government borrowing at the time) and loan guarantees issued for up to an additional $3 million. Petitions soared from less than 100 firms in 1975-76 (the first year of the programme) to over 700 in 1979-80. By early 1980, 224 clothing firms had been certified.[88] While the time between petition and certification was under two months, the average period from certification to approval of financial assistance exceeded 50 weeks. Funding, therefore, lagged behind the number of petitions. While a total of $14 million had been disbursed in the first year, $94 million (nearly the maximum allowed under existing appropriations) was paid out in 1978-79.

The delays inevitable in such operations, however, increased the risk of failure. Thus, by early 1980, 47 firms that had received TAA financial support had been liquidated. This represented nearly 30 per cent of all companies that had received assistance. A major improvement in this respect was the creation of ten trade-adjustment centres in different cities throughout the country to assist applicants with their petitions and accelerate financial disbursements.

In addition to the specifically targeted TAA programme, American clothing firms had access to a number of general economic development programmes aimed either at specific areas by the Economic Development Administration (EDA) or to categories of firms by the Small Business Administration (SBA). For 1978, for instance, the EDA appropriations amounted to nearly $30 million in direct loans and $33.5 million in loan guarantees. The SBA had available $136 million for direct loans and $2.32 billion for loan guarantees. In 1975-77, $45 million of loan guarantees was made to 446 clothing companies under the SBA programme. The relative size and the marginal nature of these programmes can be judged in the context of a government budget of nearly $450 billion in 1978.

The worker-assistance programme was relatively more ambitious and costly. As of 31 January 1979, benefits totalling $637 million had been paid to 413,000 individuals. Results were, however, disappointing. A study of 963 recipients of TAA and 538 other non-trade-related unemployed individuals confirmed the impact of age, sex, experience and industrial category in re-employment delays and made other critical observations.[89] The average TAA recipient, for example, did not receive a first payment until fourteen months after the job dislocation had occurred, meaning that most recipients were already re-employed at the time the benefits began to flow. Second, the research confirmed significant disincentives to work associated with TAA benefits. Finally, there was little evidence that permanently displaced workers made any use of the training (about 9 per cent) and employment counselling and relocation services (3 to 7 per cent) available to them or that those who did obtained significant benefits from these services. Thus the programme was successful as an income maintenance scheme but little else.

In February 1979, President Carter launched a new textile programme defined in a White Paper, which promised to 'conduct a global import evaluation ... to analyze the impact of textile and apparel imports from all sources in the context of US market growth and conditions in the industry'. The idea, dear to the industry for many years, was to tie growth in imports to growth in domestic demand, effectively freezing relative market shares. In addition, the President committed his administration to much tighter controls on import surges, flexibility and violations of the trade agreements. This approach was shared by some West European countries (notably France and the United

Kingdom) so that the United States administration found itself facing a situation very different from that which had prevailed in 1973. The domestic industry was now allied to other importing-country governments, and the United States was practically alone in trying to avoid too fast an escalation of trade restrictions against developing-country exporters. The White Paper was the price to pay, however, for industrial acquiescence in the Tokyo Round of multilateral trade negotiations then coming to an end. President Carter also promised to (i) initiate a major export drive with full government support, (ii) create a high-level tripartite group to examine problems affecting the industry's competitiveness and (iii) expand a pilot programme to enhance productivity in men's and ladies' clothing. Apart from the export drive, the other programmes were pious hopes. An analyst of the 1979 Tokyo Round and 1981 MFA negotiations commented that

> 'although the White Paper did include concessions to the industry with respect to tightening import restraints, it did not require a fundamental policy change on the part of the United States'.[90]

In the end, the policy of the United States towards the clothing industry during the last ten years has largely been limited to offering a fair degree of protection. Neither the funds available for adjustment nor the programmes themselves (now being dismantled by the Reagan Administration) have played a major role in bringing change to the industry. Certain programmes, such as the joint Department of Commerce/Apparel Manufacturers Association export drive (a $3 million programme half financed by the Government to encourage clothing companies to venture abroad), are laudable but modest steps in the right direction. The size of the domestic market and the strength of some of the leading companies should, though, guarantee the survival of a large proportion of the industry under any external circumstances.[91] There is little else the Government can do or appears to be disposed to do.

Japan: Positive Adjustments

The Japanese Government has had a long history of involvement in the affairs of its textile and clothing industries. The Government reacted as different segments of the industry lost competitiveness to low-cost producers in the South-east Asian basin or saw their exports threatened, either by trade restrictions in the United States and Western Europe or by local import-substitution policies in the developing countries. Its adjustment strategy consisted of (i) encouraging a shift of resources to higher value-added segments, (ii) facilitating the scrapping of excess capacity and an upgrading of production facilities and (iii) promoting the introduction of new technology.

The first major government initiative addressed specifically to the industry was the creation in 1956 of the Textile Industry Advisory Board, a joint business/Ministry of International Trade and Industry (MITI) planning group. It was established to deal with the problem of excess capacity in cotton fabrics resulting from the recently agreed export restraints negotiated with the United States Administration and to promote the development of synthetic-fibre and textile production as an alternative. The industry was, at that time, characterised by a multitude of independent small firms at the middle and end stages of the production chain and by a score of large producers of chemical fibres and spinners. They were linked to each other by a multiple-layer distribution system which tended to isolate producers from final consumers. Excess loom and spindle capacity was thus maintained as a hedge against large market swings and added to the industry's instability and financial difficulties.

Over the next 22 years a total of 52.5 billion yen (about US$10 million per year) was spent by MITI to purchase and scrap excess capacity in the industry.[92] This was done through five consecutive textile acts (see Figure 4.2) which attempted to deal with the short-term problems presented by foreign restrictions on Japanese exports and the more basic structural issues which resulted from the rise in Japanese wage costs relative to those in other South-east Asian countries. In aggregate terms the structural shift was relatively successful. Japan's textile and clothing industries (particularly the former) had been a major pillar of the country's recovery after World War II. In 1955, they accounted for 19 per cent of industrial production, 23 per cent of the manufacturing workforce and 37 per cent of its exports. By 1980, these ratios had declined to 12 per cent, 6 per cent and 5 per cent, respectively. While exports accounted for 39 per cent of the industry's output in 1955, they were down to 24 per cent in 1980; but import penetration had climbed from 0.8 per cent to 18 per cent of domestic demand during the same period. Japan had gone from being the main textile exporter in South-east Asia to a situation analogous to that prevailing in Western Europe and the United States. But her adjustment problems had been compounded by having experienced in 30 years what in most other industrialised countries had taken nearly a century.

The first two textile acts had the quite limited objectives of providing financial incentives for the scrapping of facilities and encouraging production of synthetic textiles. While no data are available on the success of the former, the LTA and MITI's coaching contributed to an increase in man-made fibre production in Japan from 239,000 tons in 1963 to over 1 million tons in 1970. The Special Textile Act of 1967 was more ambitious in its goals. Motivated by Japan's perception that currency convertibility and membership in the

FIGURE 4.2

Chronology of Trade and Adjustment Assistance Policies Affecting Japan's Textile Industry

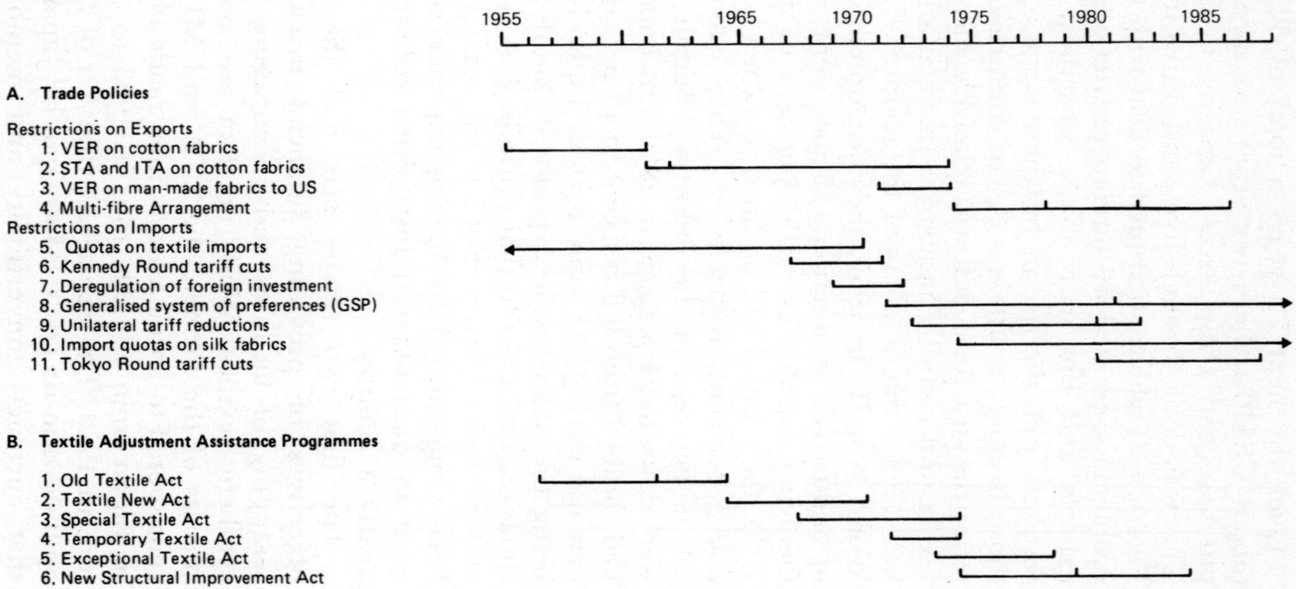

C. General Industrial or Related Policies

1. Act for Promotion of Rationalisation
2. Act for Joint Activity by Small Enterprises
3. Act for Modernisation of Small Enterprises
4. Act for Enterprises affected by GSP
5. Act for International Adjustment for Small Enterprises
6. Smaller Enterprises Business Switch-Over Act
7. Structurally Depressed Industries Law
8. Depressed District Act
9. Higher Yen Act
10. Industrial Area Small Enterprise Act

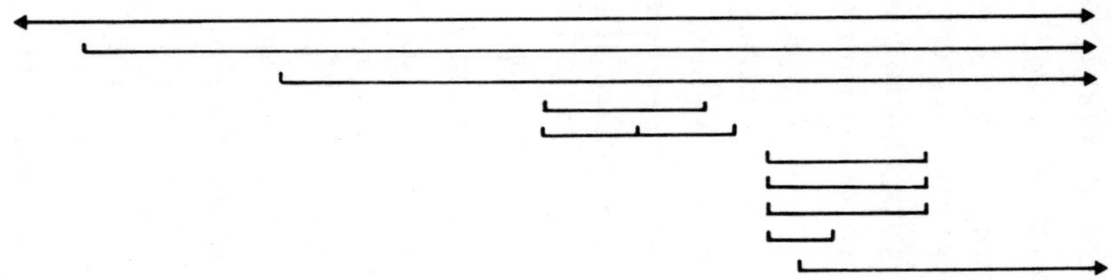

Sources: Ippei Yomazawa, 'Adjustment of the Japanese Textile Industry to the Advanced Developing Countries', Hitotsubashi University, Tokyo, mimeograph, September 1980; and Yoshie Yomezawa, *Analysis and Evaluation of the Adjustment Process and Policies of the Japanese Textile Industry* (Tokyo: Japan Economic Research Center, 1981).

Note: Short vertical strokes in the lines denote the year of renewal of the policy or programme.

OECD presaged a more competitive era to come, the Government provided ¥378 billion (most of it as low-interest loans) to the spinning, weaving, dyeing and finishing sectors of the industry to help them modernise and increase productivity.[93] The 1967 programme was also aimed at rationalising the industry, through mergers and the scrapping of old plants, and at encouraging the largest companies to invest in neighbouring countries in response to Japan's declining competitiveness. While the former aspects do not appear to have been very successful,[94] the late 1960s mark the beginning of an active foreign investment policy by the industry.

From 1970 onwards, the rising value of the yen and Japan's mounting industrial wages coincided with three developments in trade of cardinal importance for the industry. These were (i) the end of Japanese quotas on imported textile products in 1970, (ii) the introduction by Japan in 1971 of preferential tariff concessions to developing-country producers and (iii) the establishment of a 'voluntary' export-restraint agreement on man-made fibre products with the United States. The Temporary and Exceptional Textile Acts of 1971 and 1973 were meant to deal with the short-term dislocations brought about by the VER. Similarly, the generally applicable GSP and International Adjustment Acts (C.4 and C.5 in Figure 4.2) were also intended to deal with the potential impact of these concessions on small and medium-size enterprises by encouraging them to shift to other lines of business. The results were not very satisfactory, with less than 10 per cent of the expected shifts actually occurring.[95]

The first serious attempt to change the structure of the industry, particularly in the clothing sector, began with the Structural Improvement Act of 1974. In 1971, MITI's Industrial Structure Council published its first 'Long Term Vision' document, which emphasised the shift to knowledge-intensive sectors that would be necessary in the years ahead. Following the 1973 oil shock, MITI reconsidered its position and issued a second long-term vision in 1974, which aimed at reducing the importance of labour-intensive and energy-intensive industries by shifting these sectors to the developing countries. As applied to the textile sector, the Textile Council (the successor to the Advisory Board) reached the following conclusions:

(a) Demand would begin to slow down and shift to high-quality and more fashionable clothing as incomes rose.

(b) Knowledge about market trends and consumer preferences should be promptly communicated upwards in the textile chain; this would require greater integration and cooperation between textile and clothing companies.

(c) Low-value-added textiles would be left to the developing countries.

(d) Companies that could not adapt must switch to other industries with greater potential.

(e) Government policy should promote these adjustments by undertaking several measures to help small and medium-size firms and should maintain a free-trade policy that would encourage a better international division of labour and benefit Japanese consumers.[96]

The main aspect of the 1974 Act, which embodied these principles, was that it shifted the emphasis from productivity as the solution to a more subtle view that the industry needed to 'respond' either by shifting resources abroad and to other industries or by moving to more fashion-intensive ('knowledge-intensive' in their view) production. At the same time, the Japanese Government felt that, by keeping trade pressures on the industry, the value of the available financial incentives would be highlighted by the continuing threat of extinction.

After 1970, Japan's import regulations on textile products became among the most liberal within the industrial world. Following the abolition of all remaining quotas regulating textile imports, Japan embarked on a policy of gradual tariff reduction and encouragement of imports from developing countries. The country was among the first to adopt a generalised system of preferences for developing-country exports in 1971 and extended it for ten years in 1981. Between 1972 and 1978, for example, imports of textile products (mainly clothing) from GSP countries increased four-fold from 20.5 per cent to 43.2 per cent of total textile imports. Approximately 11-15 per cent of these imports entered duty-free under the GSP provisions. Japan has also accelerated the tariff reductions agreed upon at the Kennedy and Tokyo Rounds of multilateral trade negotiations so that, by 1980, her trade-weighted average tariff rate on textile products was 11 per cent versus 14 per cent for the European Community and over 23 per cent for the United States.[97] On outer-wear since 1981 Japan has already been putting into effect the rates she agreed to reach by 1987, which place it between 15 and 50 per cent below comparable rates of the United States and the European Community.[98]

Following the surge in imports in 1973-74, protectionist sentiment arose in the industry. Industry representatives asked that Japan approach the 1977 renegotiation of the MFA as an importer and not as an exporter, which had been the case until then. The Textile Council re-examined the issue in 1976 and reconfirmed their earlier position that the maintenance of a liberal trade policy was the best option available given the necessity to shift to higher value-added goods. As has been pointed out, however, this attitude can be partly attributed to the facts that (i) Japan is a net exporter of textile products (especially fibre), (ii) her imports come mainly from countries in East and South-east Asia (60 per cent of the total) plus China (12 per cent), with which Japan has an enormous positive overall trade balance ($9.4 billion in 1980), (iii) Japan has considerable direct investments in the textile industries of these same countries and (iv) Japan has been very conscious of her economic interdependence with the Asian-Pacific region.[99]

Nonetheless, the evidence is that of mild protectiveness rather than protectionism. As distribution channels for imported clothing and textile products diversify, the level of import penetration and accompanying tensions will surely rise. There are more than 2,000 importers of textile products in Japan, all scrambling for a piece of the action. Also, larger retailers, such as department stores and supermarket chains, have moved aggressively into direct buying abroad, to the point where 32 per cent of imported consumer goods sold by department stores and 20 per cent by large supermarkets were direct foreign purchases.[100] It is in this active and competitive atmosphere, exposed to the latest fashions from Western Europe and the United States and the fast-reacting and low-cost suppliers of South Korea and Hong Kong, that MITI plans to breed the worldwide ready-to-wear houses that will assure Japan a place in the international textile industry.

There has also been a number of general industrial-assistance programmes that benefited clothing and textile companies (C.1-C.10 in Figure 4.2). With one partial exception, most of these initiatives were aimed at small and medium-size enterprises. The Government has reasoned consistently that large diversified firms can handle whatever adjustment problems they encounter by applying their substantial human and financial resources to solve them or by shifting resources to other activities. In assisting the smaller companies, the main tools employed are preferential financial terms, government-financed scrapping programmes and access to the designated industries' credit fund. The agency primarily responsible for carrying out the policies is MITI's Small and Medium Enterprise Agency. As the title of the various acts reveal, the intended result is to bring about modernisation, concentration or shifts in resource allocation among the large mass of small companies that constitutes Japan's secondary industrial sector. Little is known about the impact of these programmes on clothing firms, but they do not vary much in concept and substance from those operated by similar agencies in West Germany or the United States.

Beginning in the mid 1970s, however, a number of large and significant industries in Japan got into considerable economic trouble, among them, open-hearth steel, aluminium refining, shipbuilding and synthetic fibres. In order to deal with these major problems, the Government passed the Structurally Depressed Industries Law in 1978.[101] The key elements of the programme seem to be (i) to establish clear recognition that there is a need to restructure the sector, (ii) to keep industry and labour essentially responsible for the final outcome and (iii) to maintain a certain amount of external (import) pressure to assure that the aid offered will be put to good use.[102] Of course, Japan has been fortunate in having had a number of expanding industrial sectors capable of assimilating redundant workers from depressed industries. In the case of the spinning sector, for example, the presence of rapidly-growing automotive firms in the Nagoya district facilitated the reductions in employment that were agreed upon in a compromise restructuring and scrapping plan.[103] Whether this situation will continue is a separate but important question.

The Government has paid little attention, however, to worker-adjustment measures. Between 1974 and 1980, the total workforce in the textile and clothing industries diminished by 323,000, or 25 per cent of total employment. The major declines were in cotton spinning

(47 per cent) and man-made fibres (44 per cent), while the clothing industry appears to have held its own. In most of these cases, worker adjustment, retraining and re-employment were undertaken by the firms themselves (in the case of synthetic fibre, through intra-company transfers of workers); elsewhere, adjustment occurred as the result of inter-industry shifts, as in the case of the spinning sector. No labour-tracking studies were available, but MITI officials presumed that, since many workers in the industry were women (71 per cent), they had shifted either to the services sector or dropped out of the labour market altogether.[104] Other than maintenance payments, no special adjustment programmes were available to redundant clothing and textile workers in Japan.

One final aspect of the Japanese approach towards the industry concerned the hopes discussed earlier for a major technological revolution that would reverse (or at least diminish) the current competitive disadvantage of domestic clothing firms. These hopes are anchored in the robotisation of clothing assembly. Since the passage in 1978 of the Machinery and Information Law providing special tax advantages to buyers of robots, 24 manufacturers and ten insurance companies have banded together to create the Japan Robot Leasing Corporation. The Corporation is geared primarily towards supplying small companies, is backed by the Japan Development Bank and can provide engineering and consulting services in addition to hardware. In 1983, MITI's Agency for Industry, Science and Technology, plus ten robot, computer and machinery manufacturers, joined in a general research-and-development effort to create a new generation of computer-aided manufacturing (CAM) systems for which the Government's contribution will amount to ¥17 billion. Fundamental obstacles yet remain to such a development: pattern recognition and sensory capacity is not yet sufficiently developed for the needs of the clothing industry and the financial cost of such equipment may very well outweigh its labour-saving capabilities. The only thing certain at this stage is that no major change in the economic structure of production on the scale envisaged by some Japanese officials appears likely before the next decade.

In summary, Japan's strategy seems to be to use the clothing industry as the leading sector for a transformation of the entire textile chain. While each sector obviously has different problems requiring different solutions, the aim is to move the industry towards higher fashion-content and higher valued-added sectors of the market while conceding the bottom end to the developing countries. Thus one sees a progressively more open import policy linked with extensive assistance to small and medium-size enterprises. Coupled with a general trimming and modernisation of the fibre and textile sectors and with more encouragement of foreign direct investment in the Asian-Pacific basin, this is expected to yield a smaller but highly competitive industry in the long run.

Lessons of a Decade of Intervention

The history of public intervention in the clothing industries of all eight countries in the study is summarised in Table 4.8. Prior to 1970 (with some notable exceptions), intervention was confined for the most part to government support for industrial development programmes of a general nature and to the orderly marketing agreements negotiated since 1955 to limit imports from Japan and, later, the developing countries. The United States attempted to ease the impact of import competition through an innovative programme of trade adjustment assistance, an initiative that failed because of bureaucratic obstacles. Japan, on the other hand, succeeded in reducing capacity in some of its most sensitive sectors, but not in bringing about major shifts in the allocation of resources. In Western Europe, only Italy, paradoxically the most successful producer in the European Community, was actively involved in trying to salvage a number of important textile and clothing companies for political reasons.

In general, this was a period of relatively painless adjustment in the industry: clothing employment was rising in many countries and significant opportunities existed in other areas to absorb any job losses that might occur in declining sectors of the clothing or textile industries. All of this changed drastically in the next five years. A rise in the intensity and scope of import competition, coupled with sustained gains in productivity and the virtual end to growth in demand in most developed countries, resulted in a rapid decline in employment in clothing and a shift in government policy towards massive job-support schemes. It also became evident after 1975 that general industrial development programmes were relatively ineffective in dealing with the underlying competitive problems of the clothing industry. Elaborate and selective schemes began to emerge in all countries, characterised by a diversification of assistance to include research and development, management consultancy, marketing and exports, in addition to the more traditional capital incentives associated with previous programmes.

Prodded by the Commission of the European Community, MITI and the American Economic Development Administration, the latter half of the 1970s witnessed efforts by all grant-giving agencies to make explicit linkages between investment, assistance and sectoral restructuring. The scope of intervention appeared to have shifted once again: first, from a general development to a sectoral orientation and, second, from providing relief to facilitating a more permanent solution through restructuring.

TABLE 4.8

Comparative Chronology of Public Intervention in the Clothing Industry Pre-1970

Belgium	*France*	*West Germany*	*Italy*	*Netherlands*
			•Acquisition of Lanerossi Group by the State (1962) •Established GEPI as a state salvage operation for bankrupt companies (1968)	
United Kingdom	***United States***	***Japan***	***All countries***	
•First VER with Hong Kong (1969)	•First with Japan on cotton products (1956) •Kennedy Plan (1962) sets up trade adjustment assistance (TAA) for workers and firms: ineffective	•MITI sets up textile Advisory Board (1956) •Scrapping and modernisation acts aimed at cotton sector	•STA (1961) •LTA (1962-74)	

Table 4.8 (cont.)
Comparative Chronology of Public Intervention in the Clothing Industry 1970-73

Belgium	*France*	*West Germany*	*Italy*	*Netherlands*
•Support for technological progress through CETIH and CIRIT: direct and para-fiscal tax contributions	•Law 1101 reduces social-security contributions (1970). Later struck down by EC (1975) •Acceleration of GEPI interventions to over 100 firms in sector (1970-75)			•Rotterdam consultants report on the future of the industry (1972)
United Kingdom	***United States***	***Japan***	***All countries***	
	•Soften conditions for TAA eligibility •VERs negotiated on man-made textiles	•Import quota ended •Encourages outward investment in Asian LDCs •Temporary and Exceptional Acts continue scrapping and modernisation support to all textiles sectors	•Support builds up for more comprehensive trade agreement, particularly in the United States	

TABLE 4.8 (cont.)

Comparative Chronology of Public Intervention in the Clothing Industry, 1974-75

Belgium	*France*	*West Germany*	*Italy*	*Netherlands*
•Pressure mounts for government intervention •Interest-free loans granted against employment guarantees	•Regional and small-enterprise subsidies used extensively by industry	•Provincial assistance to the industry grows	•Peak of GEPI activities	•Steering Group recommends heavy public support for the industry •Emergency subsidies to firms to preserve jobs •Wercon and Strucon tripartite advisory bodies are created
United Kingdom	***United States***	***Japan***	***All countries***	
•Temporary employment subsidies go into effect to preserve employment; clothing industry is major beneficiary •Clothing EDC launches industry-development scheme with state funding	•New Trade Act simplifies eligibility rules for TAA and expands scope of progamme to include affected communities	•Structural Improvement Act shifts emphasis of government intervention to a total response based on high-value-added clothing sector as main target for development	•First MFA goes into effect (1974-77). EC delay in arranging bilaterals causes imports surge	

TABLE 4.8 (cont.)

Comparative Chronology of Public Intervention in the Clothing Industry 1976-77

Belgium	*France*	*West Germany*	*Italy*	*Netherlands*
•Safeguard (Claes) Plan is outlined based on more strict import controls, second interest-free loans and export support	•Emergency Plan is enacted for cotton sector •Clothing firms make extensive use of existing regional and general aid programmes		•Law 675 creates CIPI and provides it with $3 billion industrial reconversion fund. EC opens procedures against it •GEPI activities are turned down and limited to the South	•NEHEM-sponsored plan to restructure the Dutch industry is backed by significant public support •EC reacts to subsidies and opens investigation procedures
United Kingdom	*United States*	*Japan*	*All countries*	
•EC intervenes to limit TES funding given the programme's repeated renewal	•TAA payments to firms and workers begin to grow		Leadership for re-negotiation of MFA shifts to Europe, particularly France and the United Kingdom	

TABLE 4.8 (cont.)

Comparative Chronology of Public Intervention in the Clothing Industry 1978-80

Belgium	*France*	*West Germany*	*Italy*	*Netherlands*
•EC attacks plan on the basis that it lacks selectivity •Government sponsors major study of the industry as the foundation for targeting aid •Study suggests 20-30,000 jobs can be saved at a public cost of over BF9 billion	•FSAI is created to provide alternative employment in depressed regions. EC reacts to cumulative nature of aids •Emergency plans are enacted successively for yam, texturising and wool filament industries •Codis plan includes textiles as one of 'key' industries for public support		•CIPI publishes Sistema Moda study. Federtessile publishes its own study of the industry. Both conclude that high social charges are a problem; industry criticises state-owned sector subsidies •Fiscalisation of social charges agreed by government. EC intervenes to standardise rates for both sexes	•Employment Fund is exhausted for worker compensation •Breakdown of consensus between labour, industry and government. NEHEM and Strucon collapse •Government shifts to high-technology strategy and limits support to industry

United Kingdom	United States	Japan	All countries
•EDC launches project for technology development and diffusion •CIPRA	•Carter Administration issues White Paper in support of industry as precondition for Congesssional approval of Tokyo Round tariff cuts and other agreements	•Law for Structurally Depressed Industries is enacted: synthetic-fibre sector is major recipient •Robotisation gains public support	•Restrictive MFA succeeds in slowing down import growth from LDCs

Table 4.8 (cont.)

Comparative Chronology of Public Intervention in the Clothing Industry Post-1980

Belgium	*France*	*West Germany*	*Italy*	*Netherlands*
•Government modifies Claes Plan substantially and EC objects strenuously	•Socialist government launches textile plan. EC opens investigation singling out reductions in social-security charges			
United Kingdom	*United States*	*Japan*	*All countries*	
	•Reagan Administration begins to dismantle TAA programme	•Heavy investments and hopes put in robotisation of industry	•MFA renewed in 1981 with equally restrictive provisions as in 1977	

Note: In the table 'nil' signifies 'nothing to report'.

This change in the nature of public intervention in the industry implied that governments would have to play a more active and discriminating role as economic agents relative to the more impartial role they had assumed in the past as distributors of subsidies for the promotion of industry. To cope with these new responsibilities, new structures and institutions were needed and the post-1975 period was also characterised by a multiplication of new government; tripartite or quasi-government bodies entrusted with the difficult decisions concerning allocation of resources and eligibility for assistance.

By the end of the decade, there was evidence of a further shift in the approach of public authorities to the adjustment problem. The collapse of consensus mechanisms and the frustration created by the complexity of the task of allocating aid to the industry drove public officials away from the quest for solutions specific to individual industries towards better ways to improve overall allocation of resources in the economy. Not all countries experienced the same evolution nor was the same timetable followed by those that did. Five basic models of intervention emerge, whereby one can trace the general outlines of this evolutionary process.

Market-led Industry Adjustment

Throughout the 1950s and 1960s, most governments paid relatively little attention to their clothing industries, relying on market forces (partially constrained by tariffs and quantitative restrictions on certain products) to shape the process of adjustment. The prevailing rates of economic growth and industrial expansion meant that displaced workers could find alternative employment in other segments of the industry or in other industries. After 1975, only West Germany maintained this position in the face of the dramatic contraction of her industry, although the United Kingdom and the Netherlands let employment in their clothing sectors shrink by 40 and 60 per cent, respectively, of their pre-1970 peaks before taking direct remedial measures. Japan, which moved assertively in the direction of a more open market from the late 1960s onward, did not have to cope with such a reduction in employment in the clothing sector until much later and neither did the United States.

The resistance of some of these countries to intervention may be due to certain common traits. In most cases there was a strong and expanding industrial base which allowed large numbers of redundant clothing workers to move into other branches of industry, at least until the general level of employment deteriorated badly in 1975. Also, being highly dependent upon exports, they were unwilling to foster the spread of protectionist feelings among their trading partners, particularly the developing countries with which all had large and positive trade balances. With relatively strong currencies and a diversified industrial export base, none of them had much to gain by reverting to restrictive, domestically-oriented policies. For the United States, in spite of a lower rate of import penetration, the enormous size and diversity of its domestic market allowed for a high degree of competition in the industry.

Under such conditions, successful firms pursued the kind of adjustment strategies discussed in the previous chapter. They moved aggressively to follow market trends, to specialise in the higher-fashion end of the market and to offer retail clients a range and quality of services which were in every way (except price) superior to those provided by low-cost foreign producers. They also invested heavily in productivity and manufacturing efficiency and transferred abroad those product lines or production processes most vulnerable to competition or least amenable to automation. But, as unemployment increased and the balance of trade deteriorated, the willingness to maintain an open competitive system collapsed, first in the United States with the MFA and then in Western Europe when employment issues became paramount.

Job Preservation

One by one, in the midst of economic recession, balance-of-payments difficulties and rising unemployment, four of the six European Community members in the sample abandoned their market-oriented 'neglect' of the clothing industry and switched to policies for preserving jobs. The rationale in all cases was that unusual times required unusual remedies and that, given enough time, the industry could undertake the necessary efforts to restructure itself along more competitive lines. As the crisis deepened and results were not forthcoming, temporary job measures took on a more permanent character.

In Belgium, job-support grants in the form of interest-free loans were offered as a 'once only' emergency measure for 1975, but a second and similar package was proposed a year later. In the Netherlands, the rapid contraction of the domestic industry led to massive intervention to support existing jobs on an unprecedented scale. But, in terms of the size and duration of job-support schemes, Italy and the United Kingdom clearly led the field within the European Community. Italy began public take-overs of troubled firms in the early 1960s and control was eventually extended to more than 10 per cent of total employment in the industry by 1977. In that year, Italian state holdings in the industry suffered losses of $65 million, or about $3,500 per employee. In the United Kingdom, the temporary employment subsidy became the mainstay of her textile and clothing industries. Nearly half of all TES applications received by the end of July 1978 came from these two sectors, and payments to them under job-support schemes totalled more than £100 million in the scheme's first three years.

It is difficult to uncover any common causal traits that might lead to countries adopting this policy. To some extent its origin lies in the frailty of governments in Italy, the United Kingdom and, to a lesser degree, Belgium and the Netherlands. Between 1973 and 1976, the British Government was not in a position to take strong measures in an industry that employed so many people. Political difficulties in Italy, coupled with problems of regional disequilibrium, created strong pressure for intervention in the interests of stability and equality. Belgium's deep cultural split and the industry's predominantly Flemish base called for political wariness as regards any decision affecting employment. In the Netherlands, the case was simply one of too much decline, too quickly and at the wrong time. Underneath a few superficial similarities, though, are significant differences in performance, strength and industry characteristics.

On balance, the job-preservation strategies proved to be extremely costly and ineffective in maintaining employment, without even taking into account the negative effect they probably had on healthy segments of the industry. As Table 4.9 shows, the Netherlands, the United Kingdom and Italy spent significant sums on what were no more than direct subsidies to employment.[105] More important is the fact that these programmes served to remove any urgency for workers to seek alternative employment or for the industry to face tough decisions about rationalisation or restructuring. Furthermore, healthy companies suffered, since, as the Italian private sector correctly claimed, the existence of state-supported companies made their task much more difficult, given that they had to compete not only with imported products but also with heavily subsidised national ones. It seems clear that the levels of expenditure committed to this approach could not be sustained indefinitely and that continuing pressure from the Commission of the European Community for their

TABLE 4.9

Average Yearly Financial Subsidies per Worker, 1975-77[a]
(US$ million)

	Belgium	*France*	*West Germany*	*Italy*	*Netherlands*	*United Kingdom*
Employment						
Assistance	40[b]				200[c]	150
Creation		30				
Investment						
Specific				35	60	30
General	10	1	0.5	4		5
Regional		6	1.5	7		15
Marketing and export		4		7	40	
Research and development		0.5		1		
Specific intervention		4.5		248[d]		
Totals	50	46.0	2.0	302	300	200

SOURCE: José de la Torre, 'Public Intervention Strategies in the European Clothing Industries', *Journal of World Trade Law*, March-April 1981, Table 7.
NOTE: Where no figure is given in the table there was 'nothing to report'.

[a]The corresponding figures for Norway and Sweden were $2,130 and $2,250 per worker respectively.

[b]Discontinued since 1977.

[c]A second programme of similar magnitude was put into effect for 1978.

[d]Represents losses incurred in the nationalised firms (that is, an average of $2,480 per worker for 1975-77) which accounted for about 10 per cent of clothing-industry employment.

elimination in fact provided countries such as the United Kingdom with an excuse for freeing themselves from such onerous responsibilities.

Technological Advance as Industrial Strategy

France was, perhaps, unique in basing her early policy towards the clothing industry on the increases in productivity that might result from extensive research into manufacturing processes. In this case, state involvement was primarily limited to providing the necessary funds for research and to taking a restrictive line in trade negotiations. Throughout the 1970s, France consistently took the view that clothing was an 'infant industry' in that it had never been fully industrialised and automated. Thus domestic industry should benefit, it was thought, from a certain amount of trade protection, in order to give it time to incorporate the fruits of research and development before having to confront foreign competition. Such a strategy was also an important element of the British adjustment programme for the industry established after 1978. As described above, Japan has also begun to invest heavily in technology, but her plan to automate the industry is at too early a stage of development to be evaluated. Finally, the European Community has launched a number of efforts designed to speed the flow of innovation to the industry, but the means at its disposal have been rather modest.

None of the other countries in the sample placed particular emphasis on a technological solution to the problems of the industry, although their sectoral-adjustment programmes described earlier (in Belgium, the Netherlands and the United States) did provide incentives for investment designed to modernise operations and increase productivity. The difficulties inherent in automating the clothing-assembly process and the fact that innovations could be easily adopted by any competing country may have contributed to this relatively low public commitment to process research and development in the industry. Finally, reliance on a technological cure did not appear to have been particularly successful. The message was not that technological research must be abandoned, but simply that it could not solve the industry's problems by itself. First, technology had to be integrated into a broader all-encompassing strategy that took into account the need for corporate adjustments in marketing and production location as well. Secondly, the implications for employment of increased productivity rendered more urgent the need to facilitate worker adjustment through retraining and relocation services.

Failure of Restructuring Plans

Following massive public expenditures on maintaining employment during the period 1975-77, governments began to reach for more permanent solutions to the industry's problems. Such solutions required changes in structure and improvements in competitiveness that were in line with prevailing global market and economic trends. Thus, in practically all countries, different organisations, both private and public, set out to study which courses of action seemed most promising and worthy of pursuit. The work of the Clothing Industry Economic Development Committee in the United Kingdom in 1975 and 1976, the 1978 Federtessile and CIPI studies in Italy, the 1974 report of the MITI's Textile Council, the Dutch NEHEM studies in 1977 and 1978, the studies leading to the French Codis Plan in 1978, the 1978 White Paper on the industry in the United States and the study of the textile and clothing industries sponsored by the Belgian Government in 1978-79 resulted from this need to define a suitable framework for the application of adjustment assistance. Agencies were created or adapted to implement the ambitious plans that emanated from these studies involving public officials in resource-allocation decisions to an extent and at a level of detail which exceeded previous experience in most other industrial development programmes.

The experience of these countries with their respective restructuring strategies has not been very satisfactory. For one, resources were limited and consensus was difficult to obtain on which goals were of the highest priority with respect to allocating funds to the industry. In addition, most government bureaucracies appeared ill-suited to the task of sifting through the details of corporate plans for reorganisation and redirection which involved areas of expertise (for example, finance, marketing and production) and a level of industry-specific knowledge not normally found in government. To the extent that decisions should be made, as the Belgian study recommended, on the basis of solid corporate plans rather than on sectoral and sub-sectoral considerations, this problem was amplified.

Gradually, support for these programmes eroded at all levels. The labour unions were not able to accept the sacrifices that restructuring implied and refused to share the responsibility for making them. Industry was more interested in obtaining a strengthening and extension of import protection through a renewed MFA than in the meagre resources that could be committed to restructuring. And, finally, governments came to realise that the complexity and political costs of dealing with a fragmented industry at such a level of detail were more than that for which they had originally bargained.

Neo-liberal Approach

Both the public debate in certain countries, as well as actions by the Japanese, American and Dutch governments since 1980, point to a new style of public intervention in the clothing industry: one that shuns the complexity of restructuring decisions while recognising that the present economic environment cannot assimilate the large number of potential job-seekers that would result from a liberal market-oriented policy.

Thus the outlines of a new 'neo-liberal' approach seem to be emerging based on a mix of the following three principles:

(a) A certain degree of protection is still necessary to guarantee an orderly evolution of competition in an industry which is both highly fragmented and employs a large proportion of the industrial labour force.

(b) The principal task of government should be to provide alternative employment opportunities in sectors where high-wage developed countries can produce a competitive advantage and not to sustain employment where that advantage is lost or in decline.

(c) Since the burden of such adjustment is to a large extent borne by the workers, government should try to minimise the private costs of adjustment by facilitating employee mobility, retraining and job-search services in the event of trade-related displacement.

Historical experience is such that reasonable doubts can be formulated about the potential success or impact of policies based on each of these three principles. But, taken together, they represent a more realistic view of what the role of the state can be in facilitating adjustment and of the costs and benefits associated with non-neutral intervention policies. In terms of the classification defined in Table 1.1 and reproduced in Table 4.10, the evolution of public policy towards the industry has come nearly full circle. Whether this new approach will succeed where the others have failed depends primarily on whether it fully takes account of the international competitive trends described in Chapter 2 and the relative effectiveness of the private-response strategies discussed in Chapter 3. By matching these multiple strands of analysis, as the study

TABLE 4.10
Evolution of Public Policy towards the Clothing Industry

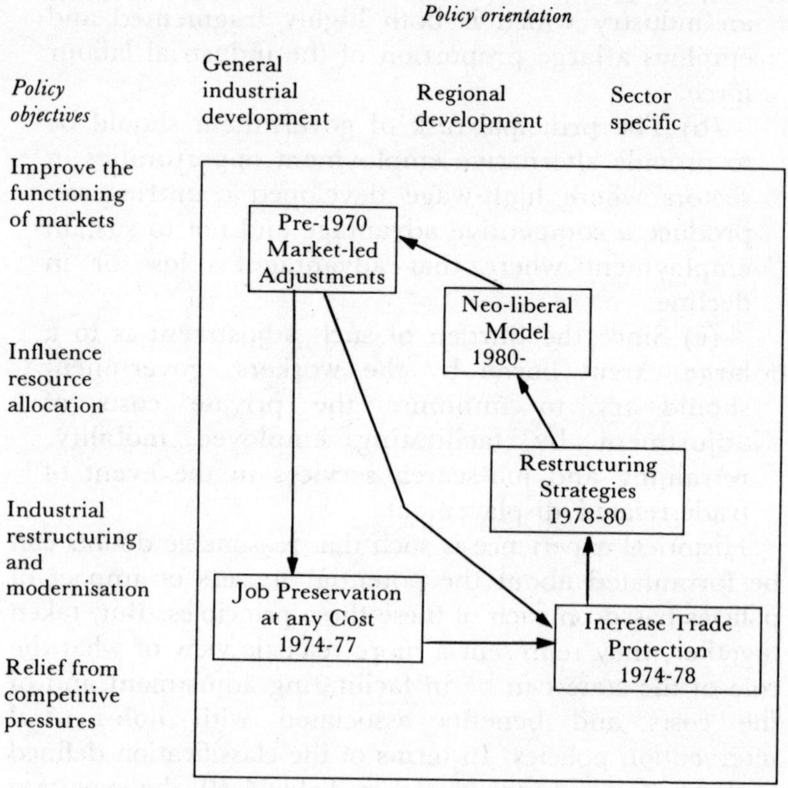

attempts in the following chapter, one can arrive at a handful of reasonable recommendations to guide private and public strategists in the next decade.

NOTES AND REFERENCES

1. The early history of protection in the United States actually did not concern clothing directly. The establishment of a price-support system for cotton producers in 1933 marked the beginning of a process in which each successive stage of production was forced to seek protection for its domestic component. Thus by 1956, the two-price system for cotton was estimated to increase raw-material costs to American fabric producers by 25 per cent. Once these textile firms sought and obtained protection from foreign suppliers (who had access to cheap American cotton), the clothing industry joined the bandwagon out of fear of the consequences of buying higher-priced American fabrics. For a detailed discussion of these developments see Vinod K. Aggarwal and Stephen Haggard, 'The Politics of Protection in the US Textile and Apparel Industries', in John Zysman and Laura Tyson (eds), *American Industry in International Competition* (Ithaca: Cornell University Press, 1983) pp. 249-312.

2. See *The History and the Current Status of the Multi-fiber Arrangement* (Washington: US Government Printing Office, for the International Trade Commission, 1978) for an historical perspective on these negotiations.

3. For a detailed account of the negotiations leading to the 1977 agreement and the various positions of the main parties, see Chris Farrands, 'Textile Diplomacy: the Making and Implementation of European Textile Policy — 1974-1978', *Journal of Common Market Studies*, Oxford, September 1979, pp. 22-39; Stephanie Lenway, 'Textiles: the Politics of Protection', University of Washington, mimeograph, March 1982; and Aggarwal and Haggard, *loc. cit.*

4. Many of these job losses occurred in the synthetic-fibre sector (particularly in France, Holland and West Germany) as a result of over-investment and excess capacity, while other losses were the direct result of depressed levels of demand throughout Europe. Nonetheless, from 1973-77, American employment in textiles and clothing remained constant while the European Community lost 17 per cent of its workforce. Equally, American imports of textiles and clothing (in dollar value) increased by 19 per cent and 17.5 per cent, respectively, while comparable figures for the European Community were 75 per cent and 126 per cent. West European sentiment was thus much more protectionist than that of the American delegation, reversing the attitudes held at earlier negotiations.

5. See Keesing and Wolf, *op. cit.*, pp. 59-87.

6. 'La communauté européene, et les échanges de produits textiles', *Europe Information*, No. 44/81, Commission of the European Community, Brussels, pp. 8-9.

7. *Textile and Clothing Industries: Structural Problems and Policies in OECD Countries*, *op. cit.*, p. 123.

8. For the text of the protocol extending the Arrangement and incorporating a set of mutually agreed understandings on its implementation, together with the conclusions of the Textile Committee adopted simultaneously, see 'Extension of Multi-fibre Arrangement Agreed', *GATT Press Release*, Geneva, No. 1304, 22 December 1981.

9. For two evaluations see *Le Monde*, Paris, 19 January 1982, p. 23; and *The Economist*, London, 14 August 1982, p. 14.

10. As an indication of the limited impact of preferential agreements in fostering exports of textiles and clothing products from developing countries, the proposals of the Reagan Administration for preferential access to the market of the United States to goods from Caribbean countries specifically excluded such items as textile products and footwear.

11. *Europe Information*, No. 44/81, p. 4.

12. *First Report on Competition Policy* (Brussels: Commission of the European Community, 1972) pp. 131-32.

13. *Bulletin of the European Communities* (hereafter cited as *Bulletin*), Luxembourg 9/10-1971, part 2, No. 78. For a detailed analysis of the Community's competition policies towards the textile industry, see J.S. Chard and M.J. MacMillan, 'Sectoral Aids and Community Competition Policy: the Case of Textiles', *Journal of World Trade Law*, March-April 1979, pp. 132-57.

14. One of the first cases reviewed by the Commission concerned not the nature of the aid itself but its financing. The French Government has imposed a 'para-fiscal', supplementary tax on the sale in France of certain textile products (irrespective of origin) in order to finance a research-and-development programme for the industry. The Commission argued that such a levy was incompatible with the free-trade provisions of the Treaty of Rome. While the cost was proportionally distributed between imported and domestic production, the benefits accrued mainly to French manufacturers. Furthermore, any increase in foreign sales in France would result in a larger share of the programme being financed by non-French companies. Eventually, the Commission's position was upheld by the European Court on 25 June 1970, setting a major precedent against the indiscriminate use of 'para-fiscal' taxes. *Bulletin*, 9/10-1969, ch. V, point 15; *Bulletin* 8-1970, part 2, point 15; and *First Report on Competition Policy*, *op. cit.*, pp. 142-44.

15. *Bulletin*, 8-1970, part 2, point 17.

16. It should be noted that indirect labour costs (that is, social-security charges and pay-roll taxes, paid holidays, vocational training and other benefits) as a percentage of direct wage costs varied enormously from country to country. The actual percentages in the clothing industry for selected countries are:

	1967	*1978*
Belgium	48.3	62.0
Canada	12.5	19.1
France	56.6	63.9
West Germany	39.2	60.2
Italy	90.5	92.7 (1977)
Netherlands	45.8	56.7 (1972)
Sweden	22.8	61.5
United Kingdom	16.0	20.3
United States	21.0	21.3

See *Textile and Clothing Industries: Structural Problems and Policies in OECD Countries*, *op. cit.*, Table 38, p. 80.

17. *Bulletin*, 9-1972, part 2, point 23. Three months later, an objection was also raised to the application of the extraordinary-aid procedures to all textile firms, particularly those employing more than 500 workers, *Bulletin*, 12-1972, part 2, point 19.

18. *Bulletin*, 7/8-1973, point 2114.

19. *Bulletin*, 3-1975, point 2117.

20. *Bulletin*, 2-1973, points 1401-8.

21. *Bulletin*, 6-1974, point 2120.

22. *Bulletin*, 6-1980, point 2.1.34.

23. *Bulletin*, 7/8-1982, point 2.1.52.

24. *Bulletin*, 12-1982, point 2.1.47.

25. *Bulletin*, 3-1976, point 2116; *Bulletin* 4-1976, point 2112, and *Bulletin* 9-1976, point 2108.

26. *Bulletin*, 12-1975, point 2133, and *Bulletin* 1-1976, point 2111.

27. *Bulletin*, 9/1974, point 2229, and *Bulletin* 4-1975, point 2256.

28. *Commission Policy on Sectoral Aid Schemes*, COM (78)221 final (Brussels: Commission of the European Community, 1978). The previous month, the *Seventh Report on Competition Policy* had severely attacked state aid as a major obstacle to maintaining competition in the Community.

29. *General Guidelines for a Textiles and Clothing Industry Policy*, COM (78)362 final (Brussels: Commission of the European Community, 1978) p. 6.

30. *Bulletin*, 4-1979, point 2.1.20.

31. *The 1980s: the Decade for Technology*, *op. cit.*

32. *Bulletin*, 4-1982, point 2.1.103, and *Bulletin* 7/8-1982, point 2.1.184.

33. *Europe Information*, No. 44/81.

34. *Bulletin*, 7/8-1981, points 1.4.1-1.4.9.

35. The issues of regulation of 'outward-processing' trade and markings of origin have caused considerable debate within the European Community, since different countries had different stakes in outward processing. Regulation of quotas was eventually approved by the Council of Ministers in February 1982 (*Bulletin*, 2-1982, point 2.2.8). The quotas were allocated to clothing manufacturers and the use of textiles originating from the Community made mandatory. Some countries, notably the United Kingdom, objected to the additive nature of outward-processing quotas and have refused to put the regulation into effect. The debate on markings of origin has been equally divisive. After discouraging national legislation on this issue, the Commission was forced to present a proposed directive to the Council in October 1980, which was, however, later withdrawn when found wanting. A new regulation proposed in December 1981 (*Bulletin*, 12-1981, point 2.1.16) remains inoperative.

36. The situation was quite different, however, with respect to the Economic Expansion Law first proposed in 1969 in order to replace two earlier acts dating from 1959 and 1966. The law provided for low-interest loans, subsidies and special premiums to promote investment and job creation. Due to its general applicability, the Commission of the European Community opened proceedings under Article 93-2 in June 1970. Since the programme was defined without reference to specific regions, and the Belgian Government did not want sectoral specificity to remove the instrument's subtle flexibility, the Commission agreed to operate on the basis of a system of previous notification for any significant usage (over 15 per cent subsidy or more than an 3 million EUA investment). The law adopted in December 1970 provided assistance through partial subsidies to investments worth BF635 million in 1971 and BF438 million in 1972 in the clothing sector alone. After a drop

in use during the recession, the expansion law was again made use of by the clothing industry in 1976 and 1977 (aiding projects which represented total investments of BF363 and BF129 million respectively), which gave rise to significant concern as to its adherence to the stated guidelines laid down by the Commission. By 1982, however, no action reflecting this concern had been taken by the Commission.

37. *Bulletin*, 3-1978, point 2.1.27, and *Bulletin* 3-1979, point 2.1.30. It should be noted that the European Commission raised no objection to the creation of an Industrial Redevelopment Fund on 7 September 1979 whose objective was to assist industrial conversion towards new- and high-technology sectors in regions affected by declining industries. On any loans for restructuring, the Belgian Government agreed to abide by procedures established by the Commission whereby:

— if no restructuring plan were drawn up, assistance would be limited to six months and no interest-free loans under the 1970 Economic Expansion Act allowed;

— if a plan existed, any assistance had to conform to the terms of the plan; and

— prior notification had to be given to the Commission whenever the affected firm employed more than 300 people, or 150 people in 'sensitive' sectors such as textiles, clothing and footwear.

See *Bulletin*, 12-1978, point 2.1.44, and *Bulletin* 9-1979, point 2.1.28.

38. McKinsey & Co., 'Vers le redressement de l'industrie belge du textile et de la confection', Report submitted to the Ministry of Economic Affairs of the Belgian Government, Brussels, June 1980.

39. *Bulletin*, 4-1980, point 2.1.29, and Bulletin, 9-1980, point 2.1.21.

40. Bulletin, 12-1981, point 2.1.46. There had been considerable opposition within the Commission to the Claes Plan, particularly on the part of the West German Government which considered it too far-reaching.

41. *Bulletin*, 7/8-1982, point 2.1.43, *Bulletin*, 9-1982,point 2.1.26, and *Bulletin*, 2-1983, point 2.1.40.

42. *Bulletin*, 2-1983, point 2.1.39.

43. The main beneficiary of FSAI was initially the automotive industry; 15,000 jobs were thus created in the first two years at a cost to the State of FF131,000 per job. See Green, *op. cit.*, p. 38.

44. Jacques de Bandt, 'France', in Renshaw (ed.), *op. cit.*, p. 168. The schemes included those administered by the Fond de Développement Economique et Social (FDES), created in 1955, and the Comité Interministériel pour l'Adaptation des Structures Industrielles (CIASI), founded in 1974.

45. *Bulletin*, 9-1980, point 2.1.20.

46. *Bulletin*, 12-1979, point 2.1.50.

47. *Bulletin*, 5-1982, point 2.1.19, and *Bulletin*, 1-1983, point 2.1.25.

48. *Le Nouvel Economiste*, 7 February 1983, pp. 38-9.

49. Ulrich Hiemenz and Kurt von Rabenau, 'Effective Protection of German Industry', in Corden and Fels (eds), *op. cit.*, p. 18.

50. Neu, *loc. cit.*, p. 181.

51. For an indication of their views, see Farrands, *loc. cit.*, p. 37. He states that: 'The German solution, strongly emphasised by Count Lambsdorff

[then West Germany's Minister of Economics] to the embarrassment of colleagues who wished to tread more softly, is a return to a more liberal market [in the 1981 MFA negotiations].' This was later confirmed by Count Lambsdorff in an address to the Trade Policy Research Centre in London on 17 December 1979. See Count Otto Lambsdorff, 'Goals for the 1980s: Competition, Price Stability and Adjustment', *The World Economy*, London, February 1980, pp. 415-25.

52. See Klaus-Werner Schatz and Frank Wolter, 'The Federal Republic of Germany', in Renshaw (ed.), *op. cit.*, pp. 181-208; and Horn, *op. cit.*

53. As reported and discussed in detail by Horn, *op. cit.*

54. *Ibid.*, p. 55.

55. Chard and MacMillan, *loc. cit.*, p. 149. Neu, *loc. cit.*, states, however, that 'there is no evidence that they [the clothing and textile industries] received more support than other industries' (p. 165).

56. Indirect support for this view can be obtained from the fact that, from 1972 to 1976, employment in the clothing sector in Bavaria decreased by 16,000 workers (or 15 per cent of total industry employment) while the national average was more than 30 per cent. One study reported that, in 1975, at least seven of the top 49 textile firms were receiving *Land* subsidies; cited in Shepherd, 'Public and Private Strategies for Survival in the Textile and Clothing Industries of Western Europe and the United States', *op. cit.*

57. For the following seven years, the company lost an additional L24 billion, an indication of things to come for the record of state intervention in the industry. For a detailed account of this record, see F. Coltorti and G. Mussati, *GEPI e TESCON: Due Interventi delle Participazione Statali* (Milan: Franco Angeli, 1976).

58. In a document published in 1976, the Italian Industry Association (AIIA) warned:

> 'There is an immediate danger that the clothing sector will acquire in a short time a structure consisting of, on one side, industrial enterprises kept artificially alive through public salvage operations and, on the other side, enterprises operating at the margin on the basis of black labour and fiscal tax evasion.'

59. Personal interview with former GEPI official in Milan, 1979.

60. Law No. 1011, the subject of the long-running dispute between the European Commission and the Italian Government described above, was finally abrogated in August 1977. During nearly six years of operations, L29 billion of subsidised loans were granted to the clothing sector for 121 projects and L265 billion for 890 projects to the textile sector.

61. *Bulletin*, 12-1976, point 2130, and *Bulletin* 12-1977, point 2.1.59.

62. Simultaneously, the Textile and Clothing Industries Association (Federtessile) released a voluminous study confirming the competitive performance of medium-size firms (200-500 employees) in the clothing sector. Among various recommendations, the study proposed increasing training assistance for displaced workers, greater support for an aggressive export promotion policy, the fiscalisation of social-security charges and a stop to government take-overs of bankrupt companies. See *Progetto Tessile* (Rome: Federazione fra l'Associazioni delle Industrie Tessili e Abbigliamento [Federtessile], 1978); and *Sistema Moda* (Rome: Comité Interministeriale de Politica Industriale [CIPI], 1978).

63. *Bulletin*, 12-1979, point 2.1.47, and *Bulletin* 9-1980, point 2.1.19.

64. Tunisia alone was the recipient of nearly US$1 million of Dutch foreign investment in the clothing industry in 1973; 1,869 new jobs were created in that country. See *Herstructurering Nederlandse Confectie-Industrie: deel 1 Herenbovenkleding-Industrie* and *deel 2 Damenbovenkleding-Industrie*, *op. cit.* As discussed earlier (Chapter 3), this development continued to the point where the volume of outward-processing trade exceeded total domestic production in 1980.

65. Krekel, van der Woerd and Wouterse, 'Perspectief onderzoek Confectie-Industrie', Rotterdam, mimeograph, 1972.

66. The two most important studies were those by NEHEM, *op. cit.*, dealing with the men's and women's outer-wear sectors.

67. *Bulletin*, 10-1977, point 2.1.26, and *Bulletin*, 10-1978, point 2.1.46.

68. In May 1977, the European Commission acted against two proposed programmes for the Netherlands — WIR and a regional-aid scheme known as IPR — for being incompatible with the Commission's guidelines on general and regional aid programmes. Regions were defined too widely, premiums for different sectors overlapped and the aid was also available to old investments which rendered it 'operational aid' in the Commission's view. Both programmes were eventually modified to suit Commission objections. *Bulletin*, 5-1977, points 2.1.19-2.1.21, and *Bulletin*, 5-1978, point 2.1.28.

69. *Annual Report*, NEHEM, 's-Hertogenbosch, various years.

70. Many of the data in this section were taken from Ben Evers and Gerard de Groot, 'The Netherlands', in Renshaw (ed.), *op. cit.*, pp. 124-37.

71. It should be noted that the Netherlands is probably the only OECD country that has attempted to link industrial readjustment with a prospective view of the interests and growing competitiveness of the developing countries. (It may be argued that in Japan, MITI's guidelines for industrial restructuring, included in its various 'visions', have performed, at least implicitly, the same role.) Beginning in 1974, the Ministries of Economic Affairs and Development Cooperation of the Dutch Government launched an active and forward-looking policy that aimed to anticipate the shift in restructuring needs this view would imply at home, and to provide assistance to the developing countries to foster their industrialisation in these areas, presumably with the aid of foreign direct investment by Dutch firms. The policy has been generally judged to have failed and the government appears since to have adopted a more conventional approach in its commercial relations with the developing countries, promoting industrial exports through aid and credits and facilitating foreign investment by Dutch corporations whenever exports are not possible. For more details, see Ben Evers, *Industrial Restructuring and Development Cooperation in the Netherlands*, Occasional Paper No. 6 (Tilburg: Development Research Institute, University of Tilburg, 1979); and Evers and de Groot, *loc. cit.*, pp. 128-31.

72. Evers and de Groot, *loc. cit.*, pp. 127-28.

73. For an analysis of these early programmes, see Miles, *op. cit.*, and Miles, 'Protection of the British Textile Industry', in Corden and Fels (eds), *op. cit.*, pp. 184-214.

74. *Bulletin*, 12-1975, point 2132.

75. *Bulletin*, 1-1978, point 2.1.16, and *Bulletin*, 3-1978, point 2.1.24.

76. A few months later, for example, the European Commission approved Ireland's Employment Maintenance Scheme without specific conditions (*Bulletin*, 7/8-1978, point 2.1.41). When it was renewed a year later, however, the Commission imposed four conditions: it limited the budget to £4.5 million and assistance to less than 50 per cent of workers; it required prior notification when more than 125 workers were to be covered; and it declared the synthetic-fibre sector ineligible for the programme. *Bulletin*, 7/8-1979, point 2.1.32.

77. *Clothing Industry Development Proposals*, Report of the Economic Development Committee on the Clothing Industry (London: National Economic Development Council, 1975).

78. There were thirteen different industry schemes negotiated over several years by the NEDC and the Government involving an allocation of £268 million. The schemes were managed by the Department of Industry which was responsible for processing applications and controlling the disbursement of funds. The Wool Textile Industry Scheme had already been introduced in 1973 and renewed in 1976 with grants subordinated to the scrapping of excess capacity. A study by the Department of Industry concluded that the funds made available (£24 million in both stages) had an important leverage on investment and had 'brought about a most encouraging improvement in the performance of the industry in all major respects'. See *Wool Textile Industry Scheme: an Assessment of Selective Assistance Under the Industry Act of 1972*, *op. cit.* It has been estimated that, of the 4,500 jobs lost in the sector pursuant to the scheme, only 4 per cent remained unemployed when tracking efforts were stopped by the end of 1977. See Vincent Cable, Jeremy Clarke and Mary Sutton, 'The United Kingdom', in Renshaw (ed.), *op. cit.*, p. 229.

79. J.T. Lambert, *Clothing Industry Scheme: an Assessment of the Effects of Selective Assistance Under the Industry Act of 1982*, Government Economic Service Working Paper No. 61 (London: Department of Trade and Industry, 1983).

80. See Miles, 'Protection of the British Textile Industry', in Corden and Fels (eds), *op. cit.*, pp. 193-95; Cable, 'British Protectionism and LDC Imports', *ODI Review*, London, No. 2, 1977; and Farrands, *loc. cit.*

81. Marks and Spencer, for example, purchased over 90 per cent of its clothing requirements in the United Kingdom and had an explicit corporate commitment to do so. They also purchased 40 per cent of all shirts manufactured in the United Kingdom and had spurned low-cost foreign suppliers even though such a policy had obliged the firm to upgrade its shirt line in order to compete in the higher price ranges. The firm had, in most cases, dealt with the same suppliers for over twenty five years, purchased more than 50 per cent of their output (and often 100 per cent) and guaranteed stable production runs and long lead times in ordering.

82. J.L. Juvet, 'The Cotton Industry and World Trade', *Journal of World Trade Law*, September-October 1967, p. 553.

83. For an excellent discussion of these issues, some of which are cited extensively in this section, see Aggarwal and Haggard, *op. cit.*

84. *Ibid.*, p. 276.

85. *The History and the Current Status of the Multi-fiber Arrangement*, *op. cit.*, p. 7. For a discussion of the plan and its various elements, see Aggarwal and Haggard, *op. cit.*, pp. 280-83.

86. For an assessment of this earlier programme, see Harold A. Bratt, 'Assisting the Economic Recovery of Import-injured Firms', *Law and Policy in International Business*, Washington, Vol. 6, No. 1, 1974, pp. 1-36; and Charles Frank, *Foreign Trade and Domestic Aid* (Washington: Brookings Institution, 1977).

87. Aggarwal and Haggard, *op. cit.*, p. 298.

88. This and other data on the company TAA programme come from Harold W. Williams, 'Trade Adjustment Assistance', in *Domestic Apparel Program* (Washington: United States Department of Commerce, 1980).

89. The analysis that follows is based on Walter Corson, Walter Nicholson, David Richardson and Andrea Vayda, *Survey of Trade Adjustment Assistance Recipients*, Report prepared by Mathematica Policy Research (Washington: United States Department of Labor, 1979).

90. Lenway, *op. cit.*, p. 4.

91. This is, obviously, a view not shared by the industry. In a 1977 submission to the Ways and Means Committee of the House of Representatives in the United States Congress, Burlington presented an analysis carried out by the econometric consultants Data Resources Inc. which claimed that increases in textile imports between 1978 and 1985 would cause a direct loss of 384,000 jobs (1.4 million if secondary effects were counted) in both the textile and clothing sectors. If accompanied by a tariff reduction of 50 per cent, the estimates climbed to 592,000 direct job losses and a total employment drop of 2.2 million. See 'L'industrie textile aux USA', *op. cit.*, p. 43.

92. Ippei Yomazawa, 'Adjustment of the Japanese Textile Industry to the Advanced Developing Countries', Hitotsubashi University, Tokyo, mimeograph, September 1980. He estimates that 93 per cent of this figure was given in return for the industry's compliance with the various agreements restraining textile exports to the United States.

93. Van Tho, 'Industrial Policy and the Textile Industry: the Japanese Experience', *Journal of Contemporary Business*, Seattle, Vol. 11, No. 1, 1982, pp. 123-24.

94. Yoshie Yomezawa, *Analysis and Evaluation of the Adjustment Process and Policies of the Japanese Textile Industry* (Tokyo: Japan Economic Research Center, 1981). Yomazawa, *op. cit.*, on the other hand, claims that the unique system for making these cuts (the weaver's association in each district would submit a plan specifying optimal capacity for the area and then allocate plant expansion and scrapping quotas to its members on the basis of their 'prospective competence') resulted in 70 per cent of the planned figures being reached between 1967 and 1971 (p. 14).

95. Yomazawa, *op. cit.*, p. 14.

96. Van Tho, *loc. cit.*, pp. 124-25.

97. *Ibid.*, p. 121.

98. Yomazawa, *op. cit.*, Table 5, p. 20.

99. Van Tho, *loc. cit.*, p. 127. Again in 1979, the industry tried unsuccessfully to get the Japanese Government to negotiate a bilateral agreement with South Korea. See Yomazawa, *op. cit.*, p. 40.

100. Yomazawa, *op. cit.*, pp. 23-4.

101. For a detailed description of the programme, see *Industrial Policy: Japan's Flexible Approach*, GAO/ID-82-32 (Washington: US General Accounting Office, 1982) pp. 68-69.

102. The synthetic-fibre industry has been one of the major beneficiaries of this programme. Following a major drop in volume since 1974, MITI issued a set of guidelines in 1977 to cut back production by 25 per cent in certain lines. These were generally observed with the result that prices recovered within six months. In April 1978, Japan's FTC approved the creation of an anti-recession cartel and, shortly thereafter, the industry was designated 'structurally depressed'. A major scrapping and moth-balling programme followed which has been considered a model for other depressed sectors to follow. See *Industrial Policy: Case Studies in the Japanese Experience*, GAO/ID-83-11 (Washington: US General Accounting Office, 1982).

103. *Industrial Policy: Japan's Flexible Approach*, *op. cit.*, p. 71.

104. *Ibid.*, pp. 75-76.

105. The level of employment support in Norway's and Sweden's clothing industries far exceeded any commitments made by the members of the European Community. In both countries, in spite of very large grants and subsidies amounting to an average of $2,130 and $2,250 per worker, respectively, for each year during the period 1975-77, employment continued to drop precipitously. See de la Torre and Bachetta, 'Decline and Adjustment: European Policies Towards Their Clothing Industries', *op. cit.*, pp. 73-81.

CHAPTER FIVE

Decline, Adjustment or Resurgence? the Shape of Things to Come

ULTIMATELY workers, the owners of capital and management must take (or be forced to take) the steps that will gradually alter a country's industrial structure in response to changing competitive conditions. They can be left alone to read and interpret the signals that anticipate changes in their environment, they can be shielded for a time from the consequences of their actions or inaction; or they can be prodded, subsidised, motivated or otherwise encouraged to adapt. In the end, though, their responsibility cannot be shunned forever in a market-oriented system without fundamentally altering the tenets of democratic society.

To the extent that firms and workers undertake the shifts and bear the costs associated with adjustment, the rest of society benefits from a more efficient allocation of resources and a competitive and lower-price supply of goods at little or no social cost. The process should, in theory, be smooth and continuous, involving a myriad of marginal decisions by the owners of the factors of production, with only a fraction of the economy affected at any time. But if large, discrete or rapid movements are required, or rigidities exist which hamper the efficient transfer of resources from one activity to another, the costs can be significant. The burden of adjustment then falls on those who, presumably, have reaped past benefits and have now been slow or reticent to react in a changing world.

This essay has been about a decade of decline and adjustment in the clothing industries of the world's largest, most industrially advanced economies, the causes of this transformation and the policies pursued by both private-sector and public-sector participants in response. But what of the next decade? What further changes can be expected to occur and what are the chances that private and public actors can manage a smooth, if not totally painless, transition to a new global competitive environment?

Private Adjustment Towards the 1990s

Projections are inherently risky. The last decade has shown both the folly of extrapolation as well as the economic value of flexibility. Yet decisions on investments or careers cannot be postponed simply because the world has become less predictable. Moreover, there are many basic trends, whose foundations are anchored in socio-economic phenomena that can be extrapolated with some degree of certainty. While the risk of error obviously remains, it would be as foolish to ignore the strength and direction of these forces as to claim they are immutable.

It is unlikely, for instance, that real growth in demand for clothing in the developed countries will exceed 2 per cent per annum over the next ten years, irrespective of economic conditions. Significant growth in demand will, however, occur in most of the developing world where population growth continues to exceed 3 per cent per annum and income growth is also pulling more and more people into the cash economy. Thus, the shifts in world production and consumption of clothing towards the Third World which characterised the past fifteen years are almost certain to continue.

More important, perhaps, for the developed countries is the continued pressure that developing-country producers will exert on world markets. Barring a near-magical discovery that may drastically alter the manufacturing process (or, indeed, the nature of the garments themselves), the economics of clothes production will continue to favour producers in low-wage countries. As a result, manufacturers based in developed countries will retain their current domestic-market shares only through the sustained use of quantitative restrictions imposed on imports from developing countries. The developed countries' share of world employment and exports in the industry will therefore probably follow the decline in their share of production and consumption, but at a faster rate. The loss of competitiveness in export markets, combined with the productivity gains induced by this continued competitive pressure, will tend to ensure this outcome.

The prognosis would be rather gloomy, if it were not for one other trend of great importance to the industry: the emergence in the 1970s of a global consumer demand for clothes with a high-fashion content. By the end of the decade, a few large international houses were deriving considerable profit from the privileged market position they had obtained in most of the developed countries, as well as in the principal urban centres of the middle-income countries. Design, style and colour, as well as exclusive distribution, were the hallmarks of these firms. They aimed their market strategies of product value and differentiation at a new segment of the market for clothing: the relatively affluent consumer who is willing to pay for the intangible qualities of a limited degree of exclusivity and excellence in design. The crucial fact is that such customers can be found in many countries regardless of age or nationality. This 'global' segment of the industry was expanding rapidly with important implications for the survival and prosperity of any firm based in the developed countries.[1]

Thus, one can distinguish two broad sections of the industry where international competitive conditions will differ.[2] One is the relatively more functional end of the market which accounts for the bulk of sales in the developed countries and an overwhelming proportion in the developing world. These are the price-sensitive product groups, with low growth in demand and extensive distribution which have felt import competition most severely. Firms still operating in these areas in high-wage countries are likely to see their competitive position irrevocably eroded over the next decade. Some will, of course, survive as they provide insurance against the vagaries of international supply and the difficulties inherent in serving a very large market from a considerable distance, or by mastering capital-intensive, mass-production and marketing techniques. But import penetration in these product groups could reach (or even exceed) 50 per cent under free-trade conditions in most developed countries.

The situation is very different in the other 'global' segment of the market. The keys to success here are only partially related to cost. Quickness of reaction, the ability to incorporate new trends and designs into production schedules, flexibility of operation, relatively good access to quality fabric suppliers, proximity to major centres of demand and intimate and service-intensive relationships with distribution channels are among the factors that determine success in these product markets. Location near the principal and wealthier consumer markets is, therefore, essential, even though some manufacturing and assembly may in fact be carried out in low-wage countries. For these product lines, the bulk of the value added, from fibre production to final sale, will accrue to citizens of the developed countries. As this 'designer' segment of the clothing industry's market is growing rapidly in developed countries and is also expanding into the middle-income developing countries, the opportunities for successful adjustment strategies in this direction would seem to be plentiful.[3]

In Chapter 3 the adjustment strategies that had been followed by developed-country firms were discussed as well as the impact they have had on their performance. The next decade should see an even greater trend towards global specialisation and, therefore, a greater urgency to adopt global strategies for survival.

The issues of technology, size and scale of production, automation and modernisation will continue to dominate public debate. But the critical decisions firms will have to make for survival are centred on product policy and manufacturing location. The former is intimately related to the trends discussed above: only by moving to those segments of the market where product attributes other than those of a purely physical nature are important to the consumer can high-cost firms hope to remain in business. The latter is related to the shift in world consumption and production patterns that has already been discussed.

The successful clothing companies of the next decade will have to become truly international. First, they must seek to serve the same type of customer throughout the world, in order to capitalise on their investments in design and product image. Thus the establishment of international distribution and marketing operations is a prerequisite for assuring domestic success. Secondly, manufacturing operations will tend to reflect conflicting requirements of scale, proximity of market and fabric suppliers and competitive labour costs. How best to balance these claims will be a function of the product and market circumstances of each firm. But what is certain is that the next decade will require considerable investment outside the home market by successful firms as they seek both to extend their market coverage and balance their cost structures. The 'global' market segment will therefore be characterised by globally-oriented companies much more than they have been in the past.

Issue of Protection

The implications of these trends for employment in the industrial countries are unequivocal. The number of jobs in the industry will continue to contract in response to changes in import penetration, productivity and export competitiveness, particularly when coupled with low demand growth.[4] To the extent that a broader distribution of the costs of adjustment is deemed desirable, the state will intervene to assure it. How, then, can such intervention be made compatible with the inevitable long-term evolution of the industry?

The justifications given for intervention are many. One could argue, for example, that the market is far from perfect; that, in such an atomistic industry, information concerning technical or fashion changes may not flow either soon enough or rapidly enough among its many units; that mobility of resources is constrained by such barriers to exit as social, community or family pressures; that government regulations and social-security charges based on broad political considerations and a complex industrial base affect this particular industry pervasively; and so forth. Alternatively, arguments can be made that, given the large labour force in the industry, the adjustment cost is too large and adjustment itself too disruptive to be left totally to the private sector; that the associated social costs are too significant; or that the process is too rapid for the factors of production to be able to respond in an orderly fashion; in sum, that the short term overwhelms the long term. Finally, income distribution and social-welfare considerations might lead governments to intervene directly, particularly if there is a serious regional problem associated with the industry's downturn. In any event, and almost irrespective of the validity of the argument, governments are led to make the attempt to absorb into public spending a part (if not all) of the private costs citing reasons of efficiency or equity, or both.

The West European, American and Japanese experiences in the clothing industry show that there are a number of strategies pursued by national governments when trying to reapportion the costs of adjustment. The most widely used has been to tighten the provisions of existing trading arrangements. There are some significant advantages in this. For one, the effective level of protection can be manipulated to sustain only those firms with some chance of success in the long term, while letting the marginal ones disappear. Protection is also relatively easy to implement, enjoys a clear and vociferous constituency and the costs associated with it are widespread, difficult to evaluate and of no immediate consequence to policy makers. It becomes difficult to argue in favour of an efficient long-term allocation of resources when unemployment levels are high and the adverse consequences of protection apparently remote.

But the costs associated with protection are present and real. For one, protection delays inevitable adjustments to the point where their magnitude makes them extremely difficult to absorb within the prevailing socio-political structure. This, in turn, results in either the potential for significant disruption later or, because of a fear of this, in further postponement of adjustment through additional protection. Secondly, protection diverts the energies of the efficient firms in the industry from the necessary reorientation towards a global market, by encouraging them instead to serve vulnerable domestic markets. Finally, the costs of providing special measures of protection to the industry will grow as more and more low-cost producers try to enter (but are excluded from) the market.

In short, protection has both an allocative and a distributive cost that, however difficult to measure, cannot be ignored. It is precisely this characteristic of protectionism that makes it perverse: it is an unquantified, long-term tax, imposed on society without an explicit process of political review that takes account of the public's interest. Lacking transparency but supported by closely-knit constituencies of special interests, protection, however justifiable in the short term, tends to extend its lease on life almost unchallenged. The textile industries have proved this over the last 22 years, as the 'temporary' levels of protection given the industry since the first sign of difficulties, have, if anything, strengthened.[5]

It can be argued that past extensions and the escalation of measures of protection have become endemic to the present system. Expectations of automatic renewal of trade protection are self-fulfilling in that they remove the incentive to design and implement an appropriate adjustment programme and so establish the bases for further renewals of the arrangements. If adjustment and an end to artificial barriers of protection are both desirable objectives, it might be preferable to negotiate one last MFA in 1986 with a longer duration (perhaps ten to twelve years), but one that incorporates a gradual but irrevocable commitment to an eventual removal of all quantitative trade barriers against imports of clothing into the developed-country markets. This in itself would provide firms both with the long-term horizon on which to plan their adjustment strategies and the certainty that, in the absence of adjustment, survival would be in question.[6]

Challenge for Public Policy

What else can governments do, if anything, to promote positive adjustment in this industry? When protection proved inadequate, direct employment subsidies were applied widely. One country after another plunged into the direct defence of employment through a variety of policies ranging from outright subsidies to state ownership of bankrupt firms. These policies, however well intentioned, soon proved to be both extremely expensive and ineffective in maintaining employment. The remaining alternative was to bring about a restructuring of the industry that would simultaneously achieve the elusive goals of maintaining employment, enhancing competitiveness and attaining a reasonable external balance. The lessons of the last decade in various declining sectors, as well as the experience of the clothing industry, have clearly pointed out the difficulties inherent in any restructuring programme.

The Dutch programme failed to win the support of industry and labour because it asked for too many compromises and detailed negotiations. It was too ambitious to succeed. The British scheme, while considerably more modest, appears to have at least nudged the industry in the right direction, while the American trade adjustment assistance programme delivered too little, too late, for it to have had any major impact. Finally, the various programmes of technological diffusion, while generally supportive of improvements in quality and efficiency, were insufficient to bring about major turnarounds in the industry.

If public assistance is to facilitate positive adjustment, it must act to induce companies to make the kind of choices that have been shown to lead to success; that is, policies which are in tune with global market trends. Among the most promising areas for government action in support of industry's adjustment strategies, could be the following:

(a) There could be increased government support for the internationalisation of major producers or groups of companies. Existing export promotion schemes and investment assistance programmes should be made available to the industry on a targeted basis, at least concurrently with the gradual decrease of protection suggested above. Companies competing in well-defined product areas on a broad geographical basis have the best chances of success and government support should be used to reinforce this tendency.

(b) Promotion of complementary foreign manufacturing facilities by domestic clothing manufacturers could be fostered. 'Outward processing' keeps the bulk of the total value added at home and makes maximum utilisation of the possibilities for an international division of labour. Quotas for outward processing should not be included within the MFA quotas since this considerably limits their appeal. In addition, government assistance programmes aimed at supporting foreign investment in developing countries should be used to stimulate the establishment of such offshore assembly affiliates in conveniently located, low-wage countries: the Caribbean, the Mediterranean and South-east Asian basins for the North American, West European and Japanese markets, respectively.[7]

(c) Size of firms continues to be a significant determinant of success in the industry, particularly as access to the high-income markets will require sophisticated design and management skills that small specialised firms cannot easily obtain. Fiscal policy and investment incentives should be made consistent with a policy of promoting larger firms capable of functioning in a highly competitive and geographically diverse market.

(d) Vigorous opposition could be mounted against protection in the developing countries on the grounds that it is inconsistent with a progressive international division of labour within the industry. Progress towards freedom of access to developed-country markets should be made contingent on a similar process of liberalisation of the clothing markets of major world exporters, especially of the more developed of these countries. A graduation scheme can be implemented within the next MFA whereby the rate and speed at which specific-country quotas in the importing countries will be dismantled is made contingent upon both the level of income of each exporting country and its own protective barriers. Thus little liberalisation of access would be granted to relatively more developed countries, such as South Korea or Brazil, unless they undertook to liberalise their own clothing markets, while access to OECD markets could be granted under any circumstances to the poorest countries, such as Sri Lanka or Haiti, or to those which maintain open markets, such as Hong Kong or Singapore.

(e) Active support could be afforded any effort that is designed to improve quality and/or design content, such as trade shows and design schools, and that would stimulate the exchange and ferment of ideas necessary for creativity and innovation to prosper.

These specific programmes might help to facilitate intra-industry adjustments as well as improve the competitiveness of the entire textile chain, as Japan has come to understand. But, whatever the path chosen, the clothing labour force will continue to shrink in most developed countries. Other programmes, therefore, of general applicability may be necessary to complement the sectoral policies outlined above. Of these, two deserve special mention:

(a) The most urgent programme would contain measures that could assist displaced clothing workers to adapt through education, training and relocation assistance. This is no easy task given the age and skill distribution typical of the industry and the general reluctance of female workers to move. But these measures are necessary to lower the resistance of labour to making inter-industry shifts and to reduce the hardships that a broad adjustment effort might impose on workers. In fact, the cost to the nation of early retirement or separation payments may be significantly lower than the costs of keeping unemployable workers on the job through increases in the marginal rate of protection.

(b) Finally, to the extent that sectoral problems, in clothing, textiles or elsewhere, have a regional dimension, adjustment can be accelerated through regional policy instruments.

The suggested approach offers several advantages. First, it is 'positive' adjustment in that whatever subsidies are offered are designed to encourage new activities and not just to support the old. Secondly, it breaks the unholy alliance of management and labour on protection by offering differentiated alternatives to both. Finally, it can be largely decentralised, thus avoiding the rigidities of centrally-managed programmes and allowing for better coordination between local interests and national resources.

Conclusion

The historical record of private and public strategies for adjustment in the clothing industry is rich with lessons for the future. It is perfectly clear that many firms *can* and *have* managed to adapt and profit from changing market and cost conditions. They have pursued aggressive policies of increased product value and have reduced costs through the use of modern technology and investment in offshore manufacturing. It is also clear that the main activity of government in the past has been to finance and support resistance to change, largely through subsidisation of employment and trade protection. This has not prevented a considerable decline of employment nor a significant reduction in the number of firms active in the industry, trends which are likely to continue under practically any set of foreseeable circumstances.

After this long history of largely futile and certainly costly intervention, the time has come for a planned programme of liberalisation. In such a context, a leaner, more competitive and ultimately healthier industry will undoubtedly emerge. Having failed to prevent change, it is perhaps time for governments to show confidence in the ability of private firms to manage it.

NOTES AND REFERENCES

1. For an interesting discussion of the same trend in other industrial sectors, see Theodore Levitt, 'The Globalisation of Markets', *Harvard Business Review*, May-June 1983, pp. 92-102.

2. This ignores, of course, the fact that each sub-sector or product category in the industry will, for a variety of specific technical and market reasons (for example, labour content, possible automation, fashion cycle, distribution system and so on), exhibit different inherent propensities towards internationalisation. The argument made here is simply that, irrespective of these *a priori* conditions, the emergence of a global market in segments of the ready-to-wear clothing business adds a different and important dimension to internationalisation.

3. As an indication of the size of this segment, the 'designer houses' in France, represented in the Fédération de la Couture, du Prêt-à-Porter de Couturiers et de Créateurs de Mode (which includes all related accessories as well), employed 47,000 people in 1981 and had a turnover of 6.2 billion French francs. In addition, the members of the Fédération Française du Prêt-à-Porter Feminin employed 70,300 people and had a turnover of FF9.1 billion. These two groups, therefore, alone represented about 40 per cent of total employment in the industry. Their shares of value added and exports would be considerably larger.

4. For example, if imports accounted for 20 per cent of domestic consumption and increased at 6 per cent per annum, consumption itself grew at 2 per cent per annum, productivity increased at 4 per cent per annum and exports, representing 25 per cent of production, grew at 4 per cent per annum, domestic employment would decrease by nearly 22 per cent in a decade.

5. For two excellent discussions of the evidence on the costs associated with protection in this industry, see Martin Wolf, Hans Hinrich Glismann, Joseph Pelzman and Dean Spinanger, *Costs of Protecting Jobs in Textiles and Clothing*, Thames Essay No. 37 (London: Trade Policy Research Centre, 1984), and *Textile and Clothing Industries: Structural Problems and Policies in OECD Countries*, *op. cit.*, pp. 120-28.

6. The debate on what proportion of the clothing industry in the developed

countries would survive such a gradual process of import liberalisation is highly inconclusive. For two sets of opposite views, see, on the side of gloom, *The Future of the Man-made Fibre Industry in Western Europe* (Paris: Comité International de la Rayonne et des Fibres Synthétiques [CIRFS], 1976) p. 10, and *Information on Man-made Fibres*, CIRFS, Paris, pp. 46-50, and the Burlington submittal cited above, 'L'industrie textile aux USA', *op. cit.*, p. 43; while, on the side of boom, see Keesing and Wolf, *op. cit.*, pp. 131-40, and Renshaw, *op. cit.*, pp. 82-87. Their estimates for all OECD countries range from a maximum loss of nearly 1 million clothing workers (nearly 40 per cent of current levels) within ten years to only 168,000.

7. A good example of misguided public policy in this area is the specific exclusion of textile and clothing products from the recent American initiative to bring investment to the Caribbean basin as a major stimulant to economic development in that area.

List of References

THIS bibliography lists works cited in the text apart from standard statistical sources and those of minor relevance which may have been cited only once or twice. Not all references, therefore, have been listed here and the reader should refer to the Notes and References at the end of each chapter and to the sources of the Tables and Figures for more complete bibliographical information. It is divided into books and articles, official publications and the publications of private organisations.

VINOD K. AGGARWAL and STEPHEN HAGGARD, 'The Politics of Protection in the US Textile and Apparel Industries', in John Zysman and Laura Tyson (eds), *American Industry in International Competition* (Ithaca, New York: Cornell University Press, 1983).

JEFFREY S. ARPAN, MARY BARRY and TRAN VAN THO, 'The Textile Complex in the Pacific Basin: the Patterns and Textures of Competition and the Shape of Things to Come', mimeograph, University of South Carolina, undated.

JEFFREY S. ARPAN, JOSÉ DE LA TORRE and BRIAN TOYNE, *The US Apparel Industry: International Challenge — Domestic Response*, Research Monograph No. 88 (Atlanta: Georgia State University, 1982).

BELA BALASSA, *Structural Change in Trade and Manufactured Goods between Industrial and Developing Countries*, World Bank Staff Working Paper No. 396 (Washington: World Bank, 1980).

P.W. BAREERSEN, *The Border Industrialisation Program of Mexico* (Lexington, Mass.: D.C. Heath, 1971).

DEREK BLADES, 'The Hidden Economy and National Accounts', *OECD Economic Outlook*, Paris, June 1982.

HAROLD A. BRATT, 'Assisting the Economic Recovery of Import-injured Firms', *Law and Policy in International Business*, Washington, No. 1, Vol. 6, 1974, pp. 1-36.

VINCENT CABLE, 'British Petroleum and LDC Imports', *ODI Review*, London, No. 2, 1977.

VINCENT CABLE, JEREMY CLARKE and MARY SUTTON, 'The United Kingdom', in Geoffrey Renshaw (ed.), *Employment, Trade and North-South Cooperation* (Geneva: International Labour Office, 1981) pp. 209-59.

J.S. CHARD and M.J. MACMILLAN, 'Sectoral Aids and Community Competition Policy: the Case of Textiles', *Journal of World Trade Law*, London, March-April 1979.

F. COLPORTI and G. MUSSATI, *GEPI e TESCON: Due Interventi delle Partecipazioni Statali* (Milan: Franco Angeli Editore, 1976).

W.M. CORDEN and GERHARD FELS (eds), *Public Assistance to Industry: Protection and Subsidies in Britain and Germany* (London: Macmillan, for the Trade Policy Research Centre and the Institut für Weltwirtschaft an der Universität Kiel, 1976).

GERARD CURZON, JOSÉ DE LA TORRE, JUERGEN B. DONGES, ALASDAIR I. MACBEAN, JEAN WAELBROECK and MARTIN WOLF, *MFA Forever? Future of the Arrangement for Trade in Textiles*, International Issues No. 5 (London: Trade Policy Research Centre, 1981).

José de la Torre, 'Public Intervention Strategies in the European Clothing Industries', *Journal of World Trade Law*, London, March-April 1981.

José de la Torre and Michel Bacchetta, *Decline and Adjustment: European Policies Towards their Clothing Industries* (Fontainebleau: Institut Européen d'Administration des Affaires [INSEAD], 1979).

José de la Torre and Michel Bacchetta, 'The Uncommon Market: European Policies towards the Clothing Industry in the 1970s', *Journal of Common Market Studies*, Oxford, December 1980.

José de la Torre, M.J. Jedel, J.S. Arpan *et al.*, *Corporate Responses to Import Competition in the US Apparel Industry*, Research Monograph No. 74 (Atlanta: Georgia State University, 1978).

George Eads and Edward M. Graham, 'Transparency: Prerequisite for Positive Adjustment', *OECD Observer*, Paris, November 1982.

Ben Evers, *Industrial Restructuring and Development Cooperation in the Netherlands*, Occasional Paper No. 6 (Tilburg: Development Research Institute, University of Tilburg, 1979).

Christopher Farrands, 'Textile Diplomacy: the Making and Implementation of European Textile Policy, 1974-78', *Journal of Common Market Studies*, Oxford, September 1979.

J.M. Finger, 'Trade and Domestic Effects of the Offshore Provision in the US Tariff', *American Economic Review*, Menasha, Wisconsin, September 1976.

J.M. Finger, 'Offshore Assembly Provisions in the West German and Netherlands Tariffs: Trade and Domestic Effects', *Weltwirtschaftliches Archiv*, Kiel, No. 2, Vol. 113, 1977.

CHARLES FRANK, *Foreign Trade and Domestic Aid* (Washington: Brookings Institution, 1977).

PAOLO GIUIUZZA and SERGIO MARIOTTI, *Economies of Scale and Multi-plant Operations in a Branch of the Italian Clothing Industry*, Working Paper 80-3 (Brussels: European Institute for Advanced Studies in Management, 1980).

GERALD K. HELLEINER, *Intra-firm Trade and the Developing Countries* (New York: St Martin's Press, 1981).

ERNST-JEURGEN HORN, *Management of Industrial Change in Germany*, Sussex European Paper No. 13 (Brighton: Sussex European Research Centre, University of Sussex, 1982).

J.L. JUVET, 'The Cotton Industry and World Trade', *Journal of World Trade Law*, London, September-October 1967.

DONALD B. KEESING and MARTIN WOLF, *Textile Quotas Against Developing Countries*, Thames Essay No. 23 (London: Trade Policy Research Centre, 1980).

O. KREYE, 'World Market Oriented Industrialization of Developing Countries: Free Production Zones and World Market Factories', in *The New International Division of Labour* (Starnberg: Max Planck Institut für Sozialwissenshaften, 1977).

WILHELM KURTH, 'Textiles and Clothing: a National and International Issue', paper presented at the International Symposium on Industrial Policies for the Eighties organised by the Spanish Ministry of Industry and Energy, in cooperation with the Organisation for Economic Cooperation and Development, in Madrid on 5-9 May 1980.

DEEPAK LAL, *Resurrection of the Pauper-labour Argument*, Thames Essay No. 28 (London: Trade Policy Research Centre, 1981).

Sanjaya Lall, 'Offshore Assembly in Developing Countries', *National Westminster Bank Quarterly Review*, London, August 1980.

Count Otto Lambsdorff, 'Goals for the 1980s: Competition, Price Stability and Adjustment', *The World Economy*, London, February 1980.

Theodore Levitt, 'The Globalization of Markets', *Harvard Business Review*, Boston, May-June 1983.

McKinsey and Company, *Vers le redressement de l'industrie belge du textile et de la confection*, Report submitted to the Ministry of Economic Affairs, Belgian Government, Brussels, 1980.

Caroline Miles, *Lancashire Textiles: a Case Study of Industrial Change* (Cambridge: Cambridge University Press, for the National Institute of Social and Economic Research, 1968).

David Morawetz, *Why the Emperor's New Clothes are Not Made in Colombia*, World Bank Staff Working Paper No. 368 (Washington: World Bank, 1980).

Samuel Rosenblatt, 'Trade Adjustment Assistance Programs: Crossroads or Dead End?', *Law and Policy in International Business*, Washington, No. 4, Vol. 9, 1977.

A.J. Sarna, 'International Guidelines for Industrial Adjustment Policies', *Journal of World Trade Law*, London, December 1981.

Uwe Schwarting, 'Strategies for Survival: the Example of the Clothing Industry', *Intereconomics*, Hamburg, January-February 1979.

Geoffrey Shepherd, *Textile-industry Adjustment in Developed Countries*, Thames Essay No. 30 (London: Trade Policy Research Centre, 1981).

Tran Van Tho, 'Industrial Policy and the Textile Industry: the Japanese Experience', *Journal of Contemporary Business*, Seattle, No. 1, Vol. 11, 1982.

Martin Wolf, Hans Hinrich Glismann, Joseph Pelzman and Dean Spinanger, *Costs of Protecting Jobs in Textiles and Clothing*, Thames Essay No. 37 (London: Trade Policy Research Centre, 1984).

Stephen Woolcock, 'Textiles and Clothing', in Louis Turner and Neil McMullen (eds), *The Newly Industrializing Countries: Trade and Adjustment* (London: Allen & Unwin, 1982).

Ippei Yomazawa, 'Adjustment of the Japanese Textile Industry to the Advanced Developing Countries', mimeograph, Hitotsubashi University, Tokyo, 1980.

Yoshie Yomezawa, *Analysis and Evaluation of the Adjustment Process and Policies of the Japanese Textile Industry* (Tokyo: Japan Economic Research Centre, 1981).

Official Publications

This is divided into signed and unsigned publications cited within the book.

Signed Official Publications

Antoine Basile and Dimitri Germidis, *Politiques d'attractions des investissements étrangers orientés vers l'exportation: le rôle des zones franches industrielles d'exportation* (Paris: OECD Development Centre, 1982).

John Bragg, 'Assessment of New Technology', in *Domestic Apparel Program* (Washington: International Trade Administration, United States Department of Commerce, 1980).

Vincent Cable, Jeremy Clarke and Mary Sutton, 'The United Kingdom', in Geoffrey Renshaw (ed.), *Employment, Trade and North-South Cooperation* (Geneva: International Labour Office, 1981) pp. 209-59.

Walter Corson, Walter Nicholson, David Richardson and Andrea Vayda, *Survey of Trade Adjustment assistance recipients*, Report prepared by Mathematica Policy Research (Washington: United States Department of Labor, 1979).

Diana Green, *Managing Industrial Change? French Policies to Promote Industrial Adjustment* (London: Her Majesty's Stationery Office, for the Department of Industry, British Government, 1980).

E. Jahan, C. Jaedlicki, M. Lanzzarotti and J. Massini, *La stratégie des investisseurs fransçais face à la concurrence des pays à bas salaires* (Paris: OECD Development Centre in conjunction with the Institut de l'Entreprise, 1980).

J.T. Lambert, *Clothing Industry Scheme: an Assessment of the Effects of Selective Assistance Under the Industry Act of 1982*, Government Economic Service Working Paper No. 61 (London: Department of Trade and Industry, 1983).

Geoffrey Renshaw (ed.), *Employment, Trade and North-South Cooperation* (Geneva: International Labour Office, 1981).

P. Tandon, *The Case of India*, Report within the Free Trade Zone Project (Paris: OECD Development Centre, 1981).

Harold W. Williams, 'Trade Adjustment Assistance', *Domestic Apparel Program* (Washington: International Trade Administration, United States Department of Commerce, 1980).

Unsigned Official Publications

CLOTHING ECONOMIC DEVELOPMENT COMMITTEE, *Clothing Industry Development Proposals* (London: National Economic Development Council, 1975).

'La communauté européenne et les échanges de produits textiles', *Europe Information*, Brussels, No. 44, 1981.

Commission Policy on Sectoral Aid Schemes, COM (78)221 final (Brussels: Commission of the European Community, 1978).

Economic Factors Affecting the Use of Items 807.00 and 806.30 of the Tariff Schedules of the United States (Washington: US Government Printing Office, for the Tariff Commission, 1970).

First Report on Competition Policy (Brussels: Commission of the European Community, 1972).

General Guidelines for a Textiles and Clothing Industry Policy, COM (78)362 final (Brussels: Commission of the European Community, 1978).

The History and the Current Status of the Multi-fiber Arrangement (Washington: US Government Printing Office, for the International Trade Commission, 1978).

Industrial Policy: Case Studies in the Japanese Experience, CAO/ID-83-11 (Washington: US General Accounting Office, 1983).

Industrial Policy: Japan's Flexible Approach, GAO/ID-82-32 (Washington: US General Accounting Office, 1982).

Policies for Adjustment: Some General Orientations (Paris: OECD Secretariat, 1978).

Positive Adjustment Policies: Managing Structural Change (Paris: OECD Secretariat, 1983).

Report on the Labour Force Tracking Project: Costs of Labour Adjustment Study (Ottawa: Department of Industry, Trade and Commerce, Canadian Government, 1980).

Textile and Clothing Industries: Structural Problems and Policies in OECD Countries (Paris: OECD Secretariat, 1983).

The 1980s: the Decade for Technology, Report prepared for the Commission of the European Community (Washington: Kurt Salmon Associates, 1979).

Wool Textile Industry Scheme: an Assessment of Selective Assistance under the Industry Act of 1972 (London: Her Majesty's Stationery Office, for the Department of Industry, British Government, 1978).

Private Organisations

Die Bekleidungsindustrie in der Bundesrepublik Deutschland im Jahre 1977 (Cologne: Bundersverband Bekleidungs-industrie, 1978).

Guide de la formation continue dans l'industrie de l'habillement (Paris: Centre d'Etudes Techniques des Industries de l'Habillement [CEITH], 1972).

Herstructurering Nederlandse Confectie-Industrie: deel 1 Herenbovenkleding-Industrie, 1977, and *deel 2 Damenbovenkleding-Industrie, 1978* ('s-Hertogenbosch: Nederlandse Herstructureringsmaatschappij [NEHEM]).

Industrial Adjustment in the Netherlands (Tilburg: Development Research Institute, University of Tilburg, 1975).

I Problemi dell'Industria dell'Abbigliamento, Working Paper on the Clothing Industry (Milan: Associazione Italiana Industriali Abbigliamento, 1976).

Progetto Tessile (Rome: Federazione fra l'Associazioni delle Industrie Tessili e Abbigliamento [Federtessile], 1978).

Sistema Moda (Rome: Comite Interministeriale de Politica Industriale [CIPI], 1978).